In the real world, the foundation of everything we think about and do is data. Our brains organize data by patterns, which is another way of saying sets. In the virtual world of programming, it's still all about data. But now we have to build and manage the sets of data ourselves. We can and should use the SQL language as our means of communication, but even before that, we've got to make sure the data is organized so that it accurately captures entities and expresses the relationships between them. Skip or do a poor job at database design, and everything else in your application development process will suffer. Do it right, and everything that follows is more intuitive, easier to build, and much easier to maintain.

With long and deep experience, Heli has written an ideal guide to both database design and Oracle SQL Developer Data Modeler.

—Steven Feuerstein
Architect, Oracle Corporation

Working as a database administrator and developer, one of the hardest problems you encounter is coming late to a project that is suffering from performance problems. In many cases the problems are caused by fundamental flaws in the database design. Identify these too late in the development process and the job of redesigning the database and refactoring the associated code can be a huge problem.

Over the last 30+ years programming paradigms have come and gone, but data has remained king. Regardless of your chosen development methodology, if you are planning to use a relational database, you have little choice but to spend time on the design phase. Trying to cut corners will always results in problems later.

—Tim Hall
Oracle ACE Director
Database Administrator, Developer, and Author
http://oracle-base.com

Data modeling is critical to success. Data modeling and data design are now more important than ever. With the onslaught of big data, our job is even more critical; turning data into information is a necessary task and cannot be accomplished without understanding what the structure of the data really is. If we do not turn our focus to understanding the structures of the data, then we cannot properly identify it or make sense of it, much less turn it into information that the business can utilize.

—Dan Linstedt
Founder and CEO
http://LearnDataVault.com

Enterprise applications are used to enable business. A great application not only supports a process but allows the organization to understand what is happening and allows it to respond. Key to all this is the data, and a well-designed database allows that access and flexibility.

My reality is that whenever I have struggled to get the information I need from an application, it has been because of poor database design. This book will help reinforce the need for good-quality database design.

—Debra Lilley
ACE Director

The idea of producing a formal database design is regarded by many as being old-fashioned these days. However, from my 25+ years' experience of working in the field of database performance, I do see a clear correlation between the time spent designing a database up front to meet the functional requirements and the chance of success of the project. The correlation in the other direction is even clearer; if time is not invested in understanding the requirements of the application system and in understanding the database that stores its data, then the chances of building a system that meets user requirements is small, and the probability of heading off on a tangent from the core requirements is greatly increased. Performance cannot be retrofitted to a system; it has to be designed in.

Using tools to help automate the design process, as recommended in this book, reduces the time needed for the design stage and makes it less likely that there will be a temptation to short the design stage. And that has to be better for everyone.

—Graham Wood
Architect
Oracle Corporation

ORACLE®

Oracle Press™

Oracle SQL Developer Data Modeler for Database Design Mastery

Heli Helskyaho

LSE / IMT

Mc
Graw
Hill
Education

New York   Chicago   San Francisco
Athens   London   Madrid   Mexico City
Milan   New Delhi   Singapore   Sydney   Toronto

Library of Congress Cataloging-in-Publication Data

Helskyaho, Heli.
 Oracle SQL developer data modeler for database design mastery / Heli Helskyaho.
   pages   cm
   ISBN 978-0-07-185009-4 (alk. paper)
1. Oracle (Computer file).   2. Database design.   I. Title.
   QA76.9.D26H44   2015
   005.75'85—dc23

                                                    2015009597

McGraw-Hill Education books are available at special quantity discounts to use as premiums and sales promotions, or for use in corporate training programs. To contact a representative, please visit the Contact Us pages at www.mhprofessional.com.

Oracle SQL Developer Data Modeler for Database Design Mastery

1 2 3 4 5 6 7 8 9 0   DOC DOC   1 0 9 8 7 6 5

ISBN   978-0-07-185009-4

MHID   0-07-185009-0

Sponsoring Editor	Technical Editors	Production Supervisor
Paul Carlstroem	Kent Graziano	Jean Bodeaux
Editorial Supervisor	Jeff Smith	**Composition**
Patty Mon	**Copy Editor**	Cenveo Publisher Services
Project Manager	Kim Wimpsett	**Illustration**
Kritika Kaushik,	**Proofreader**	Cenveo Publisher Services
Cenveo® Publisher Services	Paul Tyler	**Art Director, Cover**
Acquisitions Coordinator	**Indexer**	Jeff Weeks
Amanda Russell	Jack Lewis	

To my loving family: Marko, Patrik, and Matias.
And to my grandparents, Laura and Matti Luukkainen,
Marja Lehto and Harri Holmikari. I will miss you always!

About the Author

Heli Helskyaho has a master's degree in computer science from Helsinki University and specializes in databases. Heli is an Oracle ACE Director and has been a frequent speaker at many conferences. She has worked in IT since 1990 and with Oracle products since 1993. She has been in several positions, but each role has always included database design. Heli has been an Oracle Designer user since 1996 and an Oracle SQL Developer Data Modeler user since 2010. Heli is an active member in the Oracle user groups community, including Oracle User Group Finland as well as EMEA Oracle user groups community (EOUC) where she has served as their spokesperson/ambassador since 2007. Heli is also the CEO for Miracle Finland Oy. Heli believes that creating good database design and documentation reduces performance problems and makes solving them easier. You can follow her on Twitter @helifromfinland or read her blog on helifromfinland.wordpress.com.

About the Technical Editors

Kent Graziano is the owner of Data Warrior LLC and a lifetime member of Rocky Mountain Oracle Users Group (RMOUG) and ODTUG. He is an award-winning author and speaker, Oracle ACE director, certified Data Vault Master (DVDM) and Data Vault 2.0 Architect, and expert data modeler and data warehouse architect with more than 30 years of experience, including more than 25 years using Oracle (since version 5) and Oracle tools and two decades doing data warehousing. He is a recognized expert in Oracle*CASE, Oracle Designer, and Oracle SQL Developer Data Modeler. Kent has written numerous articles, authored one Kindle book (available on Amazon.com), coauthored four books, and done many presentations, nationally and internationally. Most recently, he was voted the second-best presenter at OUGF14 in Helsinki, Finland. You can follow Kent on Twitter @KentGraziano or on his blog Oracle Data Warrior (http://kentgraziano.com).

Jeff Smith is the product manager for Oracle SQL Developer Data Modeler and is thrilled to have true design experts, such as Heli and Kent, help Oracle Database customers build their applications right, the first time. Jeff has a bachelor's of science in computer science from West Virginia University and for the past 14 years has focused on database development and administration tools. You can follow Jeff at @thatjeffsmith on Twitter or read his productivity tips and tricks for Oracle SQL Developer Data Modeler at www.that jeffsmith.com.

Contents at a Glance

Contents

Forewords

What Is Database Design, Anyway?

Databases lie at the heart of so much of what we do in the IT world that it's surely obvious that they need to be properly designed. Yet neither design theory, nor design best practice, appear to be very well understood in the industry at large. (You only have to look at the Wikipedia article on database design to see the truth of these claims.) With this state of affairs in mind, therefore, I offer the following definitions:

Database design   Either logical database design or physical database design, as the context demands—though the unqualified term *database design,* or sometimes even just *design,* is usually taken to mean logical database design specifically (unless the context demands otherwise).

Logical database design (or just logical design)   The process, or the result of the process, of deciding what tables some database should contain, what columns those tables should have, and what integrity constraints those tables and columns should be subject to. The goal is to produce a design that's independent of all considerations having to do with either physical implementation or specific applications (this latter objective being desirable for the very good reason that it's generally not the case that all uses to which the database will be put are known at design time). Overall, the logical design process can be summed up as one of (a) pinning down the table predicates and other business rules as carefully as possible, albeit necessarily somewhat informally, and then (b) mapping those informal predicates and rules to specific tables, columns, and integrity constraints— preferably in such a way as to ensure that the result of the process involves no uncontrolled redundancy. (I'll explain in a few moments what I mean by the terms *table predicate, business rule,* and *uncontrolled redundancy.*)

Physical database design (or just physical design) The process, or the result of the process, of deciding, given some logical design, how that design should map to whatever physical constructs the target DBMS happens to support. Observe, therefore, that the physical design should be derived from the logical design and not the other way around; ideally, in fact, it should be derived automatically.

For the remainder of this brief discussion, I'll concentrate on logical design specifically. The first thing I want to say is that there does exist some science that can help with the logical design process; I refer, of course, to such matters as the principles of further normalization and the principle of orthogonal design. Thus, if you're a designer, you owe it to yourself—as well as to your clients, which is to say the people who are going to have to live with the databases you design—to be thoroughly familiar with those principles and to know how and when to apply them. (As an aside, I note that there's quite a bit more to the science than many people seem to realize. It's certainly not just a matter of making sure the tables are all in third normal form. However, this isn't the place to go into details.)

The second thing I want to say is that although the science is important, there are, sadly, numerous aspects of design that the science doesn't address at all. And that's where practical experience comes in. If you do have a lot of personal experience in the design field, well, good for you—you'll have learned (possibly the hard way!) what works and what doesn't. But if you don't have much experience of your own to fall back on (and maybe even if you do), then you'll need sound advice you can follow, advice from someone who does have such experience. A good book on design, by a suitably qualified professional, can help meet that need. A word of caution, though: Books on database technology (as opposed to books on design specifically) might *not* be what you need here. Such books do often describe design concepts but fail to give much guidance on how to apply those concepts to the practical task of design. *Caveat lector.*

Let me now elaborate as I promised on those terms *table predicate, business rule,* and *uncontrolled redundancy.* First, the table predicate for a given table is simply a reasonably precise, but informal, statement in natural language of what the table in question means—in other words, how that table is meant to be understood by users. For example, suppose we have a table called EMP ("employees"), with columns called ENO, ENAME, DNO, and SALARY. Then the predicate for that table might look something like this:

> *The person with employee number ENO is an employee of the company, is named ENAME, works in the department with department number DNO, and is paid salary SALARY.*

ENO, ENAME, DNO, and SALARY are the *parameters* to this predicate, and of course they correspond to the columns of the table.

Second, a business rule is also a reasonably precise but informal natural language statement, one that captures some aspect of how the data in the database is supposed to be constrained. (Actually, some writers regard table predicates as a special case of business rules; however, there's more to business rules in general than just the table predicates as such.) To start with, there'll certainly be rules that specify what type of information is denoted by the parameters to those table predicates; in the case of employees, for example, there'll be a rule to the effect that the SALARY parameter ("salaries") denotes money values, expressed in, let's say, euros or U.S. dollars. Then there'll be rules that constrain the values those parameters can take for a given employee considered in isolation (for example, a rule that says salaries mustn't be negative and must be less than some specified upper limit). There'll also be rules that constrain the set of employees taken as a whole, independent of other "entities," such as departments, that might be represented in the same database (for example, a rule to the effect that employee numbers must be unique). Finally, there'll be rules that constrain employees considered in combination with such other entities (for example, a rule to the effect that every employee must be assigned to some known department, or a rule to the effect that no employee can earn more than the manager of the department the employee in question is assigned to).

I'd like to say a bit more about this issue of business rules, because it's important—also because in practice it does tend to get somewhat overlooked. As the foregoing discussion should be sufficient to suggest, business rules can be quite complex (as complex as you like, in fact). As I've already said, however, they're necessarily somewhat informal. Their formal counterpart—i.e., the thing they map to in the logical design—is *integrity constraints* (constraints for short), which thus need to be stated in some formal language and enforced by the DBMS. In other words, I depart here from certain other writers in stating categorically that database design isn't just about choosing data structures—integrity constraints are crucial as well. (Of course, it's true that other writers do talk about key and foreign key constraints—sometimes cardinality constraints too—but those particular constraints are really nothing but important special cases of a much more general phenomenon.) In this connection, I'd like to draw your attention to some remarks (somewhat paraphrased here) from *The Business Rule Book* by Ron Ross (2nd edition, Business Rule Solutions Inc., 1997):

> Even though business rules (like the data itself) are "shared" and universal, traditionally they haven't been captured in database design. Instead, they've usually been stated vaguely (if at all) in largely uncoordinated analytical and design documents, and then buried deep in the logic of application programs. Since application programs are notoriously unreliable in the consistent and correct application of such rules, this has been the source of considerable frustration and error.

I couldn't agree more. Moreover, note the implicit but strong criticism of DBMS products that fail to provide adequate support for integrity constraints! (Interestingly, the support provided in this area by the SQL standard is actually not too bad; but SQL products have been rather slow, to say the least, in implementing this aspect of the standard.)

Finally, what about that matter of uncontrolled redundancy? Well, we can say, loosely, that the database displays redundancy if and only if it "says the same thing twice." And we often say, again loosely, that we don't want the database to display redundancy in this sense. But it would be more accurate to say we don't want it to display any *uncontrolled* redundancy. Uncontrolled redundancy can be a problem, but controlled redundancy shouldn't be. Let me explain. First some more definitions:

- **Controlled redundancy**   Redundancy in the database is controlled if the user is aware of it, but it's guaranteed never to lead to any inconsistencies.

- **Uncontrolled redundancy**   Redundancy in the database is uncontrolled if it has the potential to lead to inconsistencies.

- **Inconsistency**   The database is inconsistent (at least from a formal point of view) if and only if there's some integrity constraint it's supposed to satisfy but doesn't.

So if controlled redundancy means no inconsistencies, it must also mean no constraints are violated. Of course, not all constraints have to do with redundancy as such; for example, a constraint to the effect that salaries mustn't be negative doesn't. Thus, if the database were to show some employee as having a negative salary, it would certainly be inconsistent, but that particular inconsistency wouldn't be one that arises from redundancy. (It would, however, mean the database was incorrect, in the sense that it didn't faithfully reflect the state of affairs in the real world. Inconsistent implies incorrect, though the converse is false—the database can be incorrect without being inconsistent. For example, if it showed some employee as earning a salary different from that employee's true salary, it would be incorrect but not inconsistent.)

To say it again, then, constraints don't always have to do with redundancy. But redundancy does always have to do with constraints. For example, suppose—very unrealistically!—that there's a constraint to the effect that all employees in the same department must earn the same salary. Suppose further that the database shows Heli and Chris as being in the same department. Then if it were also to show Heli and Chris as earning the same salary, it would be redundant; by contrast, if it were to show Heli and Chris as earning different salaries, it would be inconsistent (and incorrect).

So to say that the database involves some redundancy is to say some constraint is supposed to apply. The constraint in the case of the "same salary" example might be formulated in SQL as follows:[1]

```
CREATE ASSERTION EX1 CHECK
    ( ( SELECT COUNT ( DISTINCT DNO ) FROM EMP ) =
      ( SELECT COUNT ( * ) FROM
            ( SELECT DISTINCT DNO , SALARY FROM EMP ) ) ) ;
```

Stating this constraint explicitly serves to inform the user that the redundancy exists; enforcing it serves to ensure that it won't lead to any inconsistencies, thereby guaranteeing that the redundancy in question is controlled. Note, therefore, that we see once again, not incidentally, how important it is to be able to state integrity constraints formally and how important it is that the DBMS should be able to enforce them.

There's one more thing I want to say here. Some readers, I'm sure, will have found the foregoing remarks on consistency and redundancy a little puzzling, especially in view of the recent interest in what has come to be known as "eventual consistency." So let me amplify and try to clarify those remarks, if I can:

■ First of all, to repeat: To say that a database is consistent merely means, formally speaking, that the database conforms to all stated constraints. Now, it's crucially important that databases *always* be consistent in this formal sense; indeed, a database that's not consistent in this sense, at some particular time, is like a logical system that contains a contradiction. Well, actually, that's exactly what it is—a logical system with a contradiction. And in a logical system with a contradiction, you can prove *anything* (for example, you can prove that 1 = 0). What this means in database terms is that if there's ever a time at which the database is inconsistent in the foregoing formal sense, you can never trust the answers you get to queries—they may be false, they may be true, and you have no way in general of knowing which they are. In other words, all bets are off. That's why consistency in the formal sense is so crucial. (It's also why, contrary to popular opinion, integrity checking must always be immediate and why "deferred checking" is a logical error.)

■ But consistency in the formal sense isn't necessarily the same thing as consistency as conventionally understood (meaning consistency as understood outside the world of databases in particular). Suppose there are two items *A* and *B* in the database that, in the real world, we believe should

---

[1] As you can see, the constraint in question is defined by means of a CREATE ASSERTION statement in SQL. For some reason, SQL sometimes (but not always!) calls constraints assertions.

have the same value. They might, for example, both be the selling price for some given commodity, stored twice because replication is being used to improve availability. If A and B in fact have different values at some given time, we might certainly say, informally, that there's an inconsistency in the data as stored at that time. But that "inconsistency" is an inconsistency as far as the system is concerned *only if the system has been told that A and B are supposed to be equal*—i.e., only if "A = B" has been stated as a formal constraint. If it hasn't, then (a) the fact that A ≠ B at some time doesn't in itself constitute a consistency violation as far as the system is concerned, and (b) importantly, the system will never rely on an assumption that A and B are equal.

■   Thus, if all we want is for A and B to be equal "eventually"—i.e., if we're content for that requirement to be handled in the application layer—all we have to do as far as the database system is concerned is omit any declaration of "A = B" as a formal constraint. No problem, and in particular no violation of the relational model.

With that, I'll conclude these brief remarks on database design. I'd like to thank Heli for giving me the chance to air my opinions on this topic, and Hugh Darwen for taking the time to comment on what I had to say (his comments led to several improvements and clarifications). And, of course, I'd like to wish Heli and her book every success in her own chosen field.

—C. J. Date
Healdsburg, California
February 2015

My name is Tom Kyte. I'm the Tom behind the http://asktom.oracle.com/ web site and column in *Oracle Magazine*. I've been doing database work for many decades going back to 1987. One of the first things I was taught was the importance of a strong design—both a software design as well as a strong database design. In any data-based application (and what useful application is in fact not based on data?), the foundation of it all is the database schema.

It has been my experience over the past 30 years to see databases and their schemas outlive their applications. When I first joined Oracle Corporation in 1993, my user interface to the expense reports database was a tablet of paper (and expense report form) and a pen. I would fill that in and mail it, and someone would transcribe that information into the database using a character mode VT100 terminal. Later, my user interface changed—an Oracle form was developed and deployed to some 10,000 people in the sales teams. Client-server turned out to be a miserable mistake long term for many reasons, but right then and there we were using the character mode screens and a newly developed GUI against the same database. The schema designed was robust enough to support both.

Then along came three-tier applications. A PL/SQL interface was developed using an early version of the PL/SQL web toolkit. One database schema…three very different applications. And then came requests for business intelligence (BI) reporting on this database (BI was just starting to become a buzzword). Same database…new applications using it in a new way. Then Java came along, and new applications written in Java sprung up. Mobile devices became all the rage, which created yet another new set of applications.

This happened all on the same database—the same database that has been supporting expense reporting for longer than I've been doing databases. Without a good design, a solid foundation from the very first days, this would not have been possible. I've seen many applications and their databases "scrapped," thrown away to be rewritten because insufficient thought was given to their design. It was easier to start over than to try to fix them.

I've seen data models where it is really easy to get data in but excessively difficult to impossible to get it back out. The developers optimized everything for getting data into the database but never gave a thought to the questions people might want to ask of that data later.

A solid data model will give you a database that will outlive your application and will outlive the newest, coolest technologies and frameworks you are using today. The tools used to build that original expensive report database mentioned earlier are museum items now, but the database itself is still going strong and still being expanded.

It is worth the time to give your data some serious thought. I know the author of this book, Heli Helskyaho, not only agrees with that sentiment but espouses it herself, and she is considered an expert in the area. I'm sure you'll enjoy her discussions on the topic.

—Tom Kyte
http://asktom.oracle.com/

Acknowledgments

I want to thank my wonderful family for all the support, specifically, my husband, Marko, and my two amazing sons, Patrik and Matias. Without your support I could have not written this book.

And thank you to my parents, Marja-Leena and Kalevi Luukkainen, who have taught me that nothing is impossible and I can do whatever I want. Not even the sky is the limit.

A very special thank-you to Philip Stoyanov and C. J. Date for all your valuable advice and support! And of course thank you to the two best technical editors in the world: Jeff Smith and Kent Graziano. I want to thank professor emeritus Seppo Sippu from University of Helsinki for teaching me so much about database design and relational theory, and for giving me the spark for databases. Thank you to my friends who were kind enough to write their opinions on database design at the beginning of this book: C. J. Date, Thomas Kyte, Steven Feuerstein, Tim Hall, Dan Linstedt, Debra Lilley, and Graham Wood. And to all my friends who have been supporting me and telling me I can do it: Thank you!

Thank you also to Paul Carlstroem, Amanda Russell, Bettina Faltermeier, and the production team at McGraw-Hill Education who made this book possible, gave me the idea to write it, and supported me all the way. Thank you to Kritika Kaushik and the team at Cenveo Publisher Services for all the help and advice.

Introduction

Designing databases is vital for any company that is serious about its data, our most valuable asset. To support efficient database design work, a designer must have a tool to be able to document the data and data usage in a formal way. This book helps people design their databases better and shows how to use a tool called Oracle SQL Developer Data Modeler in that job.

Database design consists of analyzing requirements and creating the conceptual, logical, and physical designs. This process is iterative and incremental, and all these phases will be done over and over again to get the correct and optimal design for the purpose. Database design is a process of producing detailed entity-relationship (ER) diagrams and data flow diagrams (DFDs), and it ends up producing the scripts (DDLs) for creating all the objects needed for the database. In this book, I go through the entire process of database design using Oracle SQL Developer Data Modeler.

Chapter 1: Introducing Database Design and Oracle SQL Developer Data Modeler

In this chapter, you'll learn the basics of database design and Data Modeler, and you will get some ideas on designing databases in an agile system development process.

Chapter 2: Getting Started with Oracle SQL Developer Data Modeler

In this chapter, you'll explore how to get started with Data Modeler and how to set it up to meet your needs.

Chapter 3: Introducing Requirements Analysis

Requirements analysis is the process of finding and analyzing the requirements of the future users of the application and the database. The results of this process are the specifications of user requirements. In this chapter, you will see how to do these tasks with Data Modeler.

Chapter 4: Introducing Conceptual Database Design (Logical Model)

Conceptual database design consists of translating the requirements into a formal conceptual data model and process models. The result of conceptual database design is a conceptual schema and process models. In this chapter, you will see how to create a logical model with Data Modeler.

Chapter 5: Introducing Logical Database Design (Relational Model)

The logical database design process consists mainly of transforming the conceptual model (logical model) into a relational model. The result of this phase of database design is a relational database schema, a set of relational schemas, and their constraints. In this chapter, you will see how to create a relational model with Data Modeler.

Chapter 6: Introducing Physical Database Design

The physical database design is the phase in which you decide the technology and version of your database. Data Modeler supports different versions of Oracle, Microsoft SQL Server, and IBM DB2 databases. In physical database design you design physical database elements related to the selected technology and add physical properties to elements from the relational model. In this chapter, you will learn how to create the physical design with Data Modeler.

Chapter 7: Generating DDL Scripts for Creating Database Objects

A data definition language (DDL) is for creating database objects. Generating DDL scripts with Data Modeler is quite simple, and it can be done over and over again to find the right settings to get the right kinds of scripts. The DDLs are based on the relational model and one of its physical models. In this chapter, you will learn how to generate DDLs with Data Modeler.

Chapter 8: Designing a Data Warehouse Database

In this chapter, you will briefly see the most common methods of data warehouse design: star schema, snowflake, and Data Vault. You will also learn how to design a data warehouse database using Data Modeler.

Chapter 9: Using Version Control and Working in a Multiuser Environment (Subversion)

Subversion can be used for both version control and to enable a multiuser environment when working with Data Modeler. In this chapter, you will learn how version control (Subversion) works with Data Modeler, including how to add designs to version control and how to work with them. You will also explore how to solve possible conflicts. In this chapter, you will also learn how Microsoft Excel can be used to enable a multiuser environment.

Chapter 10: Documenting an Existing Database

It is important to have documentation for your databases. If you do not understand your data, you cannot keep it up to date, secure, of good quality, and so on. In addition, changing the data structures based on the current requirements is impossible if you do not understand what you are changing. Documentation is also vital when solving problems related to data such as performance. With Data Modeler you can document an existing database by reverse engineering the database from the data dictionary or from existing DDLs, you can use the documentation you might have from a third-party modeling tool and import that to Data Modeler, or you can combine these methods. In this chapter, you will learn about all these options.

Chapter 11: Generating Reports and Using Search

Reporting functionality is a must when selecting a tool for database design. If you are not able to produce reports from the tool, the tool is not worth using. There are so many different needs for reporting: auditing, quality reviews, documenting, talking with end users, informing internally, and so on. Data Modeler has strong reporting functionalities, and in this chapter you will learn more about them.

Chapter 12: Comparing Designs and the Database

There are many situations when you need to compare either two designs with each other or the design with the database. In this chapter, you will learn how to do comparisons with Data Modeler and how to change either a design or a database based on the result.

CHAPTER
1

Introducing Database Design and Oracle SQL Developer Data Modeler

Database design is the process of producing detailed entity-relationship (ER) diagrams and data flow diagrams (DFDs) in order to produce the data definition language (DDL) scripts that will create the objects needed for the database. Database design consists of requirements analysis, conceptual design, logical design, physical design, and, depending on who you ask, transaction design. (This book will not discuss transaction design.) The process is incremental and iterative, meaning all these phases will be done repeatedly. The backbones of database design are logic theory and relational theory.

Database design is all about the data, namely, how to save the data and how to retrieve it. Data integrity and data quality should always be high priorities when designing a database, and you must consider future needs as well. Even though an application user interface might change every five to ten years, the database behind it must continue to perform well for years to come.

The process of database design is changing as application development processes are getting more agile and iterative. Management demands fast results, so IT projects must be completed faster than ever before. Database designers often do not have time to analyze everything well before starting to design, and sometimes systems are launched into production to be completed later in increments, without having the analysis completed. In fact, sometimes databases are created with no time spent on design and with no thought to the principles of relational theory. Even with the world seemingly getting faster every day, when designing a database, you need to know the full picture of what the database is for. That is what makes database design difficult. The only way to survive is to use a tool that meets all of today's needs, helping you create databases quickly but with the "big picture" in mind. Without a tool, you cannot be as agile as needed.

Though I've mentioned application development processes, I want to be clear that database design is not the same as application design. The database should not be designed as a side product of an application design. When trying to save time and money, people think they will design only either the ER model or the Unified Modeling Language (UML) model and then generate the other. Although it is good they realize they need two models (one for the database and the other for the application), it is not just a question of which notation to choose; the perspectives are very different and so are the goals. For example, let's look at code tables versus code files. For the application designer, it might be easier to have all the lookup information in files, but the database designer definitely will want them in tables. Why? The database person is also in charge of the data integrity, which cannot be controlled if some of the important data is in files somewhere out of the reach of the database.

I often hear people arguing about which is better, ER or UML. To me this question is irrelevant. ER diagrams are for designing databases, and UML is for designing user interfaces. If you try to design a database with UML, you can get easily distracted and want to start designing the user interface. My recommendation is that while the database designer designs the database, the application designer designs the application in cooperation with the database designer. And before the database designer moves to the logical design, the database designer and the application designer should sit down and compare their models to be sure that they really have all the requirements implemented in both the designs. There might be information in the UML model that the ER model does not have or should not have. For instance, in the UML model, there might be an attribute named AGE, but in the data model (ER), there might be an attribute called DATE OF BIRTH. There can also be some technical attributes in the data model that do not need to be in the UML model. For instance, every table might have the columns Creator, Created_Date, Modifier, and Modified_Date. The two models (UML and ER) do not have to be the same and actually rarely are, but creating and maintaining both models will guarantee a better result. But this is true only if you have a tool for both purposes; if this work is done without a tool, the dual processes take too much time and money. You want to use a tool to create designs in cooperation and take advantage of everybody's special skills and knowledge.

NOTE
The UML model and the ER model do not need to be the same and rarely are.

The importance of database design increases on agile projects. In that case, the process involves not just designing but also finding the right questions to ask and having pictures (ER models and DFDs) to use when talking to end users. You need as much information as possible from end users and business owners. You need to understand the big picture, lest you get a database totally different than you wanted. It's as simple as thinking before doing.

It's important that you understand the main concepts (*entities*) of the database and their relationships correctly because it is easy to add entities and attributes later, but it is not easy to divide them later or correct the relationships modeled wrongly. Always design the database for the right purpose and model only what is needed, starting with the most difficult task.

In Figure 1-1, you can see my version of agile database design. It starts with requirements analysis and finding the main concepts and their relationships. Next you try to model the whole conceptual model as well as you can. Then you design the conceptual model for iteration *n*, making it as detailed as possible; continue to the logical design of iteration *n*; and finally move to physical design and creating the database objects with the DDL scripts. Then you perform the whole round again for iteration *n*+1, and so on. The process is the same as it is in other projects; the only difference in an agile project is that you move from phase to phase faster, and you design in pieces, rather than as a whole.

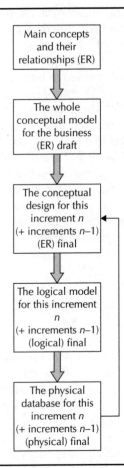

FIGURE 1-1. *Agile database design process*

If a database will hold valuable data, the database must be designed by someone who understands how the database works and knows how the data should be modeled. When designing the database, you may need all different types of subject-matter experts to give you the information you need to make decisions about the design. Additionally, if your deadline is tight, you need even more information to be sure you are making the right decisions; you don't want to have to change everything later. Prioritization is important for everybody (even the end users). Nothing is more stressful than too much work with too little time to do it. Database design means teamwork, and that's why you need a tool to do database design right in today's environment.

When selecting the tool for database design, you'll want one that supports these features: ER notation, an automatic transformation process from the conceptual design to the logical design, the ability to work in a multiuser environment, version control, reporting capabilities, scripts for generating the database objects automatically (preferably adjustable), and strong documentation tools. It would be a bonus if the tool also has support for the standardization of naming, processes, and design rules; the ability to alter scripts for changing the database to be like the design; and the ability to compare designs to each other and to compare a design to a database.

What Is Oracle SQL Developer Data Modeler?

Oracle SQL Developer Data Modeler (referred to as Data Modeler in this book) is a free tool for designing and documenting databases and data architecture. It supports not only Oracle databases but also DB2 and Microsoft SQL Server databases and, at a certain level, any standards-based database that has a Java Database Connectivity (JDBC) connector. Data Modeler supports all the steps in database design and includes easy forward and backward engineering. After you have designed your database and have a physical model for it, you can export the scripts to create the database objects. Data Modeler also supports different kinds of compares and multidimensional models. Data Modeler helps you keep your databases documented and enables you to be agile. The tool is available as a stand-alone product, but it is also integrated into Oracle SQL Developer, so you can decide which way is the best for you to use the tool. Installing the tool is simple, and support is provided by Oracle if you have a database support contract.

Data Modeler offers the following features for database designers:

- **Database design tools**   A collection of metadata about a database is called a *design* in Data Modeler. A design consists of the logical models, multidimensional models, relational models, domains, data type models, process models, business information, and change requests, as well as all the objects those models need. Every object (entity, table, diagram, and so on) is a single Extensible Markup Language (XML) file in a hierarchy that the tool creates automatically. The design itself is saved with the extension .dmd, and the .dmd file contains pointers to individual XML files.

- **Customization**   You can tweak Data Modeler to your liking. In Preferences, you can, for instance, define where to keep your working copy of designs.

- **Version control**   Data Modeler is integrated into a version control tool called Subversion. This integration allows you to have multiple users changing the model at the same time. It also gives you version control functionalities. When working with version control, the latest official version of your design is always on version control, and the one you are working with is in your local saved working copy directory.

■ **Documenting existing databases** You can import designs to Data Modeler from existing databases, from other designing tools (for example, Oracle Designer or ERwin), or from DDL scripts.

■ **Reporting capabilities** Data Modeler has built-in reporting functionalities, but you can also create your own reports and templates and use the Search functionality as a base for a report. It is also possible to use a reporting repository if you want to have reports across all your designs and use SQL to query that information. You can also print the design layouts.

■ **Documentation tools, improving quality and efficency** Data Modeler helps you standardize the design and data documentation in your company. You can use naming standards, domains, glossaries, and design rules to achieve better quality in your database design. You can also compare models and designs to each other, and you can compare a design to a database. Different compares, transformations, and notations will give you a more cost-efficient working environment with better quality.

Designing Databases with Oracle SQL Developer Data Modeler

The database design process when using Data Modeler starts with designing a logical model. In the logical model, you define entities, attributes, and relationships. The next step is to create a relational model based on the logical model. You do this simply by clicking the Engineer To Relational Model icon. When you are done with the relational model, it is time to create the physical model. You do this simply by right-clicking Physical Model in the Browser pane and selecting New. When creating a physical model, you must know what product you will use for your database (Oracle, SQL Server, or DB2) as well as its version. All the properties for the physical model depend on the chosen technology. After you have created a physical model, you should define the properties for the physical objects. After you've done that, you are ready to generate the DDLs (which are the SQL scripts for creating your database objects). You can create DDLs by selecting File | Export | DDL File. Then just run these DDLs on your database to create the objects. And all this can be done in a multiuser environment and while using version control.

You can also use Data Modeler to document existing databases (Oracle, SQL Server, DB2). You can reverse engineer the documentation from a data dictionary or existing DDLs, or you can import it from another design tool (Oracle Designer, ERwin, or a VAR file). Or, you can combine all these techniques, for example, by bringing some of the descriptions from another design tool and adding it to the physical information from the data dictionary. You can find these features by selecting File | Import.

Since an important part of database design is reporting, you might want to use Data Modeler to create your own templates and create reports based on those templates. You can also create a reporting repository; in addition to the templates, you can use SQL to query the information from there. You can also print the diagrams or use the powerful search functionality to search the information in the report.

It is also important to be able to document all the information related to the database in just one place. In Data Modeler you can document all the information needed for the database design as well as change requests, business information, and much more.

Summary

Going through the database design process is vital if you are storing important data in your database. Database design is the process of producing detailed entity-relationship diagrams and data flow diagrams to produce the DDL scripts for creating the objects for the database. Database design consists of requirements analysis, conceptual design, logical design, physical design, and, depending on who you ask, transaction design. To be able to design a database, especially in an agile system, you need Oracle SQL Developer Data Modeler. It is a free tool that supports all the needs of database designers plus some extra.

CHAPTER
2

Getting Started with
Oracle SQL Developer
Data Modeler

This chapter will cover what you need to know about Oracle SQL Developer Data Modeler before you start using it. Agreeing on and implementing certain guidelines with your team before you start working with the tool will help you streamline your work. Specifically, before starting to use Data Modeler in production or in a multiuser environment, it is valuable to decide on some standardization issues, tweak some settings in the tool, and tune the tool particularly for your needs. In many cases, it is good to start with a small project when first implementing Data Modeler into your workflow, not because it is a difficult tool to use but because there are so many decisions to make in order to use it to its full potential.

A simple way to standardize your team's workflow and to improve the quality of your database design is to use domains, glossaries, and design rules. A *domain* defines the possible values for an attribute. Creating domains is easy, but deciding what they might encompass is more difficult. A *glossary* is a pre-accepted set of terms, in other words, a vocabulary that can be used in a design. Creating a glossary will probably be even more challenging than creating a domain because agreeing on what to call certain concepts is usually difficult. *Design rules* are a predefined set of rules for the quality of design. Creating domains and glossaries for all the designers to share is worth it, and implementing domains and glossaries will increase your team's productivity and improve the quality of all your designs. In addition, using the design rules before moving to the next phase in the design process will improve the quality of the final database.

Here are some other questions to consider: Which reports do you want to use? Where will you save them? What kind of data definition language (DDL) files will you have, and where will you save them? How will you use version control, if at all? What kind of relational database management system (RDBMS) will you use? I will touch on these topics throughout this book.

Downloading and Exploring the Tool

You can download Data Modeler from the Oracle Technical Network (OTN) at www.oracle.com/technetwork/developer-tools/datamodeler/overview/index.html. After downloading the .zip file, unzip it to start using Data Modeler.

There are different versions of Data Modeler depending on your operating system and whether you want the version with or without the Java Runtime Environment (JRE). You can download the free, stand-alone product of Data Modeler or Oracle SQL Developer, which has Data Modeler integrated into it. You should agree on which version of the product will be used in your organization to avoid conflicts with different versions, especially if you are using version control in a multiuser environment.

What Is a Design?

In Data Modeler the collection of objects you create is called a *design*. A design consists of one Extensible Markup Language (XML) file with the extension .dmd (for example, Customer.dmd), a directory (for example, Customer), and subdirectories and XML files. Each element (for instance, a diagram, a table, or an entity) in a design has its own XML file and its own unique identifier (object ID). The .dmd file contains pointers to information in all these subdirectories and files. Data Modeler creates all the needed directories and subdirectories automatically when you create a design. You should not edit these XML files outside the tool unless you really know what you are doing because you risk breaking the files. Common reasons for an XML file to break is using an editor that does not support XML or using the wrong character set. If you break one of these files, Data Modeler will not be able to read it.

TIP
If you want to give the design to another Data Modeler user, just compress the .dmd file and the directories in one .zip file and pass that to the other person.

A design consists of one *logical model*, optionally one or more *relational models* that are based on that logical model, and optionally one or more *physical* models that are based on one relational model. There can also be multidimensional models, data type models, process models, domains, business information, and so on.

You need to decide at least two things before starting to use Data Modeler in production: what a design will consist of in your organization and how will you name it. A design can consist of all the databases in your organization, one database instance, one schema, or something totally different. You'll want to define what a design is so you know how you want to deal with objects that might be shared between applications, schemas, or databases. If you want to share objects, they should be in the same design since Data Modeler does not fully support sharing objects between different designs. Also, it is valuable to decide who will use Data Modeler and what they will do with it. This decision might help you to understand what a design means in your organization and to give the right privileges to the right people in your organization. In addition, you should create a naming standard for your designs. For example, you could call a design Customer or CUSTOMER or CustomerDB or CustomerData. Which one will you use? It is much more efficient if designs are named consistently and you know where to find them.

Exploring the Interface

In Data Modeler, the Browser pane shows all the elements in a design (see Figure 2-1). There are also menus for different kinds of operations: File, Edit, View, Team, Tools, and Help. Data Modeler does not save automatically, so remember to save frequently by choosing File | Save or by choosing File | Save As. Use Save As if you want to save the design in a different location or with a different name. In the File menu you'll see the option Recent Designs. This is the list of designs you have been working with; the one on the top is the one you opened last. If you want to save time when opening a design and you know it is the same design you were last working with, instead of using File | Open to browse to the file to open the design, choose File | Recent Designs. You can choose File | Close to close one design and choose File | Close All to close all the designs that are open. When using either of these, Data Modeler remains open. If you choose File | Exit, all the designs as well as Data Modeler will close.

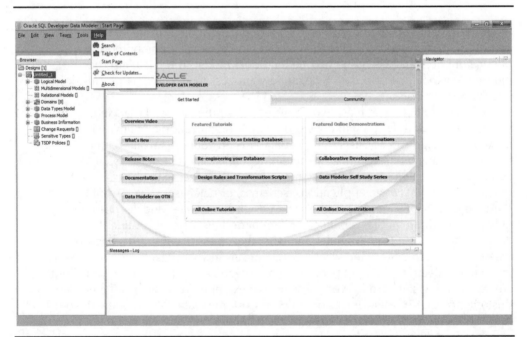

FIGURE 2-1. *Browser pane in Data Modeler*

TIP
Choose File | Exit to quit Data Modeler and close all
the designs that are open. Data Modeler will ask you
to save them all. If you click the Close (X) button in
the upper-right corner of the window, you'll be asked
if only one of the designs should be saved.

In the Browser pane you can select an entity or a table, right-click, and select Go To Diagram. You will see all the diagrams, subviews, and displays where this object is located and can select the one you want. The diagram/subview/display will open, and the object will be selected in the canvas.

If you right-click the canvas, you will see a few options. You can add to or remove objects from this diagram/subview/display by choosing Add/Remove Objects and selecting or deselecting the Include property. With View Details, you can adjust what object details will be shown in the diagram and what will not be shown. And with Show, you can add a grid, a page grid, labels, and legends to the diagram. Grids will help you align the objects and can make the diagram easier to read. The page grid shows where a page ends and another page starts. Labels are, for instance, foreign key names or source and target names in relationships. The legend shows audit information, including the name of the diagram, author, created time, modifier, modified time, design name, and type of model (logical or relational, for example).

If the Browser pane (or any other pane) disappears, you can restore it from the View menu. If you need to view the logs in order to troubleshoot something or to know what the tool is doing, choose View | Log or choose View | External Log depending on which one you need.

The best way to learn how to use the tool is to view the start page (shown earlier in Figure 2-1). On the start page, you will find links to documentation, forums, tutorials, and online demonstrations. If the start page for some reason disappears, you can get it back by choosing Help | Start Page. In fact, you can get help in any screen by pressing F1, and you can use the search and table of contents to find more information about the tool. From Help | About, you can check which version and build of Data Modeler you are using. You can also see what components, properties, and extensions are included.

You can use the Navigator pane (on the right of Figure 2-1) to go to an exact point of the diagram or to see the whole picture of it. The Navigator pane is useful especially if you have a big diagram or you cannot find the object wanted by just looking at the canvas. In Navigator, you can drag a red rectangle around the picture. Then when you move your cursor, the diagram in the logical or relational model moves accordingly. There are also diagrams with toolbars and icons for designing. By right-clicking an object, you can see the operations allowed on that object. Every object has properties, and they can be accessed either by right-clicking the object and selecting Properties or by double-clicking the object.

There is also a Messages – Log pane (on the bottom of Figure 2-1) that shows messages about what is happening in Data Modeler. Messages in red might need your attention; anything else is just for your information.

For version control, there is a Versions pane that serves as a Subversion directory and a Pending Changes pane so you can follow the incoming and outgoing changes.

Customizing the Interface

You can customize the Data Modeler user interface depending on how you like to work. You can decide which tools will be shown in the screen, you can resize them, and you can move the different panes to different places to serve you better. Just drag any panel to move it to the place you want it. You will see a red rectangle following the pane. When the position and shape is what you want, release the mouse button to drop it. The possibilities are endless, so find a combination that works the best for you. In Figure 2-2, you can see the way I prefer Data Modeler to be set up to be able to work efficiently.

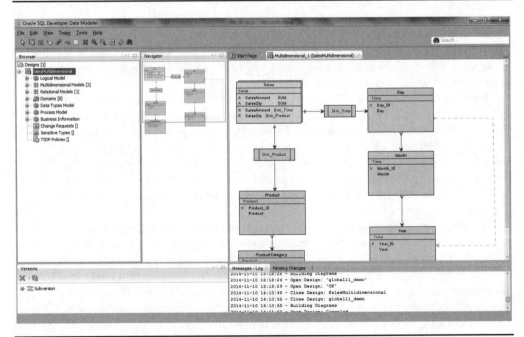

FIGURE 2-2. *My preferred layout for Data Modeler*

Tuning Oracle SQL Developer Data Modeler

Before starting to use Data Modeler in production or in a multiuser environment, it is important to set up the tool in the best way to serve your organization's needs. You could leave all the preferences at their defaults, but in time you'll find that you work in a certain way and the settings should reflect that. In the beginning, you should define at least some preferences and design-level properties and maybe create some glossaries and domains. You should also decide where those settings will be kept (preferably in version control) and how they will be shared with other users.

The tool also has design rules to help you maintain the quality of your designs. There are predefined design rules, but you can create as many of your own as needed. Having all this done will increase your productivity and the quality of your work.

Setting Preferences

Preferences are settings that affect Data Modeler behavior on an installation level, and you can share these preferences with other Data Modeler installations. Some preferences take effect immediately, but other preferences require you to close the design and reopen it for them to take effect. This is because either the preference setting is in cache memory or it has been copied to another property somewhere else in a design by Data Modeler. Since the new preference will affect only the elements created after the change, it is important to set your preferences before starting to use Data Modeler. To be sure that a change is really taking effect in the design that is open, you can close and reopen the design after changing a preference. Sometimes it is better to even close Data Modeler and reopen it.

In every new version of Data Modeler there are new preferences for the users to tune the tool to fit their needs better. See Help on Data Modeler for more specific descriptions of a certain preference. This chapter will cover the most important preferences for a user when starting to use the tool. Other chapters will cover the preferences that affect that particular phase of database design.

You can find the preferences by choosing Tools | Preferences, as shown in Figure 2-3. These preferences have an effect on only your installation of Data Modeler unless you share them with other users, as explained later in this chapter.

Preferences for Starting to Use Oracle SQL Developer Data Modeler

This section will cover the preferences that will make the tool behave the way you want, and it will explain how to share those preferences with other users after implementing them. You can change all the preferences while working on a project,

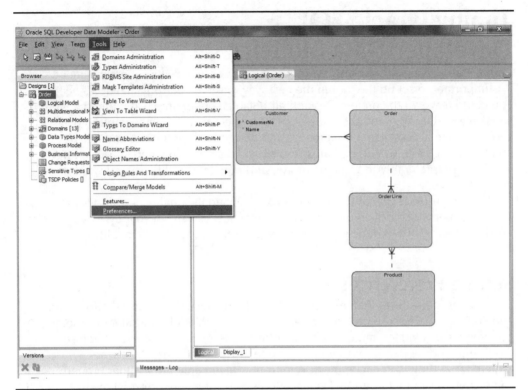

FIGURE 2-3. *Tools | Preferences*

but it is always more difficult to change settings later because it will affect all the users and possibly also the way the tool behaves.

Figure 2-4 shows the Preferences dialog, which opens after you choose Tools | Preferences, with Data Modeler selected on the left. Defining the default directories for Data Modeler to use is valuable. It is easier for you to find your files if you know exactly where they are located. You should define the directories on the Data Modeler tab as the same for all your users because it will make your life much easier, especially with version control and problem solving.

- Default Designs Directory is the directory where you will find your designs by default, and if you export or import a Data Modeler design, it will be saved here by default.

- Default Import Directory is the default directory for preferences and design-level property imports, among others.

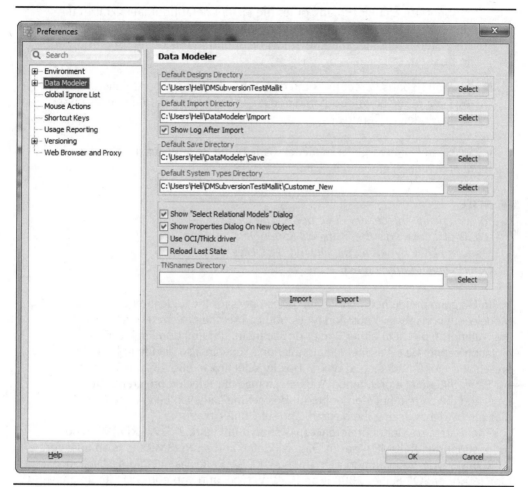

FIGURE 2-4.   *Data Modeler Preferences dialog*

■   Default Save Directory is the directory where you will save files by
     default. For example, Data Modeler will try to find exported files here
     by default.

■   Default System Types Directory is the directory where all the Data
     Modeler system files are stored by default. Typically these files are
     type definition files, default domain files, glossary files, RDBMS sites,
     customized scripts, and saved search criteria. These files affect your
     installation of Data Modeler only. Note that for domains, Data Modeler

will not use changes in any other file except defaultdomains.xml in the directory set in the Default System Types Directory preference. If changes are made in another file, they must be added to this default file in order to be used.

■ Default Reports Directory is the directory where the reports generated by Data Modeler will be stored and it can be defined in Preferences under Data Modeler | Reports.

If you expand Data Modeler in the left pane of the Preferences dialog, you will see more preferences, grouped by category.

NOTE
You can define the default directory for the DDL scripts that create database objects under Data Modeler | DDL by setting the Default DDL Files Export Directory preference.

In Diagram preferences, you'll find preferences for the logical model. Data Modeler supports several notation types. You can set the preferred notation type in the Notation Type list to either Barker or Bachman. (Information Engineering Notation cannot be set as the default notation.) You can also decide to have the presentation for inheritance as box-in-box by selecting the Box-in-Box Presentation For Entity Inheritance preference. You can change the selected preference at any time, and the current notation or box-in-box setting can even be changed for a diagram by right-clicking the diagram and selecting Notation.

There are also Model preferences, as shown in Figure 2-5. An RDBMS type is a list of supported RDBMS types in Data Modeler, and an RDBMS site is an alias for an RDBMS type. You can add as many new RDBMS sites as needed. For instance, Oracle 12c or SQL Server 2008 is an RDBMS type, and you could create an alias called TEST12c to define the RDBMS site that would be Oracle 12c in your test environment. The Default RDBMS Type preference is used for selecting the default RDBMS, and the Default RDBMS Site preference is selected by default as the RDBMS site when creating a physical model. (Chapter 6 will go into more detail about RDBMS types and sites.) The Datatype options are for defining the default for the tool to suggest as a data type for attributes (and columns). For instance, if you select Domain, domains will be suggested by default as the data type when creating a new attribute. Preferred Logical Types is a useful functionality. There are so many different logical types on the tool, and you probably need fewer than ten of them. If you define your own set of preferred logical types, it will be a shorter

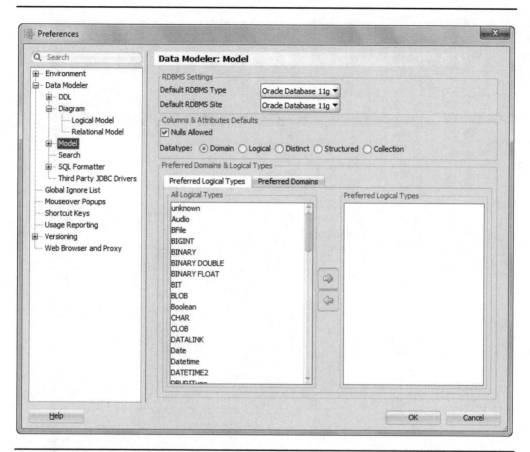

FIGURE 2-5. *Model preferences*

list for you to select from when creating a new attribute. You can add new logical types to the list at any time. You add logical types to your list by selecting the preferred logical type and clicking the arrow pointing to the right. You will see the list of selected logical types on the right side of the dialog (Preferred Logical Types).

You can also define shortcut keys to make using the tool more fluent. Figure 2-6 shows Shortcut Keys preferences. You can use the ones listed or define your own shortcut keys.

FIGURE 2-6. *Shortcut Keys preferences*

Sharing Preferences with Other Users

You can share your Data Modeler preferences with other users using the Export/
Import buttons at the bottom of the Preferences dialog when Data Modeler is
selected. To export the preferences, click the Export button. You will be asked for
the name and the location to save the XML file, and it will be saved accordingly.
This XML file can be imported to another computer with the Import button. You
need to define the settings only once, and then you can import them to other
computers in your organization. Make sure to export/import the new preferences

to all users every time you change the official preferences in your working environment.

TIP
If you realize you have failed with the import (such as importing the wrong file), do not click OK; click Cancel. The import is complete only when OK has been clicked.

Shortcut key definitions are not included in Data Modeler's exported preferences file. If you want to share the shortcut keys with other users, use the export/import functionalities from the icons, as shown in Figure 2-6.

TIP
You should save the exported file to version control like any other important file. You will learn more about version control in Chapter 9.

Introducing Design Properties

In addition to preferences that help you set up your Data Modeler working environment, there are also properties that affect only the particular design you set them for. This is a new behavior starting with Data Modeler version 4.0. Since version 4.0.3, either double-click the design name in the Browser pane or right-click and select Properties to open the Design Properties dialog. You can select the Use Global Design Level Settings option under Settings. If Use Global Design Level Settings is selected, the design properties are modified automatically based on global design-level settings from the file datamodeler\datamodeler\types\dl_settings.xml. Also, when some of the properties are changed in a design that has Use Global Design Level Settings selected, the changes are saved both to the local file and to the global file. For instance, changes to classification types, default fonts and colors, default line widths and colors, naming standard rules, and compare mappings are implemented automatically in the Design Properties dialog.

Looking at Properties to Start With

As mentioned, you can find the design-level properties either by double-clicking the design name in the Browser pane or by right-clicking and selecting Properties. You can specify new classification types and decide the colors to be used for classification and object types, as shown in Figure 2-7 and Figure 2-8. Setting up standards for colors in the diagrams makes it easier for people to read them. In the Settings | Diagram | Logical Model pane, you can select either Domain Name or Used Logical Type to have those shown for domains in a diagram (Domains Presentation).

Naming standards make designing work easier and improve the quality of your designs. For instance, you can decide how names in logical models and relational models will be separated. In a logical model, separator can be space, title case (camelCase) or a specified character. For example, if you select a space as a separator, the customer name would be "Customer name." If you select title case, the customer name would be CustomerName. If you select a specific character, let's say an underscore (_), the customer name would be Customer_name. In a relational model, you can select only a character as a separator, such as an underscore. In this example, the customer name would be Customer_name. For a relational model, you can also select Abbreviated Only, which means that only abbreviated words can be used in the relational model (see Figure 2-9). You can also define a separator character for domains and add one or more glossaries for a naming standard. The naming standards can be verified against the selected glossary or glossaries. You can find more information about glossaries in the "Introducing Glossaries" section. You can add, modify, and remove naming standards for attributes, columns, domains, entities, and tables, and these standards will be checked when you apply design rules.

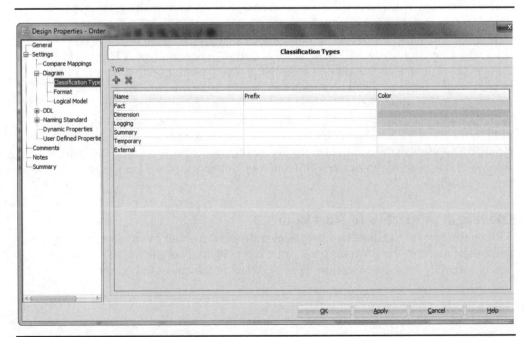

FIGURE 2-7. *Classification types*

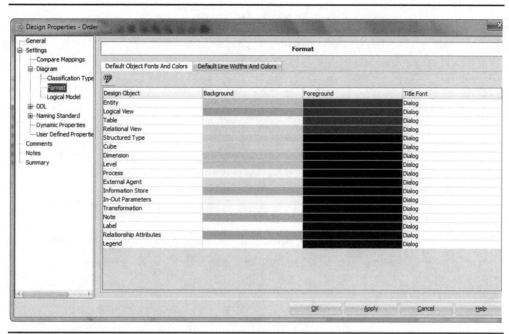

FIGURE 2-8.   *Defining formats for object types*

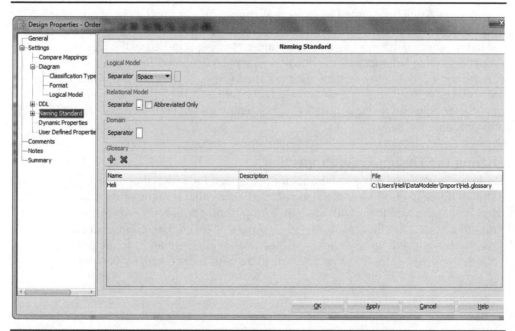

FIGURE 2-9.   *Naming Standard settings*

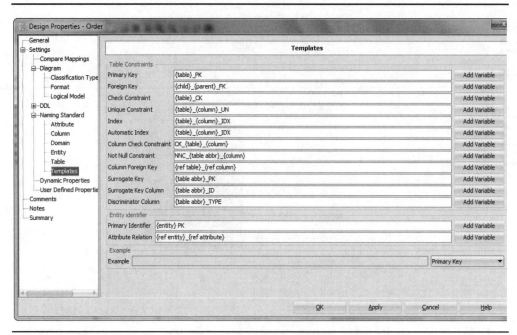

FIGURE 2-10. *Implementing naming standards by using templates*

Any violations will be reported as errors or warnings. You can find more information about design rules in the "Introducing Design Rules" section.

In my opinion, the most valuable tab under Naming Standard in the Design Properties dialog is Templates, as shown in Figure 2-10. On the Templates tab you can define how different elements such as primary keys, foreign keys, constraints, and indexes will be named. You can specify the format string for naming, and it can include variable and fixed parts of the name. Templates are used when generating elements automatically.

Sharing the Design-Level Properties

Design-level properties are valid only for the design for which they have been defined. If you want to have the same properties in other designs or used by other users, you can share them with the export/import functionality. From Design Properties, select Settings, as shown in Figure 2-11. By clicking Save, you can save the current settings. By clicking Export, you will create an XML file with your design-level properties that you can share with other users. By clicking

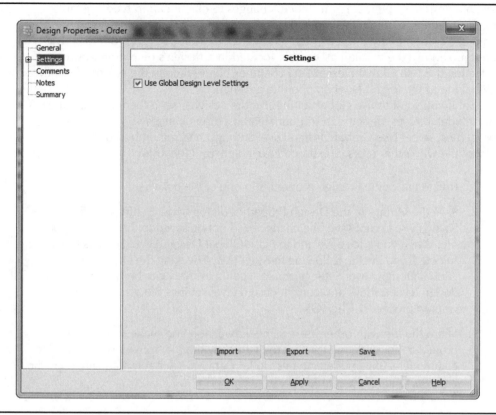

FIGURE 2-11. *Export/import functionality for design properties*

Import, you can import the properties you or somebody else has exported for
other users. The XML file, including the defined properties, should be kept in
version control and should be imported to every design whenever any of the
properties has changed.

The default directory for property exports is defined in Preferences under Data
Modeler with the Default Save Directory setting, and the default directory for property
imports is defined with the Default Import Directory setting.

Since version 4.0.3, you can also use global design-level settings. You can
select the Use Global Design Level Settings option for the current design in the
Design Properties dialog under Settings. If Use Global Design Level Settings is
selected, the design properties are modified automatically based on global
design-level settings from the file datamodeler\datamodeler\types\dl_settings.xml

when a design is opened. For instance, changes to classification types, default fonts and colors, default line widths and colors, naming standard rules, and compare mappings are implemented automatically in the design properties. The designs still use the dl_settings.xml file located in a design's own directory, but selecting the Use Global Design Level Settings box will copy the settings from the global file to the local file when opening a design.

So, if you want to use global settings for the designs, keep the file datamodeler\ datamodeler\types\dl_settings.xml updated based on changes you make to design properties, select Use Global Design Level Settings, and remember to share the global file with other users. The procedure in general is as follows:

1. Create the wanted design properties in one of the designs.

2. Save the settings in the Design Properties dialog under Settings by clicking Save. If you do not save, the changes will not be saved to the local or global file. When you click Save and the Use Global Design Level Settings box is selected, you get the following message: "By checking the checkbox 'Use Global Design Level Settings' you are going to overwrite both files – global design level settings and current design level settings file. Are you sure you want to proceed?" Click OK.

3. Share the file with other users using Subversion and make sure you have a procedure for updating the file. You can copy the file from version control to datamodeler\datamodeler\types\ to let Data Modeler automatically copy the changes to local design files.

NOTE
When you select the Use Global Design Level Settings option for one design, the default setting for all new designs is enabled as "Use Global Level Settings." Old designs are not changed automatically.

Introducing Glossaries

As mentioned, a glossary is a vocabulary of words to use in a design work. You can use them to guarantee defined design rules or to engineer between logical and relational models. You can create a new glossary from scratch, create one based on an existing logical model, or use an existing glossary. A glossary is an XML file with the extension .glossary.

Creating or Editing a Glossary

You can create and edit a glossary in the Glossary Editor (choose Tools | Glossary Editor), as shown in Figure 2-12. The default directory for saving glossaries is set in the Default Import Directory preference.

If you want to edit an existing glossary, open the Glossary Editor, select the glossary file, make your changes, and click Save. This file can be a .glossary file made with Data Modeler or a .csv or .txt file made with ERwin.

If you want to create a new glossary, start the Glossary Editor and define a filename that does not exist yet. Data Modeler will automatically create that file as a new glossary. Every glossary should have a name and a description. By selecting Incomplete Modifiers, you will allow modifiers and qualifiers to be named outside the glossary definitions, so those names do not need to be in the glossary. If you select Case Sensitive, all the validation is based on the fact that the name under validation must be written the same way as the word in the glossary. By selecting Unique Abbreviations, you will have control over the whole glossary in that all the abbreviations in the glossary will be unique. The same abbreviation cannot be used in several words, and there cannot be a word without an abbreviation. The name validation process will report these cases. With Separator and Sep. Char., you

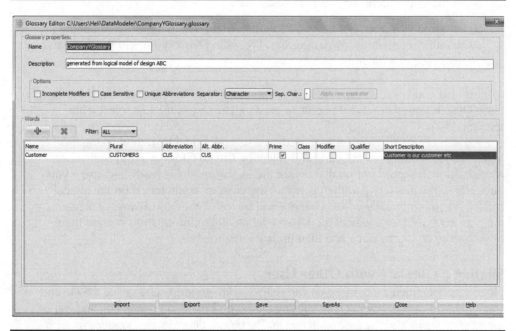

FIGURE 2-12. *Glossary Editor*

define the separator for terms that have multiple words. The separator settings are checked every time a glossary is loaded into the Glossary Editor, and a warning is given if you have any violations. Words in the list can be filtered with Filter, which restricts the display to entities by their classification: Prime Word, Class Word, Modifier, Qualifier, and Unclassified. Unclassified shows items that have no classification.

You can add new words to a glossary with the green plus button and remove them with the red X button. A name is the only mandatory element for a glossary word. A word can have a plural and an abbreviation. It can also have an alternative abbreviation (Alt. Abbr.). Classify the glossary entity as well as possible by choosing all classification types that apply to this word. Available classification types are as follows:

- A prime is the prime word for the object being defined; prime words are usually listed as keywords. Typically the word *Customer* in Customer Name is a prime word.

- Class words are usually words that identify the use or purpose of the word. *Name* in Customer Name would be an example of a class word.

- A modifier gives additional information about either the class word or the prime word. *Official* in Official Customer Name would be a modifier word. A modifier can be an adjective or a noun.

- A qualifier is a special case of a modifier that gives information about the qualification within domain values. *Weeks* in Delivery Time in Weeks is an example of a qualifier.

It is also good practice to write a description for a word, which can be done in Short Description. If you want to edit an existing glossary entry, just select it and then modify it.

You can create a new glossary based on a logical model by right-clicking the logical model in the Browser pane and selecting Create Glossary From Logical Model. But you should not do that before the logical model is ready because if you have edited the glossary and then generate the glossary again based on the logical model, all your manually edited changes will be lost. Either you always generate the glossary based on a logical model and define all the information needed there or you generate it only once and then update it manually.

Sharing a Glossary with Other Users

Once you've defined a glossary, you can share it with other users by saving the file and sharing it. You can also export it by clicking the Export button in Preferences, and you can import one by clicking the Import button. The default directory for glossary exports is the Default Save Directory preference covered earlier. The exported file is a .csv file.

Introducing Domains

As mentioned, domains are predefined data type definitions that include all the information needed for a certain kind of data such as address, money, or Social Security number. Domains and their definitions are saved in XML files.

TIP
Domains are useful for standardizing attribute and column properties and improving the design quality.

Creating a Domain

The domain definitions are Data Modeler installation-level settings. The location of a domain file is set in the Default System Types Directory preference, and Data Modeler names the file defaultdomains.xml. You can see the set of domains your installation of Data Modeler is using in the Browser pane under Domains.

You can administer domains by choosing Tools | Domains Administration; the Domains Administration dialog opens. You can select an existing file of domains by clicking the Select button and finding the file you wanted or you can create a new one by typing a filename that does not exist. If you do not select anything, the default file (defaultdomains.xml) will be used.

NOTE
Data Modeler will not use changes in any other file except defaultdomains.xml in the directory set in the Default System Types Directory preference.

To create a new domain, click Add in the Domains Administration dialog. Fill in the domain definitions (as shown in Figure 2-13) and click Apply. Then click Save. The changes will be saved in the file shown in the Domains File field in the Domains Administration dialog.

In Data Modeler you can also define other things for domains than just data types and lengths. You can define check constraints, ranges, lists of values, and rules for sensitive data. Figure 2-13 shows a domain called Boolean. You will want to use this domain whenever you have an attribute that has the values True/False. You can define those values by clicking Value List. If you want to make these changes to an existing domain definition, click Modify and then click Value List. To add new allowable values on the list, click Add. The List Of Values dialog opens, as shown in Figure 2-14. Fill in the value and the description. After you have added all the values needed, click OK.

Next you want to define a domain called Category so you can define a range for that domain. Select the domain called Category in the Domains Administration

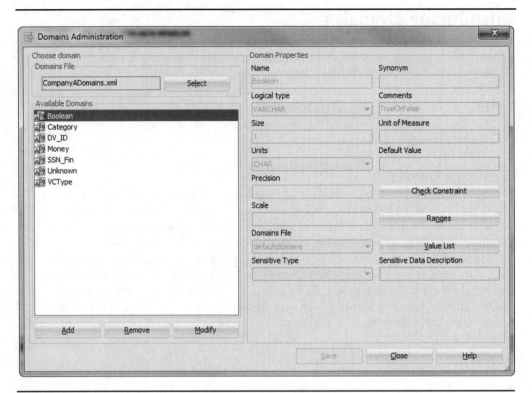

FIGURE 2-13.   *Domains Administration dialog*

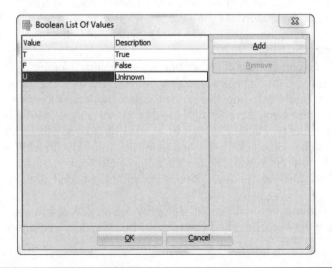

FIGURE 2-14.   *Defining a list of values*

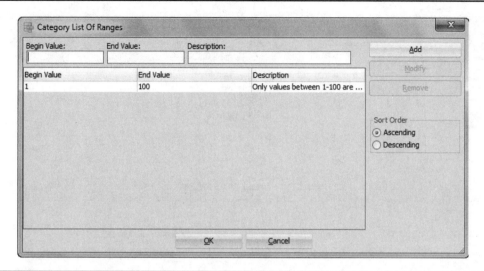

FIGURE 2-15. *Defining a list of ranges*

dialog and click Modify. Then click Ranges. In the Category List Of Ranges dialog, as shown in Figure 2-15, fill in the ranges needed and click Add. Then click OK. If you have many ranges in the list, you can sort them either ascending or descending using the radio buttons on the right.

Sharing Domains with Other Users

The only domain file Data Modeler uses is defaultdomains.xml located in the directory you set in the Default System Types Directory preference. There are two possibilities for sharing new domains to other users: You can make changes to the default file and share that with other users, or you can make changes to a separate file and share that with all users to be imported into their local default file. It is useful to have a separate file for your organization's standard set of domains to be sure everyone is using the latest version of the same file. That solution also allows users to define their own domains that will not be shared with other users.

If you decide to use the default domain file and share that, you can copy the file to all computers to the directory specified in Default System Types Directory, and all the users will have the domains available to be used in their designs.

If you decide to have a separate file for company-specific domains, you can share that file with users, but they must first import the settings to the local default file before the new domains can be used. Importing can be done with the Import functionality found in the File menu: Choose File | Import | Domains. Select Open Domain File, and select the file wanted. Select the box Import In Default Domains and click Import. If you do not check the box Import In Default Domains, you will

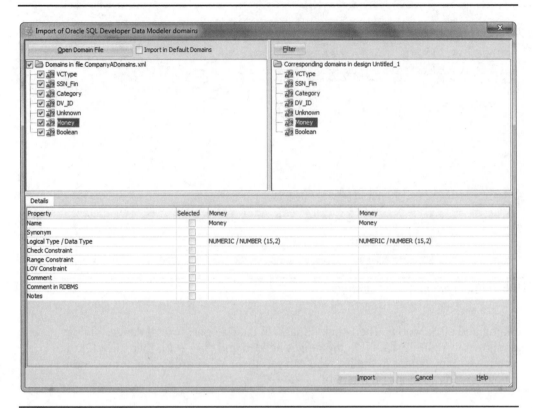

FIGURE 2-16. *Domain import*

have these domains for this one design, which is probably not what you want. See Figure 2-16 for more information on the domain import functionality.

TIP
You should save the shared domain file to version control. You will learn more about version control in Chapter 9.

Introducing Design Rules

As mentioned, design rules are an easy way of having standardized testing for the rules of database design. The testing is automatic, but you must start it manually whenever you think it is needed. There are preset design rules in the tool, and you can also create your own rules and sets of rules. Choose Tools | Design Rules and Transformations | Design Rules to open the Design Rules dialog.

Creating and Using Design Rules

There are many predefined design rules in Data Modeler, as you can see in Figure 2-17. These rules are categorized based on the model type (general, logical, relational, process model, physical) and model components (tables, views, attributes, and so on). You can always check your models against these rules, or you can create sets of rules that will be checked. You can check that your models follow one or some of the rules by selecting the rule/rules and clicking Apply Selected. Or you can check all the rules by clicking Apply All. Results are reported as either errors (red) or

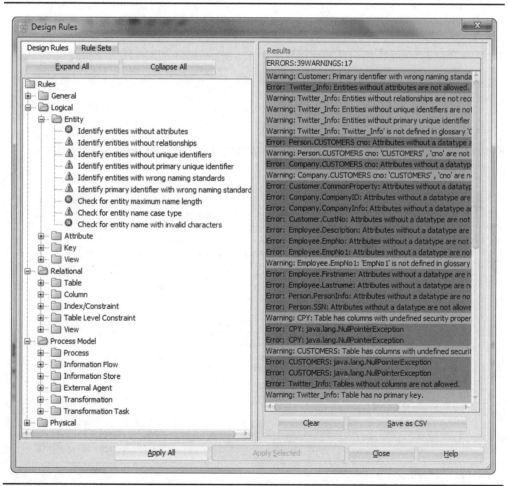

FIGURE 2-17. *Design Rules dialog*

warnings (blue). By double-clicking the error/warning message, you will be taken to the location where the error or warning occurs, and you can fix any errors or warnings immediately and one by one.

When you start using Data Modeler, you may be happy with the design rules that come with the tool, but you might come up with new ideas of rules while working with Data Modeler, so it is good to know that you are able to add them when needed as custom design rules. You can create custom design rules that are based on custom libraries. First you create a custom library as needed in the Custom Libraries dialog, as shown in Figure 2-18. Tools | Design Rules and Transformations | Libraries Then you create a custom design rule based on that custom library in the Custom Design Rules dialog, as shown in Figure 2-19, Tools | Design Rules and Transformations | Custom Rules. The custom design rules

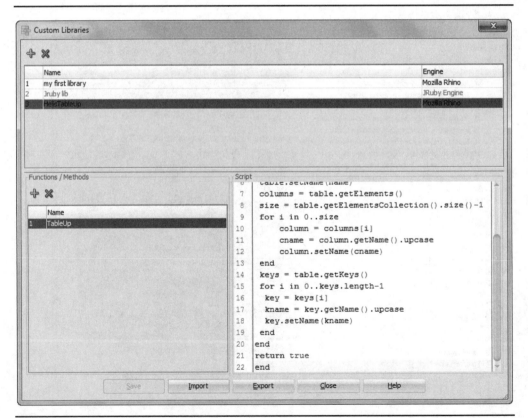

FIGURE 2-18. *Creating a library*

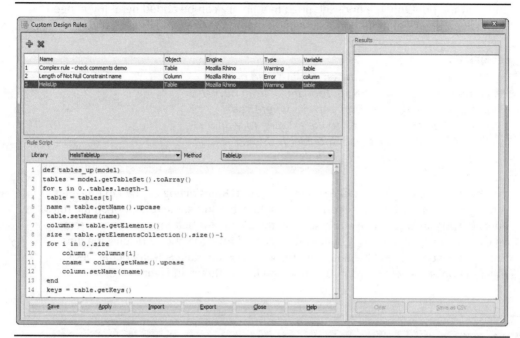

FIGURE 2-19. *Creating a custom design rule*

will be added automatically to your design rules, and they will be available for you to select on a rule set.

A library is a set of functions or methods programmed in Java, and it can be reused in custom design rules or transformation scripts. For each library, you define the name, execution engine, and one or more functions or methods to perform the functionality needed. You can add new functions and methods with the green plus sign in the Custom Libraries dialog and then program the functionality in the Script pane on the right. You can remove a function or method from a library with the red X button.

TIP
You can find some information about creating scripts in the Data Modeler directory /datamodeler/ xmlmetadata/doc. And you can always ask for help at the OTN forum.

For each custom design rule, you specify the object type it concerns, the execution engine, the severity by type (error or warning) if a violation of a rule is detected, and the variable associated with the rule. You also define the library used and the method. Only methods included in a library can be added here. If you need to modify a library or a method, you can do that in the Custom Libraries dialog.

NOTE
If you don't have the JRuby engine installed on your computer, download the appropriate kit from http:// jruby.org and install it. Find jruby.jar where you installed JRuby and copy it to the ext directory under the JDK directory that Data Modeler is using. For example, datamodeler\jdk\jre\lib\ext.

You can create your own rule sets in the Design Rules dialog on the tab Rule Sets. A rule set is useful when you frequently want to check just some rules, not all the rules defined. You can create a new rule set with the green plus button, and you can remove an existing one with the red X button. You can add rules to your set by clicking the Rule Set Properties icon (the icon with the pencil) on the Rule Sets tab of the Design Rules dialog and selecting your rules from the list, as shown in Figure 2-20.

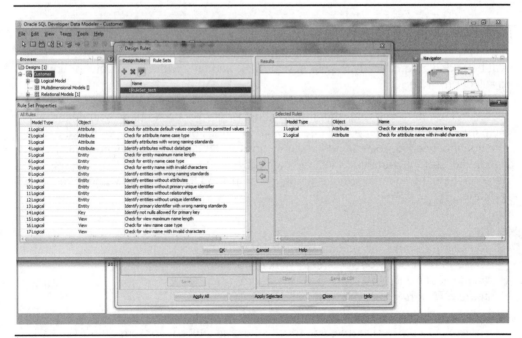

FIGURE 2-20. *Selecting a rule for a rule set*

Sharing Design Rules

The design rules that come with Data Modeler are the same for all users. But if you decide to create your own libraries and design rules, you must share them with other users to let them use them too. The sharing can be done with export/import functionality. The default folder for exporting is set in Default Save Directory in Preferences, and for importing it is set in Default Import Directory in Preferences. You can share libraries by clicking Export in the Custom Libraries dialog and saving the XML file. After that, select Import on the other user's computer and select the exported file to be imported. Likewise, custom design rules can be exported and imported the same way in the Custom Design Rules dialog.

Performance Tuning

Data Modeler is a Java Swing application that requires the Java Development Kit (JDK). Data Modeler consists of several directories and XML files that must be held in memory. If a design is large, the memory might run out, and working with Data Modeler gets too slow. You can even get a warning message (Low Memory Warning) saying you do not have enough memory. If you want to see how the memory is used and what would be a good memory setting, you can do it with a tool called Java VisualVM. If you have Oracle SQL Developer installed, you will find it named jvisualvm.exe in the JDK/bin directory. In Figure 2-21, you can see the memory allocated in Java VisualVM and how much of it has been used. If you want to change the setting in versions before 4.0, the file to change is /datamodeler/datamodeler/datamodeler.conf or /datamodeler/datamodeler/datamodeler64.conf, but since 4.0, it is a configuration setting for each user, and the file to edit is C:\ Users*username*\AppData\Roaming\Oracle SQL Developer Data Modeler*buildno*\ product.conf. The *buildno* part is the build number of your version of Data Modeler. You can still use the datamodeler.conf file, but you must remove the setting from product.conf before this setting takes effect. Remember, when editing this kind of file, Data Modeler must be closed. To change the memory setting, look for AddVMOption –Xmx. It usually has a value of 800M; you might want to change that, for instance, to 1250M or maybe even to 3GB or 4GB. But be careful because if you change the setting to be too large, it is possible that Data Modeler will not start. In that case, make the value smaller.

TIP
Using subviews might help you. Opening a diagram with 5,000 objects is definitely slower than opening a subview with 50 objects. Besides, if the diagram is too large, it is difficult to read it.

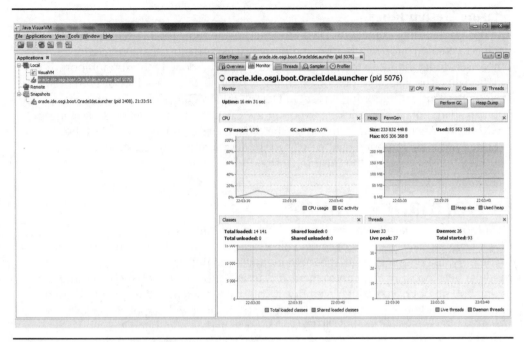

FIGURE 2-21. *Java VisualVM report for memory usage*

In Data Modeler version 4.1 there is a new design property that allows you to save the design in one or several files. It is also possible to use a mixed mode, saving some of the objects in one file and some in separate files. If you are using version control, you still need to save each object to a separate file. This functionality has been added for better performance.

TIP
Do not open physical models if not needed,
especially if the physical model is large because
opening it can affect performance dramatically.

Summary

Before starting to use Data Modeler in production with several users in your organization, it is wise to set some standards and customize Data Modeler for your needs. It is important to agree on which version of the tool to use, who will use the tool, and for what purpose. You will also want to decide what a design is in your organization and how you will name your designs.

Tuning the tool for your needs is also vital. You can set preferences and design properties and share them with all users, and you can create and share glossaries and domains to support standards. It is also important to understand that you can use design rules and set your own rules in order to check and enforce those standards. All this will improve the productivity and quality of the resulting designs. Data Modeler makes it easy to enforce standards across your organization and designers. In addition, using version control with Data Modeler for all shared and common files will raise the quality and productivity to the next level.

Data Modeler does not save designs automatically, so make sure to save frequently by choosing File | Save. You can move the different navigators, browsers, and canvases by just dragging and dropping them where you want them. Take some time to find what works for you; it is definitely worth it.

Data Modeler is a Java Swing application that requires the JDK. Sometimes you'll need to change the JVM settings to get better performance.

CHAPTER
3

Introducing
Requirements Analysis

Requirements analysis is the process of finding and analyzing the requirements that the future users of the application and database have. The results of this process are specifications of user requirements. There are at least three kinds of requirements: data, functional, and nonfunctional requirements. Functional requirements describe what the application must do, data requirements describe the data needed for the requirements and the nonfunctional requirements (for instance security and performance requirements) describe the constraints how the functional requirement must be performed. An example of a functional requirement is that the application must return the names of the customers. To data requirements that might mean a need for a Customer entity with an attribute Name and examples of nonfunctional requirement are that it can only return that information to people having permission to the information and it must be returned in 5 seconds.

The process of requirements analysis is used for specifying project goals and for planning development cycles and increments. Requirements analysis also serves as a source for planning test cases. Many times the requirements analysis also provides input to the risk analysis. It is important to find the requirements for the database. It is also important to know which requirements are mandatory, which are optional, and which will be prioritized higher than others (ranking).

The work during requirements analysis is collecting all possible data available and formalizing it into a consistent form. The work consists of conducting interviews, having meetings, reading existing documentation, and doing anything else possible to find the unwritten information. When collecting information, it is also important to verify the result with end users and business owners.

Depending on the processes your organization has and the tools you are using, the documentation of the requirements analysis may vary. This book will not go into detail on documentation; it concentrates on the work the database designer does during this phase of the database design process, if lucky enough to be involved the project at this early stage. Many times the database designer does not even know there is a new project starting because everybody thinks that the database designer has nothing to do yet, calling on the database designer only when the conceptual design starts. During requirements analysis, the database designer tries to ask all the questions needed to find out what data this new system has (data requirements) and how it is used (functional requirements). The database designer also tries to gather all the possible nonfunctional requirements for the database (related to security, performance, and so on). So, leaving the database designer out of this process is not very wise.

Mostly the requirements analysis consists of writing notes, but Data Modeler does provide logical entity-relationship (ER) models, data flow diagrams (DFDs), and transformation packages to help formalize the documentation. You can find more information about the ER model in Chapter 4. Data Modeler also lets you document business information such as responsible parties, contacts, phone numbers, e-mails, and so on. All the models created during the requirements analysis phase in Data Modeler can be used as the basis for the design work when moving to the conceptual design.

In the requirements analysis phase, the database designer is not trying to model the whole world but just the main concepts and their relationships and behavior. Still, it is good to write down anything that might be interesting when designing the database because it is possible that someone might forget to detail those things later.

All the documentation added to Data Modeler can be used as requirements documentation since it can easily be extracted from Data Modeler with the built-in or custom reports. This is one good reason to have all your documentation in Data Modeler. Another good reason is that when you have all your documentation in one place, you do not need to remember which disc or which directory you used to save your documents. You can read more about reports in Chapter 11.

Gathering Requirements for the Logical Model

In Data Modeler the entity-relationship model is called the *logical model* and can be found in the Browser pane. If the logical model is not open in the canvas, you can open it by right-clicking Logical Model in the Browser pane and choosing "Show." All the logical design with ER notation is done on this logical canvas.

Use icons on the toolbar to create new entities and relationships. When you hover your mouse over an icon, the bubble help will tell you the name of that icon. Figure 3-1 shows the bubble help for New Entity. You can create many objects of the selected type by clicking on the canvas, and when you want to stop, click the Select arrow icon on the left side of the New Entity icon.

Every object in Data Modeler has properties. You can find the properties either by double-clicking the object or by right-clicking the object in the Browser pane and selecting Properties.

An entity has several properties; Figure 3-2 shows the General properties. An entity always has a name, a synonym, and a long name. The name is used as the default for the synonym and the long name. The long name is used on screens where the entity name is combined with the attribute name (entity-name.attribute-name), and it cannot be changed; it is always identical to the name. You can also define a short name for the entity, which can be used, for instance, in foreign key names. For example, an entity name could be Customer, with a short name of Cust, a synonym of Customer, and a long name of Customer. If you select Create Surrogate Key, the surrogate key will be generated automatically for the table

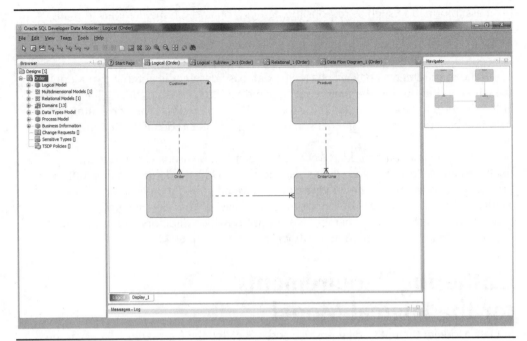

FIGURE 3-1. *The toolbar and the bubble help for New Entity*

created based on this entity. If you define the Synonym To Display setting for an entity, that is the name used in diagrams for the entity, not the Name setting. If this entity is a subentity, you can select the supertype from the list Super Type. You can learn more about subtypes and supertypes in Chapter 4.

If you already know some attributes, you can add them to your design on the Attributes tab in the Entity Properties dialog, as shown in Figure 3-3. You can add an attribute at the end of the list by clicking the green plus sign. If you want to add an attribute before the selected attribute, hold the SHIFT key and click the green plus sign. If you want to add an attribute after the selected attribute, hold the CTRL key and click the green plus sign. If your attributes are in the wrong order, select the one you want to move and click the blue arrow pointing up or down depending on which direction you want to move the attribute. If you want to modify the attribute properties, select the attribute in the list and click the Properties icon (the pencil icon) shown in Figure 3-3. For an attribute, you must define the name, and you can

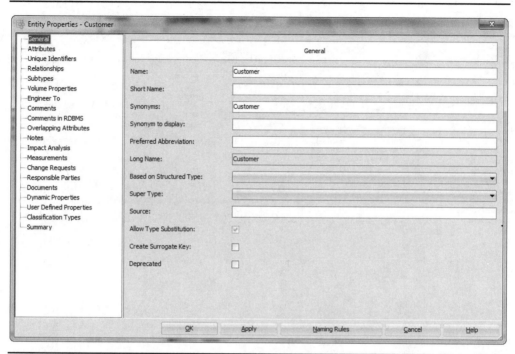

FIGURE 3-2. *General properties for an entity*

define the data type: Domain, Logical, or Structured. If you have defined your own user defined data types of collection or distinct, those can be selected for a data type as well. There are always predefined data types for structured data types in Data Modeler; therefore, that data type is available even though you have not defined any. Depending which one you select, the Type list will show you the available types for that category. If you want to see only the preferred list (defined in Preferences, as covered in Chapter 2), select Preferred. You can decide whether this attribute is the primary key by selecting Primary UID, and you can also define the attribute as mandatory by selecting Mandatory.

You can write three kinds of descriptions about an attribute: comments, comments in the relational database management system (RDBMS), and notes. Comments in the RDBMS are documentation that can be taken all the way to the database to describe an attribute that will be engineered as a column in a database. In the Comments In RDBMS field, you should enter a description that will help people use your database correctly. This text appears in the database and is the only description people not using Data Modeler or its reports can see.

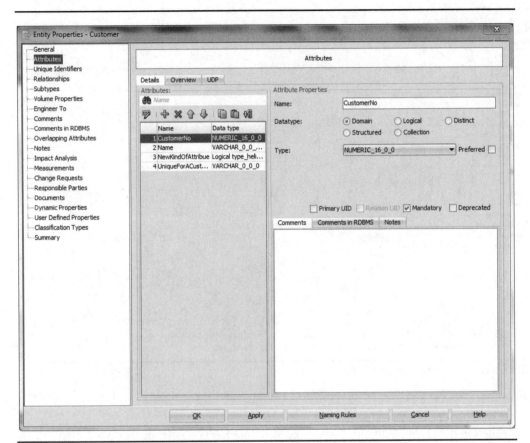

FIGURE 3-3. *Properties for an attribute*

TIP
Use Comments In RDBMS to describe how to use the database for users who do not have access to Data Modeler or its reports. Use Comments for formal documentation, and use Notes for informal documentation.

The Comments field is a description of this attribute, and people using Data Modeler can read it. This could be the official description that other users will see. Notes are usually informal notes and typically written during a planning session. Probably during the requirements analysis, the Notes field would be the best place to make notes. Afterward, you can use the descriptions in Notes and edit them to be more formal to be inserted into the Comments or Comments In RDBMS field.

TIP
You can document everything you hear in modeling sessions and meetings and put them in Notes and afterward edit and copy/move the descriptions you like from Notes to Comments In RDBMS or to Comments.

If you have any information about the volumes or growth rates of an entity, you can add that information on the Volume Properties tab. This information is only for documenting purposes; it will not be used for estimating space needed for the database (except DB2). Even though this information might not be used automatically, it is important information for the database design.

Every object in Data Modeler also has a summary. The Summary tab tells not only the object ID used in XML files but also the creator and creation time of this object and who changed it the last time and when that was. Figure 3-4 shows the Summary tab for an entity.

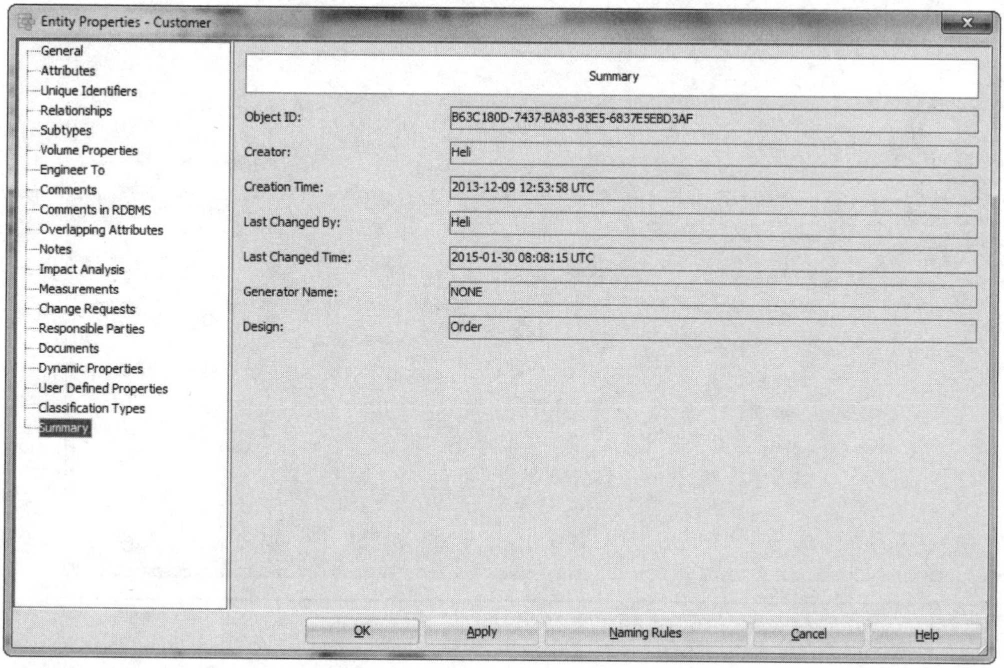

FIGURE 3-4. *Summary properties*

Relationships also have properties, which can be changed when more knowledge about the relationship becomes available. You can see and edit the properties either by selecting the relationship in the Browser pane, by right-clicking and selecting Properties, or by double-clicking the relationship on the logical model canvas. Figure 3-5 shows the general relationship properties. You can define a name for a relationship; otherwise, the default name is used. Using the default name is not best when you have many relationships similar to each other and you need to know which is which or when you have a many-to-many relationship that will be engineered to a new table with the name of the relationship. If you want to add a description for the role in a relationship, fill in the Name On Source or Name On Target field. This text will be shown in the diagram if you right-click the canvas and select Show | Labels. From the same menu you can also define the grid, the page grid, the relationship attributes, or a legend to be shown, as can be seen in Figure 3-6.

There is one more concept I would like to point out at this stage: SubViews. If you have many entities, it can be quite difficult to read a model. You might want to

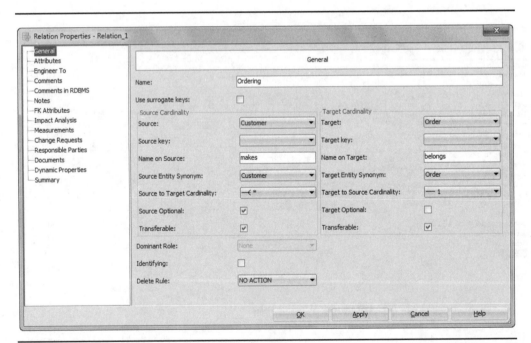

FIGURE 3-5. *General properties for a relationship*

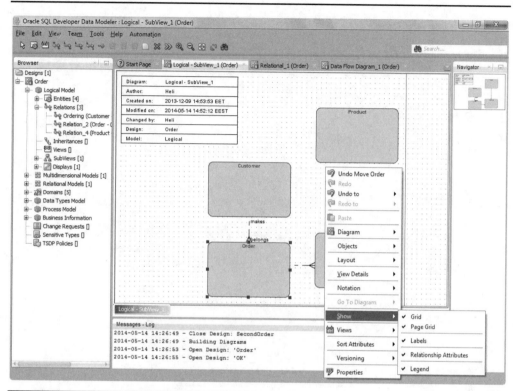

FIGURE 3-6. *Show properties for a view*

have subsets of the whole picture called *subviews*. You can create a subview in any of these ways:

- Go to the Browser pane, select SubView, right-click, and select New SubView.

- Right-click the logical model canvas and select Diagram | Create SubView. Then select the objects you want from the list shown in Figure 3-7.

- Select the objects wanted in the diagram while holding the CTRL key, right-click, and select Create SubView From Selected.

- The easiest way is probably to select the central entity in a diagram, right-click, select Select Neighbors, define the depth (*zone*) of neighbors, and then right-click again and select Create SubView From Selected.

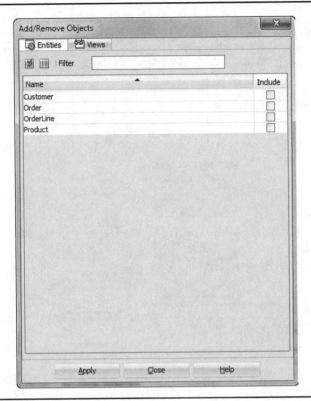

FIGURE 3-7. *Selecting objects to a subview*

You can add objects to your subview by right-clicking the canvas and selecting Objects | Add/Remove Object. You can read more about subviews in Chapter 4.

Gathering Requirements for the Process Model

During the requirements analysis, the database designer might want to document the data processes. You can do that by right-clicking Data Flow Diagrams under Process Model in the Data Modeler Browser pane and selecting New Data Flow Diagram. The processes are the functional side of the data documentation, which more or less documents the data behavior. The process model consists of data flow diagrams to design how the data flows through the system, and transformation packages, which can be used for data warehouse purposes to design extract, transform, and load (ETL). Data Modeler supports all the elements needed for process modeling: primitive processes; composite processes with unlimited levels of decomposition; transformation tasks; triggering events; information stores; external agents; external data elements;

source-target mapping for data elements; and create, read, update, delete (CRUD) dependencies between primitive process and data elements by using roles.

Introducing Data Flow Diagrams

A data flow diagram is a formal, structured notation that models a functional process. A data flow diagram consists of processes, information stores, external agents, and data flows. A *process* is an activity or a function that is performed. In an ideal case, each process should include only one activity. The difference between a primitive and a composite process is that a primitive process is a single process, while a composite process consists of several processes. An *information store* is a collection of data that is permanently stored. An *external agent* is an external effector: a role, organization, or system that is external to the system but interacts with it. External agents send information to processes and also receive information from processes. A *data flow* shows how information flows in the process. An *event* triggers the execution of a process. A note can be used in the diagram to show important information in textual format. Figure 3-8 shows an example of a data flow diagram.

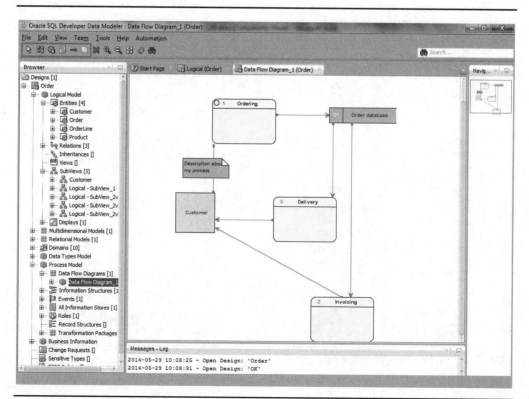

FIGURE 3-8. *Data flow diagram*

To create a new data flow diagram, in the Browser pane, under Process Model | Data Flow Diagrams, right-click and choose New Data Flow Diagram. Use the toolbar to create elements on the diagram. Click the icon of the element you want to add to the diagram and then click the canvas. When you want to stop creating elements, click the Select arrow on the toolbar. Every element in a data flow diagram also has properties.

Figure 3-9 shows the Process Properties dialog. Every process must have a name and a type (Primitive, Composite, or Use Transformation Task). A process can also have a short definition. It has a mode (Batch, Interactive, Manual, or Unknown), and depending on the mode, you can define other things such as response time. You can also define peak periods, frequency, and priority settings for a process.

Figure 3-10 shows the External Agent Properties dialog. An external agent must have a name and a type (Organization Unit, System, Role, or Other). It can have data file specifications or data elements, among other settings.

Figure 3-11 shows the Information Store Properties dialog. An information store must have a name and a type (RDBMS, File, Object, or Temporary) and, depending on the type, some other definitions.

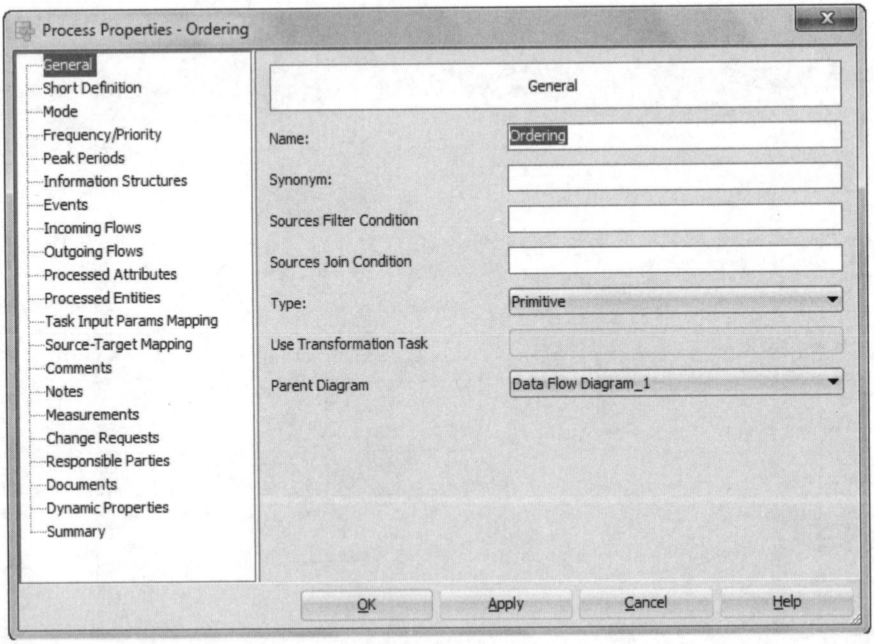

FIGURE 3-9. *Process Properties dialog*

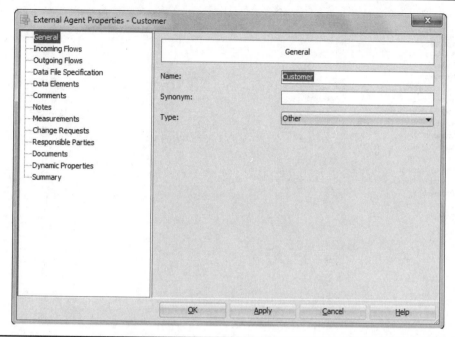

FIGURE 3-10. *External Agent Properties dialog*

Figure 3-12 shows the Flow Properties dialog. A flow has a name, a synonym, a source, and a destination. It can have a parent flow, it can be a logging flow, and it can have an event to trigger a process.

Introducing Transformation Packages

Transformations are used in data warehouse environments to change the data into the form needed. There might be different needs for different targets, for example for OLAP versus data mining, so there is definitely a need to design the ETL processes. A transformation package is a package as defined in the Object Management Group (OMG) Common Warehouse Metamodel (CWM) Specification, V1.1 (www.omg.org/spec/CWM/1.1/).

A transformation package converts different sources to different targets and allows grouping of different transformations. A transformation package can be created only if you already have defined packages that represent data sources or targets: ObjectModel (object-oriented), Relational, Record, Multidimensional, XML,

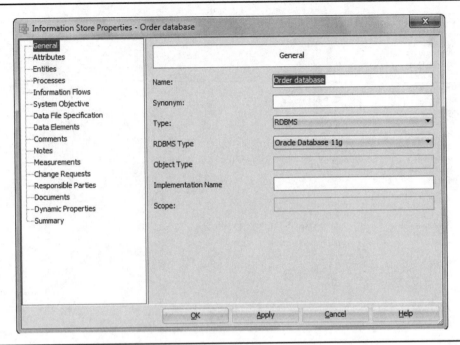

FIGURE 3-11.   *Information Store Properties dialog*

OLAP, or Data Mining. Usually you will not be able to create transformation packages during the requirements analysis phase because you need much more information to do so than you usually have at this stage. But it is good to be aware of this functionality of Data Modeler so you know to document anything interesting related to transformations.

To create a new transformation package, select Process Model | Transformation Packages in the Browser pane, right-click, and select New Package. Then right-click the transformation package name and select New Transformation Task. Data Modeler will automatically create a canvas that is named the same as your transformation task and provide an Input Parameters box. You can think of the transformation task as a function that will have an input parameter to define what the function will do and an output parameter to indicate how the function will end. The function itself (transformation task) might have several operations to do.

In the toolbar you can find the tools for designing a transformation task: New Transformation, New Information Store, New Flow, and New Note. You can also use existing information stores by dragging and dropping them from the Browser pane to the canvas.

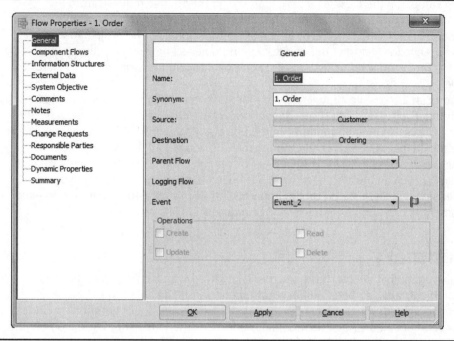

FIGURE 3-12. *Flow Properties dialog*

Adding Business Information

You can add business information to Data Modeler. Go to Logical Model in the Browser pane, double-click or right-click, and select Properties. In Logical Model Properties, you can add, edit, and remove documents and responsible parties. Responsible parties can include, for example, contacts, e-mail addresses, telephone numbers, uniform resource locators (URLs), and locations. All these can be first added to the responsible parties and then edited either by double-clicking the name or by selecting the properties symbol (the pencil icon). You can add responsible parties to elements in the design.

In addition to that, you can add change requests to objects, and you can define, for instance, the status, completeness, request date, completion date, and reason. For example, say you want to add a change request of "Add new attribute, Status" for the entity Customer. You can use the search functionality (see Chapter 11 for more information about search) to find all change requests that are not completed. You select Logical Model and then Advanced Mode. Select Change Request Logical from the Object Type list and click Add Property. Select Complete and define False as the value. On the Results tab, you can see all the change requests from the logical model that are not finished. After the search, you can run a report to .xls or .xlsx format and send it to the project manager for updates. The project manager might update the status, completion date, and notes ("I have closed this change request/Tim") and send the Microsoft Excel sheet to you to be uploaded to Data Modeler.

You can also create change requests for attributes. A change request could be, for instance, "Datatype must be changed from NUMBER to VARCHAR because the use case says that the information can include also characters." Why would you like to have the change request in Data Modeler? Well, you get all the documentation about the database in just one location. For instance, on the entity property Change Requests, you can always check what has been changed and when, and you can make impact analysis based on the Impact Analysis property. You could not do either of these tasks if you did not have change requests in Data Modeler.

Summary

It is important that the database designer is involved with the project at the stage of requirements analysis because the requirements for the database must be collected and documented. The database designer will need to ask a lot of questions to find and document all the possible information needed. The formal ways to document the requirements are usually entity-relationship diagrams and data flow diagrams. The more the documentation can be inserted into a tool in a formal way, the better it will be used in the next phases of database design. It is valuable to document everything that you hear and see during the requirements analysis. But do not worry if you cannot because luckily the same tools are available in the conceptual design phase.

CHAPTER
4

Introducing Conceptual
Database Design
(Logical Model)

C onceptual database design is the process of translating the requirements into a formal conceptual data model and process models. The result of conceptual database design is a conceptual schema and process models. Conceptual database design is similar to requirements analysis, but the difference is that the database designer must get all the information needed to be able to design the database. The main concern is the data and how it should be saved and retrieved.

This chapter will focus on entity-relationship (ER) modeling. Data flow diagrams are also important, and if they were not made during the requirements analysis, you'll need to spend some time working on them now. They are valuable for showing how the database will be used; you can learn more about data flow diagrams in Chapter 3.

A problem that arises during the conceptual database design phase is the poor quality of requirements analysis. There is usually not enough material and information to understand the whole picture, which is important when designing a database. The database designer must ask a lot of questions and demand complete answers. Modeling is a demanding job, but the fact that spoken language is not exact makes it even more difficult. In addition, end users do not always realize they should tell the database designer everything they know, even all the basic information because the designer is not a business expert. A designer should have at least an elementary awareness of basic logic to be able to formalize the spoken language and should have the courage to ask a lot of questions to be sure to understand what the end user means.

To be able to generate valuable reports, it is important to insert all the information you have into Oracle SQL Developer Data Modeler. See Chapter 11 for more information on reporting. Data Modeler has useful search features for setting common properties for several objects of the same type. See Chapter 11 for more information on those functionalities.

Setting Preferences and Properties

It is important to set some standards for the design work. Now is the time to agree on naming standards and rules, as covered in Chapter 2, if you haven't already done so. For example, will you allow Scandinavian letters? Will names always be uppercase, or can they be mixed case? There are many ways to get Data Modeler to work the way you want and to have it support your standards.

Select your design in the Browser pane, right-click it, and select Properties. The Design Properties dialog box that opens shows the *design-level properties* discussed in Chapter 2. You can specify what your diagrams will look like or set up some general naming standards and templates. You can also define a naming standard for attributes, columns, domains, entities, and tables by setting a pattern for the name. A pattern is defined with word types and their compulsions in the pattern. The word types supported by Data Modeler are Prime, Class, Modifier, and Qualifier, as defined in Chapter 2. A defined structure for an attribute could be, for instance, one optional modifier, one mandatory prime word, one optional modifier, and one mandatory class word. Examples of this structure are "Temporary Company Delivery Address" or "Company Address." You can create a structure for an object name by clicking the green plus sign on the Design Properties Settings | Naming Standard tab for that object type and selecting the word type from the list. Then you either select Mandatory to define this pattern part as required or leave it disabled to define it as optional. You can add as many word types as you need for the pattern. You can remove word types from the pattern by clicking the red X button.

These naming standards will be checked against defined glossaries when you apply design rules, and any violations will be reported as warnings. You can use this functionality to make sure that all words used in your design are defined in your glossary, and you can define one or more glossaries as validation glossaries on the Settings tab of the Design Properties dialog, as explained in Chapter 2. If you define more than one glossary, a name is considered to be valid if it can be validated using any of the defined glossaries. You can use different glossaries, for instance, to represent separate areas of interest. One glossary could be for the marketing department, another for sales, and the third one for financials. Finally, you can share the design-level properties with other users, as described in Chapter 2.

NOTE
Using several glossaries for validation may cause problems if you have the same word in two glossaries.

There are also properties that apply to the *logical model level*. Select Logical Model in the Browser pane, right-click, and choose Properties | Naming Options. You can specify the maximum length of a name and the character case (upper, lower, mixed). You can also either select a list from the Valid Characters list or specify your own list of valid characters, or you can select All Valid for all the characters to be valid. You can specify these settings for entities, attributes, and views. See Figure 4-1 for more details. If you try to create something that violates your naming options, you will get an error message immediately. For instance, if the Naming Options properties define that an entity name must be all uppercase but the designer tries to create an entity name with lowercase, an error message is given. If an element has been created before changing the naming options, the element will be checked when the design rules are applied, and any violations per the Naming Options properties will be reported as errors. In Data Modeler version 4.0.2, the Naming Options settings cannot be shared with other users, but there are plans for future releases to provide this functionality.

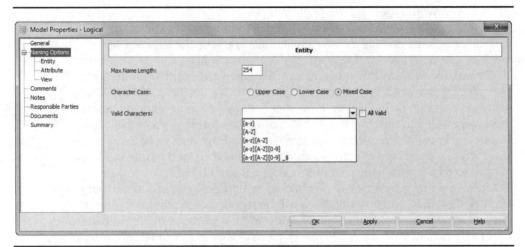

FIGURE 4-1. *Naming options for a logical model*

In addition to properties, you can set some preferences that affect the logical model. Choose the Tools | Preferences menu to open the Preferences dialog. You can make your design work easier and more comfortable by setting the preferences for the logical model the way you want Data Modeler to work. In Chapter 2 you already saw how to define the notation used and how to define the preferred types, among others. In the Preferences dialog, select Data Modeler | Model | Logical to see the settings for the logical model, as shown in Figure 4-2. By setting these preferences, you can define what the defaults will be when a new entity or a relationship is created or when you forward engineer to a relational model. You can change these defaults at any time to take effect on new elements created, and they can be changed in your logical model individually if wanted. You can define the source and target to be optional or mandatory (Source Optional, Target Optional). The source is where the relationship starts, and the target is where it ends. For instance, a Customer could be the source, and an Order would be the target. A Customer might have Orders (Source Optional, which means that the relationship line on the source side is optional; a Customer can exist without an Order), but an Order must be made by a Customer (Target Mandatory, which means the relationship line on the target side must be mandatory; an Order cannot exist without a Customer). In other words, if there is a Customer, there is no need to have an Order, but if there is an Order, there must be a Customer. You can tell Data Modeler to define the first unique identifier as the primary key by selecting Use And Set First Unique Key As Primary Key. There might be several unique keys in one entity, which helps the tool and the designer set one of them as the primary

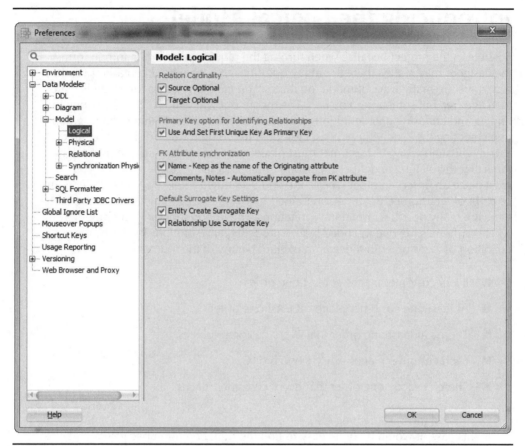

FIGURE 4-2. *Preferences for a logical model*

key. I don't recommend using this functionality since I want to define my own primary keys and be sure the right unique key will be selected, not the first one. Another problem is that a unique key can have nulls, but a primary key cannot. So, if the first unique key is set as the primary key, all its attributes must have nulls not allowed. It is not common to have several unique keys in one entity anyway. To see the preferences for a logical model for forward engineering and the preferences for the relational model, see Chapter 5.

NOTE
Changing some preferences will affect only the elements created after the change.

Introducing the Logical Model

When designing the database, it is valuable to start the design work as soon as possible in the project because when turning the requirements into a formal form, the designer may realize there are many questions that have not been asked yet. In fact, there are many ways of modeling things. You can't always say one way is better than another, but sometimes you can. The theory of logic will give you guidance in finding and choosing one definition over another. The relational theory helps when implementing the requirement in an ER model in the right way. For instance, an end user might simply say, "A customer must place an order." With that, the user might think that this statement defines a customer (that is, to be a customer at all, you must place an order). In other words, the end user might think they have defined the concept of a customer. But a person trained in logic realizes that that is not the case; there are many possible formal interpretations. The important task is to find out which of them is the one intended before modeling any solution. To clarify, the definition of a customer in the example could be any of the following:

- Every customer places at least one order.

- At least one customer places at least one order.

- There's at least one order that every customer places.

- Each customer places exactly one order.

- There's exactly one order that every customer places.

Or it could mean something else.

In this case, it would be quite easy to find the right definition because a customer is a familiar concept to most people, but you will face the same kind of assertions about concepts you are not familiar with, and you still must be prepared to ask the right questions to be able to make the right decisions when modeling. You can find more information about logic and relational theory from several books on the topic, for instance those written by C.J. Date.

It is important to be consistent on how you model, at least in one model. It is much easier to read and understand the model if the solution for the same problem is always the same. C.J. Date says, "You can be consistent or you can be inconsistent, but you shouldn't keep switching all the time between the two." It is also important to understand that the goal is to model the target, not the whole world. One reason to have a clear and simple model is that this model will be your best tool when talking with end users. You might be surprised how well they can read and understand it.

TIP
Try not to be too smart and make too complex a solution; remember that usually a simple solution is the best.

During the conceptual database design, you do not need to actively worry about normalizations, and so on, but remember the relational theory because it will help you. The important thing is to model the target as well as possible and yet simply enough so that other people can understand it too. It is important to find and model the concepts and how they are related to each other. Try to document everything you hear and learn. Be systematic in modeling. Decide where and how to document and figure out what the right level of documentation is. Make sure you have clear and easily understood ways for commenting and reviewing.

You should start the modeling with the logical model you made during requirements analysis (see Chapter 3). If you do not have anything from the requirements analysis, you must start from scratch and begin with the conceptual database design described in this chapter. At best, that means more work; it might even mean you don't have enough information to make the right modeling decisions.

A logical model consists of entities, relationships, views, inheritances, subviews, and displays. All logical model objects are displayed in the Browser pane under Logical Model. One logical model consists of one logical diagram and possibly one or more subviews and/or displays.

If you right-click Logical Model in the Browser pane, you will see the operations for a logical model.

- With Hide and Show, you can control whether the logical model diagram is open.

- You can create subviews and displays based on the logical model (more about those later in this chapter).

- You can set classification types (more about those in Chapter 8).

- You can apply naming standards and custom transformation scripts or create a glossary from the logical model (more about those in Chapter 3).

- You can search and create a report based on search results and update the data in Data Modeler with an Excel worksheet (more about that in Chapter 11).

- You can choose Engineer To Relational Model (more about that in Chapter 5) and of course view and edit the properties.

■ In every object in the Browser pane you also have the ability to select Versioning. You can find more about versioning and version control in Chapter 9.

And if you right-click the logical model diagram (or a subview diagram), you can do the following:

■ You can undo operations.

■ You can define the layout.

■ You can define what details will be shown (View Details): All Details, Names Only, or Attributes. You can also specify that classification types (the name of the classification type on an element) or comments will be shown.

■ You can select the notation.

■ You can display a page grid or a grid or make labels (source and target names) and relationship attributes visible in the diagram. Or you can specify that a legend should be shown. A legend shows the Summary properties in a diagram. All these can be selected under Show.

An Entity and Its Attributes

An entity is anything that happens to be of interest to the target of modeling, for example, a person, say Heli. Every entity is of some entity type. An entity type is a set of entities (Person) having certain properties in common (Heli, Marko, Patrik, and Matias—like all entities of type Person—have a name). An entity type is always a noun (Company, Employee, Customer). An entity set is a subset of an entity type, and it includes only those entities that belong to the target of modeling. In spoken language, entity types and entity sets are often called *entities*. In this book, we will call both an entity type and an entity set an *entity* because in the context of Data Modeler they are called entities. When referring to a single entity (Heli) of an entity set (Person), we will use a term *entity instance*. You can create an entity in Data Modeler on the logical model canvas by clicking the entity icon and then inserting the properties for the entity, as shown in Chapter 3.

An entity can be either strong or weak. A *strong* entity (for example, Customer) identifies itself without other entities or relationships; strong entities have independent existence. A weak entity (for example, Orderline) depends on other entities to identify it (Order, Customer) and has a mandatory, identifying relationship with them. The weakness of an entity is shown with a horizontal line at the end of the relationship line. You can define it in the Relation Properties dialog by selecting Identifying on the source side of the properties.

An entity has properties (for example, Person has a name) as mentioned earlier. Those properties are called *attributes*. An attribute can be *atomic,* which means it contains only a single value from a certain domain and it cannot be divided into smaller components. For example, Zip Code is an atomic attribute. An attribute can also be a *composite* attribute, which means it is a combination of two or more attributes that can be either atomic or composite. An example of a composite attribute would be Name = Firstname + Lastname. An attribute can be *multivalued* or *set-valued,* which means that the attribute will have multiple values, but the number of different values can be limited. For example, a Customer can have only three phone numbers: home, work, and mobile. Or an attribute can be a *derived* attribute. For example, Age can be derived from Date of Birth. For attributes you can specify properties in the Attribute Properties dialog, shown in Figure 4-3. You can find it by clicking the

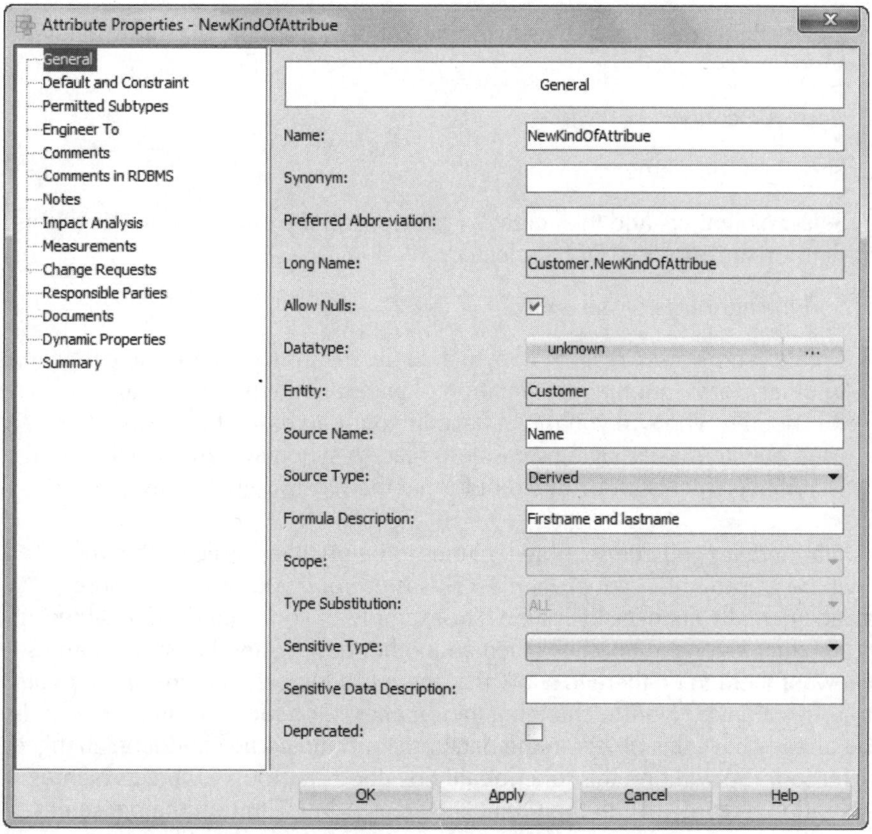

FIGURE 4-3. *Attribute Properties dialog, General tab*

Properties icon on the Attribute tab of the Entity Properties dialog, by double-clicking the attribute name, or selecting the attribute in the Browser pane, right-clicking it, and selecting Properties. In the Attribute Properties dialog, you can also define the name for the attribute source in the Source Name field and then select the preferred source type from the list. The allowable values for the Source Type list are empty (no source type), Manual, System, Derived, and Aggregate. If you want to define the formula for the derived or aggregated attribute, enter a description of the formula in Formula Description, as shown in Figure 4-3.

An attribute can be mandatory or optional. If an attribute has been defined as mandatory by selecting Mandatory when creating it, it will be shown on the canvas with an asterisk (*) in front of the attribute name. If an attribute is optional, there will be a small circle (o) in front of the attribute name in Barker notation and nothing in Bachman or Information Engineering notation.

If you right-click an entity on the canvas, you can see operations allowed on an entity. You can, for instance, do the following:

- Delete the entity totally (Delete Object) or only from the diagram (Delete View).

- Copy the entity.

- Show or hide elements.

- Select Neighbors and then create a subview on the entity and its neighbors with Create SubView From Selected.

- Sort the attributes of the entity.

- Create synonyms. Create Synonym actually means Create Visual Synonym; in other words, another presentation of an entity on the same diagram. It is not the synonym you might have in your database. It is meant to be used only to make diagrams easier to read. A synonym can have different visibility elements and a different format than the original entity.

In Data Modeler you can set object names to be unchangeable so that the name will be grayed out in the properties. This is useful if you want to be sure nobody accidentally changes the name. For example, if you want to have tables in your design that belong to another schema (another design, another system, and so on), you want them to be there to show that there is a logical relationship, but you want to prevent anybody from changing their names. Or a more common reason is that you already have this object in the database, and the name cannot be changed for any reason. You will find this functionality by choosing Tools | Objects Names Administration (Figure 4-4). In the Objects Names Administration dialog, select Fixed for all elements you want to have a fixed name. You can do this for the names of entities, attributes, relationships, identifiers, and views.

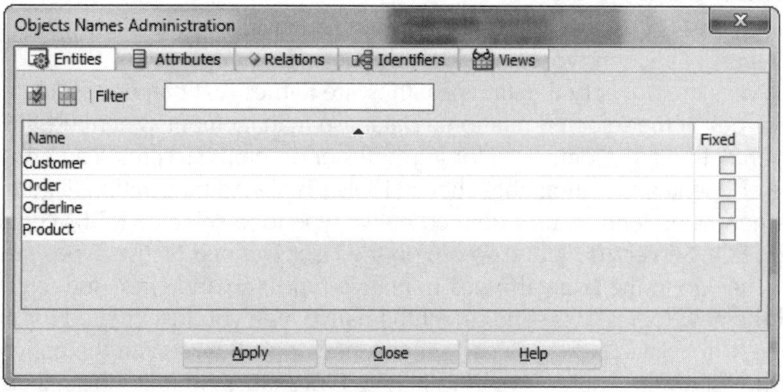

FIGURE 4-4. *Objects Names Administration dialog*

Another sometimes useful feature is to mark an object as deprecated to let other users know that this element should not be used. In many of the properties dialog boxes you can find this functionality (for instance, on the General and Attributes tabs of Entity Properties). In Figure 4-5, you can see the entity ProductGroup has been struck through, meaning that it has been marked as deprecated, as has its attribute, GroupNo.

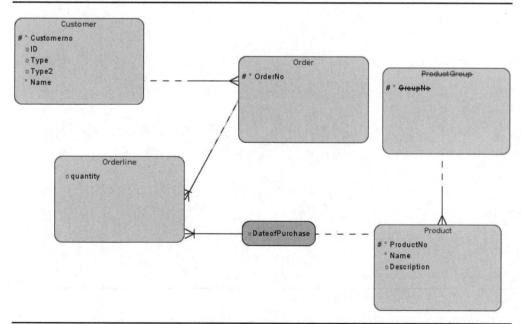

FIGURE 4-5. *An entity and an attribute marked as deprecated*

User-Defined Data Types

There are four kinds of user-defined data types in Data Modeler: distinct types, structured types, collection types, and logical types.

Logical types are not actual data types; they are names that can be associated with native types of the selected relational database management system (RDBMS) type and then defined as a data type for attributes or domains. To create a new logical type or to edit an existing one, choose Tools | Types Administration (Figure 4-6). To create a new one, define a user-defined native type for a selected RDBMS type (Oracle 12c, SQL Server 2008, and so on) on the User Defined Native Types tab. Click Save. Then go to the Logical Types To Native Types tab and click Add. Enter a name for the new logical type and select the native type you just created for the RDBMS type. Click Save. Now you can see this new logical type with the native type settings in the list on the Logical Types To Native Types tab. And it can be selected as a data type for an attribute or a domain. I have used this, for example, with a new Microsoft SQL Server version that had new data types that Data Modeler did not

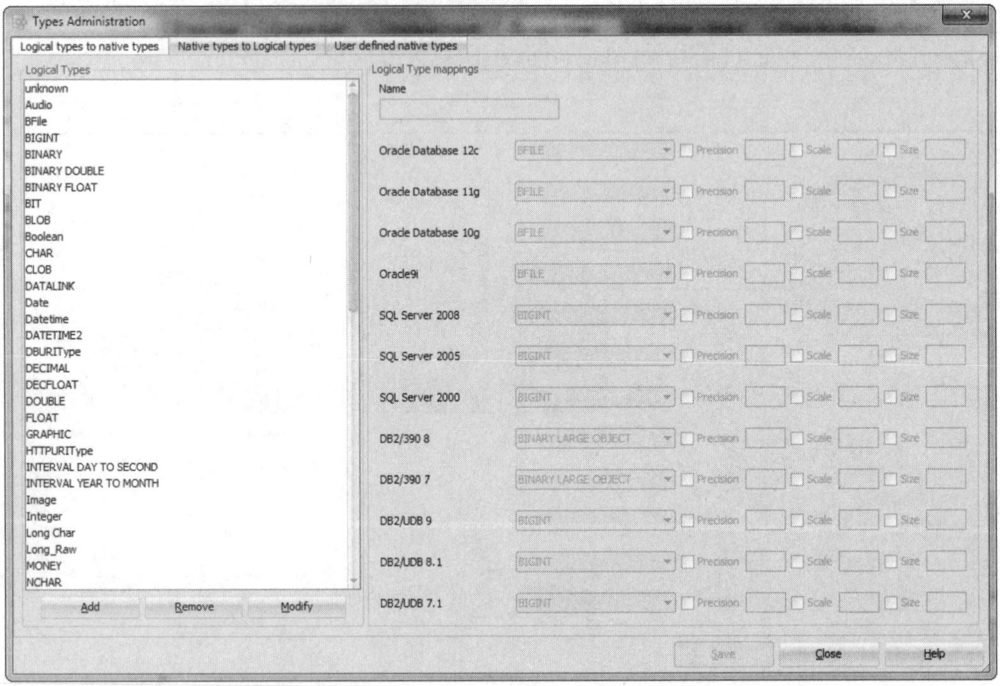

FIGURE 4-6. *Types Administration dialog*

support yet. I defined those data types as logical types and was able to use them when designing.

You can use the Types To Domains Wizard (choose Tools | Types To Domains Wizard) to create domains from data types that have been used in your design. But be careful since the domains must be carefully decided and agreed on. I would rather define them manually. Domains can be maintained by choosing Tools | Domains Administration. You can read more about domains in Chapter 2.

Distinct, structured, and collection types can be defined and managed under Data Types Model in the Browser pane. Both logical and relational models can use definitions from the data types model to specify the data type for attributes and columns. Certain structured types can also be used to define that an entity or a table is of a certain structured type. A data types model can be built manually, or you can import one from an Oracle Designer repository. You can find import functionality on the File menu, and you can read more about importing from Oracle Designer in Chapter 10.

To create a distinct or a collection type, go to the Browser pane, select the data type, and right-click. Fill in the information needed. For a new *distinct* type, you need to define the name and select the logical data type from the list of values. You can also define the size. Do not forget to comment and document your distinct type. After you have created the distinct type, it will be available in the data type list for an attribute or column. Remember to select the data type Distinct. To create a new *collection* type, you must define the name and set the collection to be either array or collection. For an array, you must define the maximum number of elements in the array; for a collection, you do not need to have this element defined. You should define the data type for your array or collection. The data type can be domain, logical, distinct, collection, or structured. You should also define the Max Size As String parameter, and do not forget to comment and document your collection type. After you have created the collection type, it will be available as a data type for an attribute or column. Remember to select the data type Collection when assigning a data type to an attribute.

A structured type is a user-defined data type that has attributes and methods. Attributes can be of type logical, distinct, structured, or collection. A structured type can also be defined as a supertype to another structured type. An entity can be defined based on a structured type. To create a new structured type, go to Data Types Model in the Browser pane, right-click, and select Show; alternatively, under SubViews, right-click, and select New SubView. Then design the structured type using icons on the toolbar. Only structured type objects are represented graphically on data type diagrams. A data type diagram consists of structured types, reference links, embedded structure links, collections of reference links, collections of embedded structure links, and notes.

From the properties of a data type, you can see whether and where this data type is used on the Used In tab.

Sensitive Data

In Oracle Database Enterprise Edition there is an optional feature (included with Advanced Security) that allows different treatment for data that has been defined as sensitive. Please read more about that in the Oracle documentation. Data Modeler supports designing sensitive data. In Data Modeler, you can define sensitive types and associate them with Transparent Sensitive Data Protection (TSDP) policies. You can create a new sensitive type in the Browser pane by right-clicking Sensitive Types and selecting New Sensitive Type. A sensitive type should always have a name. If you select Generate In DDL in the sensitive type properties, it means that the sensitive type will be created when the DDL statements are generated, and if you select Enable, you let the sensitive type be selected for association with an attribute or column. A sensitive type also has a description, comments, and notes, and on the Used tab in the properties you can see where this particular sensitive type has been used.

You can create a new TSDP policy by right-clicking TSDP Policies in the Browser pane and selecting New TSDP Policy. You must define a name for a TSDP policy and decide whether it will be included when generating the DDL. A policy can also have subpolicies that can have properties for redaction policies (in the user interface erroneously referred to as masking properties; this will be fixed in later releases of Data Modeler), as shown in Figure 4-7. You can manage redaction policies/masking

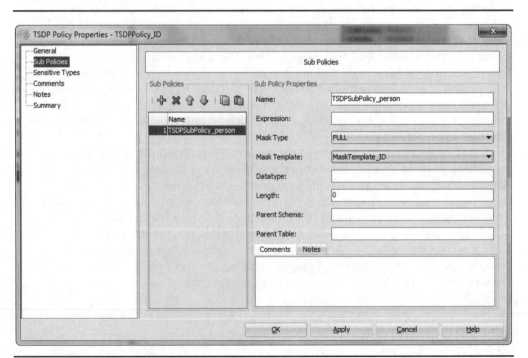

FIGURE 4-7. *TSDP Policy Properties dialog, Sub Policies tab*

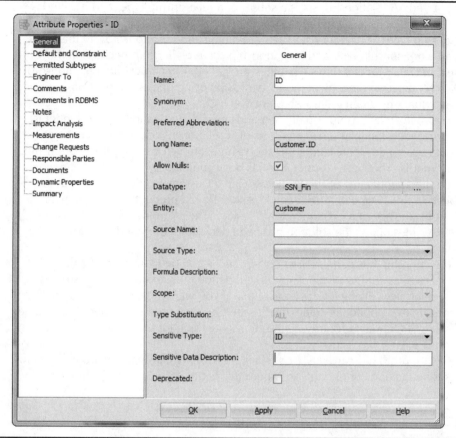

FIGURE 4-8.   *Associating a sensitive type to an attribute*

templates by choosing Tools | Mask Templates Administration. A sensitive type will be associated to a TSDP policy with the Sensitive Type property. After that, the sensitive type can be associated to an attribute in the Attribute Properties dialog (Figure 4-8).

A Relationship

A relationship is a logical association between two or more entities. The *degree* of a relationship is the number of entities involved in the relationship. If there are more than two entities in a relationship, it is called a *complex* relationship. "Heli buys an iPad" is a degree 2 (Heli, iPad) relationship (buys). A relationship type is a set of similar relationships, for example BUY (CUSTOMER, BUY, PRODUCT). A relationship type is a verb. A relationship set is a subset of a relationship type, and it includes only those relationships that belong to the target of modeling. In spoken language, relationship types and relationship sets are often called *relationships*. In this book, we call a relationship type and a relationship set a *relationship* because in the context of Data Modeler that's what they are called. You can create a relationship in Data Modeler on the logical model canvas by using one of the relationship icons in the toolbar (the green relationship arrows).

A complex relationship usually demands more investigation. An ER model is only two-dimensional, and having a complex relationship does not fit into that without raising questions. Figure 4-9 shows an example of a complex relationship. A Customer is ordering a Product that has been supplied by a Supplier. Can any of the Suppliers supply any of the Products? Can a Customer order from any of the Suppliers? Can a Customer order any Products from a product list, or are there limitations (the age of a Customer, for instance)? The ER model does not answer these questions unless the solution has been decided upon based on more questions.

A relationship has *participation constraints*: It can be mandatory (total) or optional (partial). In Data Modeler, you will define the participation constraints in the Preferences dialog on the Logical tab. If you want the source side of the relationship to be optional, select the Source Optional property; otherwise, disable it. The Target Optional property defines the same thing for the target side of the relationship.

A relationship has *cardinality constraints* (mapping cardinality, cardinality ratio) to describe the number of entity instances this entity has in a relationship. For

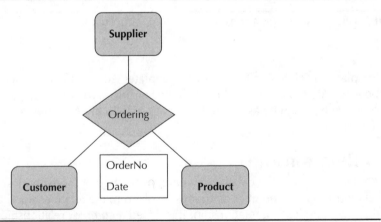

FIGURE 4-9. *Example of a complex relationship*

instance, an employee can have exactly one supervisor, no more than one supervisor, or several supervisors. In Data Modeler, there are four different kind of possible mapping cardinalities: one-to-one (1:1), one-to-many (1:m), one-to-many identifying, and many-to-many (m:n). You can also define these settings in the Relation Properties dialog by using the properties Source To Target Cardinality and Target To Source Cardinality.

The same entity can participate in a relationship several times in different roles. For instance, an Employee can be both Employee and Supervisor, which both are Employees. Figure 4-10 shows an example of an entity having a relationship to the same entity in two roles. In Data Modeler, you can create this by selecting the one-to-many relationship symbol and clicking the entity twice. If the relationship is to the entity itself, it is called a *recursion*. To avoid confusion, make sure to name different roles clearly. You can name the relationship roles in the Relation Properties dialog. Enter the name of the relationship in Name and the names for the roles in the Name On Source and Name On Target fields. To make the names visible in a diagram in Data Modeler, right-click the canvas and choose Show | Labels.

The Relation Properties dialog also has a Delete Rule list, where you can delete the rule for a child table when a row from a parent table will be deleted and rows

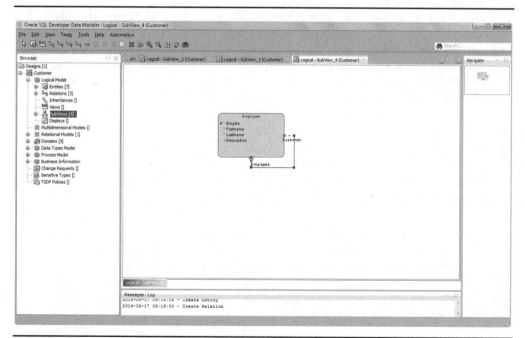

FIGURE 4-10. *A relationship to the same entity, recursion*

with that value exist in the child table. The possible choices are No Action, Cascade, Set Null, and Restrict.

- The default value No Action performs no action on these rows, which means the rows must be deleted manually from the child table before they can be deleted from the parent table.

- The option Cascade deletes these rows from the child table automatically as Data Modeler deletes the rows from the parent table.

- The value Set Null sets null for all columns in those rows in the child table that can be set to null. If there are columns that cannot be set to null, they must be handled manually.

- The value Restrict prevents any updates or deletes on the parent table on columns referred to from the child table.

Deleting a rule has no meaning in the logical model, but this is the right place to find the information needed to be able to document it. It is good that it can be documented in Data Modeler already in the logical model, and it will be forward engineered to the relational model.

A relationship can have attributes of its own. For example, a relationship between Customer and Order might have an attribute of Date of Purchase. Attributes for relationships can be defined in Relation Properties on the Attributes tab, as shown in Figure 4-11. In the diagram, the relationship attribute is shown in Figure 4-12. The relationship attributes are not shown in a diagram by default. If you cannot see them, right-click the canvas and choose Show | Relationship Attributes.

NOTE
A common mistake is to model a foreign key as an attribute. Do not do that. If you do, you will end up with duplicate columns in your relational model after forward engineering.

If the relationship line does not look the way you want, you can either select and move it or use the Data Modeler functions to move it. You can delete or hide the relationship. You can select Straighten Lines, Add Elbow, or Change The Format. If you want to change the way the relationship line looks, select Change Format and change it. You can see all operations allowed for a relationship and a relationship line by right-clicking it in a diagram.

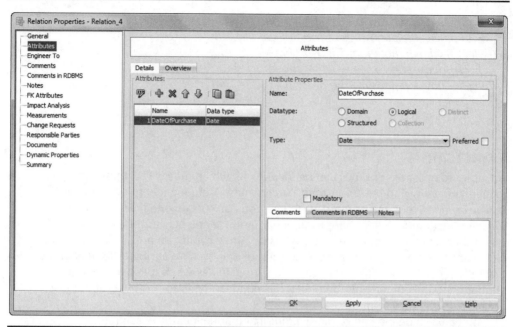

FIGURE 4-11. *Properties for a relationship attribute*

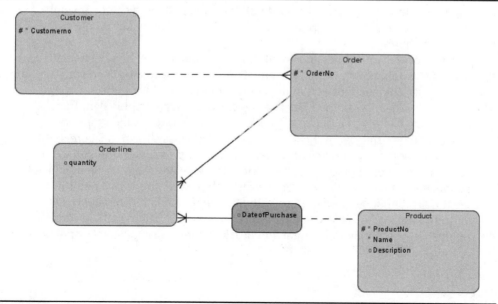

FIGURE 4-12. *An attribute for a relationship in a diagram*

TIP
If you want to see the foreign key attributes implied by the logical relationships in your logical diagram, select Bachman notation. This is a simple way to check your model to see whether the forward engineering will produce the relational model you are expecting.

Constraints

An attribute or set of attributes can be *identifying,* which means that these attributes identify the entity and are a constraint to the entity. A unique identifier for the entity can be composed of one or more attributes. You can specify one primary unique identifier that uniquely identifies each entity instance and acts as the primary key. All attributes in the primary key are mandatory; they cannot be nulls. A primary key can be a natural key, meaning that it consists of one or more attributes for that entity that truly identify that entity, or it can be a surrogate key when it consists of one attribute (usually numeric attribute) that has no meaning to the entity itself but just separates each entity from others.

You can also define one or more additional unique identifiers as unique constraints or unique keys. A unique key makes sure that there are not two entity instances in the entity that have the same values in all attributes defined for the unique key (unique constraint). The difference between a primary key and a unique key is that unique key attributes can have nulls allowed and there can be several unique keys for an entity, whereas there can be only one primary key with only mandatory attributes.

In Data Modeler you can define an attribute as a primary key by selecting the Primary UID box on the Attributes tab in the Entity Properties dialog. And you can create other unique identifiers in the Entity Properties dialog on the Unique Identifiers tab. Add a new unique identifier by clicking the green plus sign. Then double-click the name of the new unique identifier name or click the Properties icon (a pencil icon). This opens the Key Properties dialog, as shown in Figure 4-13. Add the name for the key and any other general definitions wanted. Then go to the Attributes and Relations tab to select the attributes and relationships to be used as a unique identifier. If you have named your relationships well, this is one point where you see it was worth it because it is easier to find the right relationship out of all relationships if the name is clear. You can select one by highlighting a name and clicking the arrow pointing to the right and deselect one by using the arrow pointing

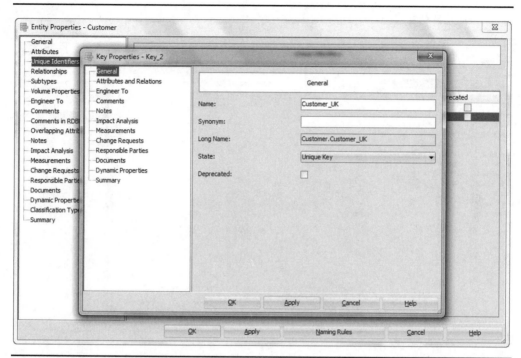

FIGURE 4-13. *Key properties*

to the left, as shown in Figure 4-14. Always remember to click Apply and Save. You can also use this same method for creating primary keys, but then you select Primary Key for the State setting. You can find the primary key in the Browser pane under Primary Keys, and you can find other unique keys under Alternate Keys. Also note that the primary key in Barker notation is indicated by the hash (#) in front of the attribute name, and the attribute in the alternate unique key is indicated by the uppercase *U*. In Bachman notation and in Information Engineering notation, the primary key is marked with an uppercase *P*, the foreign key is marked with *F*, and an identifying foreign key is marked with *PF*.

The attributes for the primary key should be identifying, stable, and not under any changes in values. For example, in many systems, a Social Security number (SSN) is defined as a primary key for a person. Is it a good primary key? No. The reasons why are as follows:

- An SSN is not unique, at least not worldwide.

- An SSN does not identify a person; in rare cases, one person can even have several SSNs.

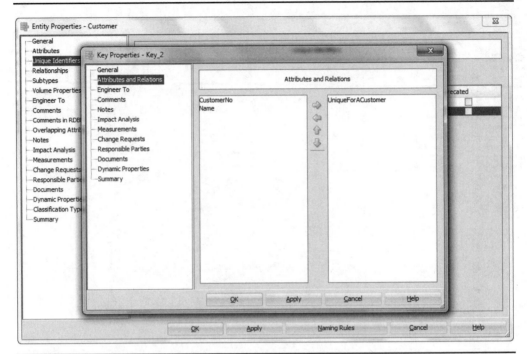

FIGURE 4-14. *Selecting entities and relationships for the unique key*

- An SSN can be changed. When you move to another country, you are given a temporary SSN. When you get citizenship, you get a permanent one. There are plenty of cases when an SSN has changed.

- An SSN is not something you can define yourself; it comes from another system and is controlled by other organizations and their rules. What if they change the rules? Do not use primary keys from another system's data (history data, and so on).

- An SSN is defined many times as sensitive data, redaction, or masking in several tables (because of foreign keys), which is not very efficient.

When selecting the primary key, you have two choices: natural key or surrogate key. Which one is better? The only correct answer to any question about modeling issues is: it depends. But deciding on the primary key is one of the most important decisions in conceptual database design. A natural key is usually more efficient; sometimes you can eliminate a join, sometimes the query optimizer works more efficiently, and so on. But there is no point trying to find a natural primary key if there is no serious candidate, though in many of these cases it indicates that there is something wrong with the model. Many times designers are too cautious to set attributes to not null and therefore are able to define only unique keys. Or the concepts are not understood well enough to really identify the entity. One of the main concerns in designing the database is the data quality. To be able to get good-quality data, you must understand what you are modeling, and you must be able to set as many attributes to not null as possible and to find all possible constraints. A surrogate primary key does not stop users from inserting logical duplicates in the database, but a natural key does, and the index for a surrogate primary key is not often used (queries are not made based on the surrogate). On the other hand, many times the best solution for data that comes from another system and is not controlled by your organization is a surrogate key because you can never be sure if the other system has changed the data you have considered to be unique not to be unique anymore. So, there is no single answer to the question. If you want to have a surrogate key, select the Use Surrogate Keys box in the Entity Properties or Relationship Properties box.

A foreign key constraint is an attribute or set of attributes that refers to the primary key of an entity, which can be another entity or the same one, as discussed earlier.

You can also define constraints for attributes. Domain constraints can define, for instance, the data type, length, allowable values, and default values. You can either predefine them in Domains to be used (see Chapter 2) or define them for every attribute separately in the Attribute Properties dialog (Figure 4-15). Define the name for the constraint and define the default value for it. If you want to use the properties defined in Domains Administration for the associated domain, select Use Domain Constraints. If this option is not selected, you can continue defining the settings. You can specify a constraint for one or more types of databases from the Constraint list. You can specify one or more value ranges for the attribute. You can specify a list of valid values for the attribute. If you select Use Domain Constraints, all the changes will automatically be done on this attribute. For instance, if a new allowable value is added to a domain constraint, it will automatically be available for this attribute as a candidate for a default value and on the list of allowable values. I recommend using the domains and their settings. That will make maintenance easier.

One more commonly used constraint is a check constraint. An example of a check constraint could be Check (Name=upper(Name)). A constraint can be immediate or deferred, meaning that it will be checked either straightaway or a bit later.

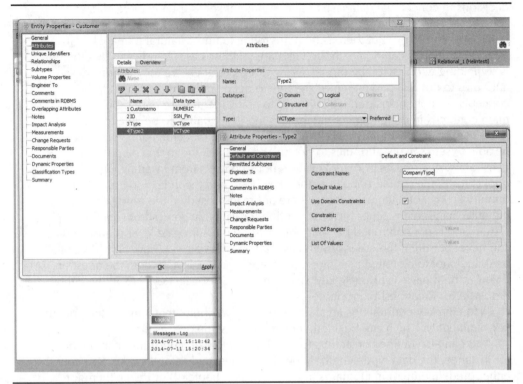

FIGURE 4-15. *Domain constraint*

Entity Views

An *entity view* is an element in the logical model that allows a designer to create a new level for the conceptual model. This level is to make the design more concrete for business owners to understand. The entity views can be combinations or subcategories of the entities in the model. An entity view can be forward engineered as a view in the relational model and as a view in the database if needed.

You can create a new entity view by clicking the New View icon beside the New Entity icon in the toolbar. An entity view appears in the Data Modeler canvas as an entity but with an orange background color. There is the name of the entity view, and then the attributes are selected in that entity view. On the bottom of the entity view figure there are the entities that are used in the entity view. In the View Properties dialog (Figure 4-16), you can name the entity view and build the view with Query Builder. You will learn more about Query Builder in Chapter 5. If you select Auto Join On Relationships, the relationships will be created for your view

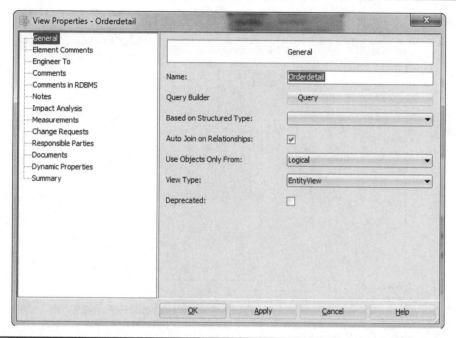

FIGURE 4-16. *Properties for an entity view*

automatically in Query Builder based on relationships in the entities selected for the view. If you disable Auto Join On Relationships, you must create relationships manually. You can select whether all objects from the logical model are available for creating the view or just the ones in a particular subview by selecting the desired one from the Use Objects Only From list. The view type can be either an entity view or a named query.

Inheritance

Sometimes you need to model a case on an entity with two or more exclusive child entities. For example, you might want to model a case where the main entity is Customer, but a Customer will be either a Person or a Company. You can solve it either by using an arc or by using the concepts of supertype and subtype.

An arc is an exclusive relationship group where only one of the relationships can exist for a given instance of an entity. To draw an arc, you must first create all the entities and relationships that you want to include in the arc. Select the entity and select all the relationship lines to be included (hold SHIFT or CTRL and click each line). Now you can see that the Arc icon in the toolbar is enabled. Click the New

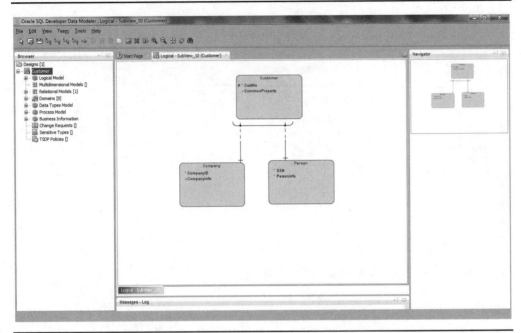

FIGURE 4-17. *An arc solution*

Arc icon. Figure 4-17 shows an arc solution where at one time there is either a relationship between Customer and Person or a relationship between Customer and Company. In other words, a Customer is either a Person or a Company but never both or neither.

All relationships included in an arc should belong to the same entity, and they should have the same cardinality. In forward engineering, an arc solution will produce one table for each entity. To be able to forward engineer this setting to the relational model, you must set all foreign key attributes belonging to the relationship to allow nulls because only one of them can have a value for each row in the table. There will be additional, optional columns in the table based on the supertype (Customer) for each foreign key referring to that table from a subtype, and an additional check constraint is needed for implementing the arc. You will learn more about forward engineering in Chapter 5. The arc solution can be a good choice when the subtypes do not have a lot in common and can be used independently.

In many cases, it is easier to model and understand the modeling target when using subtypes and supertypes to express the same need. The modeling tactic with supertypes and subtypes is usually easier for end users to read and understand, and it gives the designer the freedom to decide later how to implement this when engineering to the relational model. A hierarchy of entities based on supertypes and subtypes is called *inheritance*. All attributes and relationships of the supertype

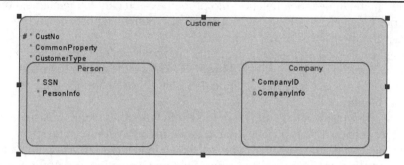

FIGURE 4-18. *Box-in-box presentation*

must belong to all of its subtypes. Subtypes are usually defined if many of the entity instances have attributes in addition to those of the supertype. A supertype is defined for an entity in the Entity General Properties dialog by selecting the appropriate entity from the list for Super Type (in the example in Figure 4-18, Customer is the supertype and Person is the subtype). The inheritance looks like the model in Figure 4-18 if box-in-box notation has been selected.

If the box-in-box notation has not been selected, the same inheritance will look like the one in Figure 4-19. In that case, the inheritance relationship properties can

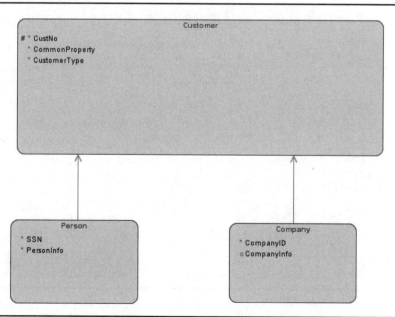

FIGURE 4-19. *Inheritance, no box-in-box presentation*

be modified in the Inheritance Relationship properties. You can define Name, Long Name, Super Type, and Sub Type fields. You can also define Engineer To and Comments, Comments In RDBMS, and Notes.

The Engineer To property page in the Entity Properties dialog is for defining which entity from the hierarchy will be transformed to a table and, if there are several relational models, to which relational model. This definition should be done for each entity.

There is a new page called Subtype in the Entity Properties dialog box since Data Modeler version 4. This page is for implementing subtypes in engineering and for setting up a discriminator column, as shown in Figure 4-20. For entity and subtypes generation, there are two decisions: Subtree Generation and Apply To Model. For the Subtree Generation field there are four choices: Do Not Preset, Single Table, Table Per Child, and Table For Each Entity. If you want to make the decision manually by setting the Engineer To property to each entity yourself, select Do Not Preset. I will discuss more about these choices later in this section. The Apply To Model selection on the same page defines whether the possible changes for the Engineer To properties will be applied to all relational models or to a specific

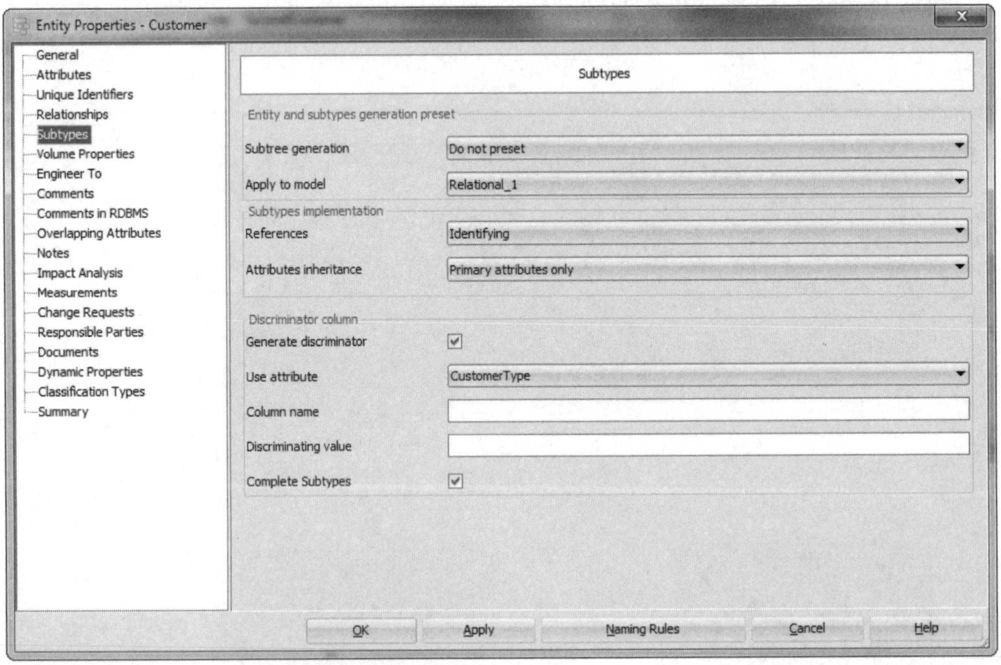

FIGURE 4-20. *Defining the inheritance*

model. For Subtypes Implementation (Figure 4-20) there are two settings: References and Attributes Inheritance. For References you have three choices: None, Identifying, and Arc Implementation. If you select None for the reference, no foreign keys are created between tables. If you select Arc Implementation, optional foreign keys from supertype to subtypes are created. Arc is mandatory if the subtypes hierarchy is complete. If you select Identifying, identifying foreign keys are created from subtype tables to supertype tables. You can also specify the attributes inheritance, and for that you have two choices: Primary Attributes Only and All Attributes. This property defines that either primary attributes or all attributes of a supertype be inherited to subtypes when implemented as tables.

For Subtypes Implementation (Figure 4-20), you can also specify a discriminator column, which is often used when generalization, a single-table implementation, has been selected. I will discuss more about that later in this section.

There are three ways to implement the inheritance in a relational model: specialization (table for each entity), generalization (single table), or neither of those (table per child). There is no one right way to model an inheritance; it always depends on what the requirements are.

Specialization of an entity means that the entity will be divided into subentity types. For instance, an entity Customer might be divided into Person and Customer. All common attributes will be in the Customer entity. Person and Customer will have only the attributes specific for those entities. This is similar to what you saw in the arc solution in Figure 4-16. In Data Modeler this is called Table For Each Entity, and you can select it by setting the Subtree Generation option in the Entity Properties dialog (see Figure 4-20) to Table For Each Entity. When Table For Each Entity is selected, all entities in the current subtree will be selected for engineering.

There are several questions you should ask to be sure that this solution is the right one. Can a Person change to a Customer or vice versa? Do you always know whether the Customer is a person or a company? Usually this is not a good solution in the sense of performance because you probably need to join these tables quite often.

Generalization of an entity means that a general supertype entity will be created for a set of entities. It is possible that a subentity has attributes that are not suitable for all entities generalized under this supertype. Let's say you have entities called Customer, Company, and Person. You can generalize all of these under a supertype called Customer. This supertype now generalizes the subtypes. The subtype inherits the attributes from the supertype and probably also has attributes of its own. In Data Modeler, this is called Single Table, and you can select it by setting the Subtree Generation option in the Entity Settings dialog to Single Table. In Data Modeler, the Engineer To property for this entity will be set, and it will be cleared for all subtypes in the current entity subtree.

In reality, you will probably need a new attribute to describe which type of Customer each customer is, such as a CustomerType attribute, because there is probably a requirement for that. In Data Modeler, you use a discriminator column for that purpose. If you select Generate Discriminator, a discriminator column will be generated for your table automatically. In Use Attribute, you can define which existing attribute will be used as a discriminator; in this case, that would be CustomerType. If you want to define a name for the column, you can do that on the Column Name property. This property defines the name of the generated discriminator column. If you do not specify a name, the template is used. You can define the discriminator value for each subtype entity in the Discriminating Value property. For instance, for Person, the discriminator value could be P, and for Company it could be C. If you do not define a value, the entity short name or entity name is used. If you want the subtypes to be complete, select Complete Subtypes. This property has impact on generated arcs and the list of possible values for the discriminator column. If the list of subtypes is not complete, then optional arcs are generated, and the value for the supertype entity is also included in the permitted list of values for the discriminator column. See Figure 4-21 for a generalization of Customer with the discriminator CustomerType. Because you have a tool like Data Modeler, you can use supertypes and subtypes and model the real case and by using the Entity Properties dialog decide how to implement it when forward engineering to the relational model.

The problem with generalization is that only the common attributes can be defined, not nulls. So, mandatory attributes in subtype entities become optional columns, and an existence dependency constraint is generated in addition to the list of value constraints for the discriminator column. In Chapter 5 you will see how forward engineering works. Generalization is probably the most popular solution, and it usually works if most of the attributes are common and the business rules are similar to all the subtype entities.

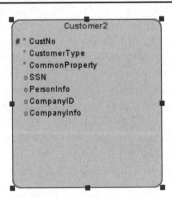

FIGURE 4-21. *Generalization with discriminator*

It is also possible to decide not to specialize and not to generalize. In that case, you will no longer have a concept of a Customer but only Person and Company. So, you will not have any information in your model that both Person and Company are Customers; you must be very sure not to have this requirement, and you must be sure that a Person cannot be changed to a Company or vice versa during its lifetime. In this case, you must define all common attributes in both entities and the specific attributes to the entity they belong to. In Data Modeler this is called Table Per Child, and you can select it by setting the Subtree Generation option in the Entity settings to Table Per Child. Selecting Table Per Child leaves entities in the current subtree selected for engineering and clears the Engineer To property for the supertype entity. In forward engineering to the relational model, only the subtype entities will be generated to tables, and they will have their own columns added with columns from the supertype entity. You will see that in more detail in Chapter 5. This solution might be good if subtype entities have little in common, if the supertype entity does not have many attributes, and if business rules are quite different in the subtype entities.

Data Modeler also supports type substitution, which complements inheritance. Type substitution is possible only if the inheritance is between structured types of entities.

Subviews

Subviews are diagrams created to represent different subject areas and to make a big diagram more readable. Any changes made to elements in a subview will be automatically made to the logical model diagram since the elements are the same. You can create as many subviews as you want by selecting SubView from the Browser pane, right-clicking, and choosing New SubView. Or just right-click the canvas and choose Diagram | Create SubView. After right-clicking and selecting Diagram, you can also delete subviews (Delete SubView). Subviews also have properties, and it is wise to name all the additional subviews to make finding the correct one easier. A subview can be named via its properties.

All new entities are automatically added to the logical diagram. Only changes that are made to an object that already exists in other subviews will be shown there. Relationships between entities that have been selected on a subview will be shown; if not all the entities needed have been selected, the relationship will not be shown. You can add new entities and relationships and make any changes in any of the subviews, and all the changes will be made automatically in all the relevant subviews. All the objects are in Data Modeler once, and subviews are just an interface to them. But there is one exception: you can delete the whole object either from your design or just from one subview. Right-click any object in any subview to see two choices: Delete Object and Delete View. Delete Object will delete the object specified everywhere, and Delete View will remove this object only from this one subview.

If you want to create a subview containing specific entities, select the entities you want in the canvas (use CTRL to select several), right-click, and select Create Subview From Selected. The easiest way to select the entities wanted is to select one entity, right-click it, and select Select Neighbors. You can specify whether only the nearest neighbors will be selected by defining the zone, or you can select all the neighbors. Then just right-click the entity again and select Create Subview From Selected. You can also drag and drop entities from the Browser pane to the subview canvas to get them included in this subview. You can also right-click in the subview and choose Objects | Add/Remove Elements to add objects to the subview or remove objects from the subview or choose Show/Hide Relationships to show or hide selected relationships.

From the toolbar you can click the icons to zoom in or out and click Fit Screen to fit the subview better in the screen. By right-clicking the subview canvas, you tune the layout (Layout), decide what details will be shown (View Details), change notation (Notation), and decide what elements will be shown in the canvas (Show).

Displays

A *display* is an independent visual version of a subview or a logical model. It has all the same elements as the original canvas, but you can change the visual as much as you want, and it will be saved as it is. You can change, for instance, the notation to be able to discuss with somebody who prefers a different notation than you usually use. Or you can change the layout or which details to show. You can, for instance, select that only names are shown from each entity. If a display is for a logical model, it can be found in the Browser pane under Logical Model | Displays. If it has been created for a subview, it can be found in the Browser pane under that particular subview. If there are displays for the model open in the canvas, they can be seen and selected below the canvas, as shown in Figure 4-22.

If you right-click the canvas, you can create displays by choosing Diagram | Create Display. Or you can create one in the Browser pane by right-clicking a subview and choosing Create Display or by right-clicking Displays in the Browser pane and choosing New Display.

Displays can and should be named to be able to find the right one when needed. You can name a display in the Properties dialog.

TIP
To find a certain element in a diagram, right-click the element name in the Browser pane, select Go To Diagram, and select the diagram you want to go to. A diagram is a logical/relational model, a subview, or a display.

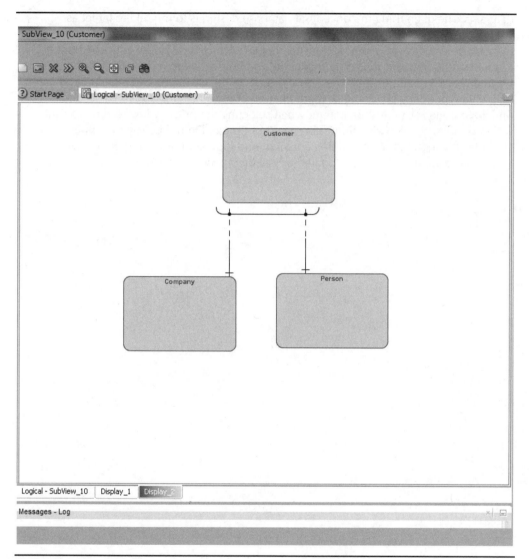

FIGURE 4-22.   *Displays*

Summary

This chapter discussed developing a conceptual database design and entity-relationship modeling and how Data Modeler supports that.

You can define the behavior of Data Modeler the way it suits you best and supports enterprise standards by setting the preferences and properties. The main tools in conceptual database design are the logical ER model and data flow diagrams. The main thing in conceptual database design is to model the target as well as possible and yet simply enough so that other people can understand it too. Data Modeler gives you many options to choose from to best model your solution. It is important to find and model the concepts and how they are related to each other via entities and relationships. You should model all the attributes you can find and their data types, lengths, domains, participation constraints, and so on. Try also to find the unique identifiers. Be careful when selecting the primary key, and be careful with redundancy; every detail must be saved just once. Do not be shy in defining attributes that don't allow nulls. Be consistent and logical in modeling. Subviews and displays are used in Data Modeler for producing more readable diagrams.

CHAPTER
5

Introducing Logical Database Design (Relational Model)

The process of creating the logical database design mainly consists of transforming the conceptual model (logical model) into a relational model. Usually that is called the *logical data model,* but in Oracle SQL Developer Data Modeler it's called a *relational model*. The result of this phase of database design is the relational database schema, which is a set of relational schemas and their constraints. If the conceptual design was done with Data Modeler, engineering to the relational model is easy. If it was done with another tool or without a tool, the first step is to insert all the data into Data Modeler to be able to use the functionalities Data Modeler provides for the transformation.

The logical database design process starts with the entity-relational (ER) model that was created in previous phases of database design. Depending on how well it was done, either you continue working on it or you move straight to transformation. Usually the model is not complete yet; you might need to add more attributes, define the data types, and so on. It's now you start thinking about whether the entities and relationships are modeled according to relational theory, and you make decisions on more difficult issues about modeling. This is the point where you must know how this database will be used (its functional models).

If it was not done earlier, it is good to start thinking about what to do with the data history, whether you need a security solution, what kind of roles there are for the users, and so on. It will be easier to implement these functionalities when there is a clear vision and understanding of the database.

Setting Preferences and Properties

There are some preferences you have not investigated yet that affect the relational model. You can find the preferences by choose Tools | Preferences. In the Preferences dialog, on the Data Modeler tab, you'll see a preference called Show Select Relational Models Dialog. If you select it, you can specify which relational models (and physical models) will be opened automatically when opening a design. If it is not selected, all relational models will be opened, but you will not be able to specify whether the physical designs will be opened, and they will not be opened automatically. My recommendation is to select Show Select Relational Models Dialog so you can control what will be opened and what will not be opened.

To define the preferences for the relational model diagram, select Preferences and go to Data Modeler | Diagram | Relational. There is only one preference here to define: Foreign Key Arrow Direction. This preference controls whether the arrow points toward the primary key or toward the foreign key in a foreign key relationship arrow.

To define the preferences for the logical model, select Preferences and go to Data Modeler | Model | Logical. (These preferences were shown in Chapter 4; see Figure 4-2.) On the Model | Logical tab, you can define the following:

- By selecting Name – Keep As The Name Of The Originating Attribute, you tell Data Modeler to keep the name specified for the attribute the same for the foreign key column in the relational model. If you want to define another name, do not select this.

■ By selecting Comments, Notes – Automatically Propagate From PK Attribute, you will get the foreign key columns in the relational model with the same comments and notes as the attribute in the parent entity.

■ Selecting Entity Create Surrogate Key tells Data Modeler to create a surrogate key for a table when the corresponding entity does not have a primary key, and selecting Relationship Use Surrogate Key tells Data Modeler to create a surrogate key as a primary key for the parent table in the relational model if there is no primary key; Data Modeler uses that column as a foreign key to the child table. In both cases, the table in the relational model will have a surrogate key as a primary key. If the parent entity has no primary key and a relationship is referring to that entity, a surrogate key is created automatically and cannot be stopped with preferences or properties.

These preferences affect only the tables and foreign keys created after setting the preference since it will be copied to the properties of the entity and the relationship, as described in Chapter 4.

To define the preferences for the relational model, select Preferences and go to Data Modeler | Model | Relational, as shown in Figure 5-1. On the Model: Relational tab, you can define the following:

■ Delete FK Columns Strategy defines the rule for Data Modeler when you want to delete a table that has one or more generated foreign key columns pointing at it. You can set it to delete the foreign key columns, do not delete the foreign key columns, or ask for confirmation for the foreign key column deletions.

■ Default Foreign Key Delete Rule specifies what happens if a user tries to delete a row containing data that is involved in a foreign key relationship. The possible values are No Action, Cascade, Set Null, and Restrict. You might have set the value already for the relationship in the logical model. In that case, that value will be used for the table created based on that entity. If you create a completely new foreign key (which I do not recommend) on the relational model, this default value is used. You can find more information about the values in Chapter 4.

■ Allow Columns Reorder During Engineering (Table's Default Value) allows Data Modeler to reorder the columns to the same order the attributes have when engineering to the relational model and to reorder the attributes to a different order of the columns when the table is engineered to the logical model. This preference will once again affect only tables created after the preference is set since the value is copied to the table properties (Allow

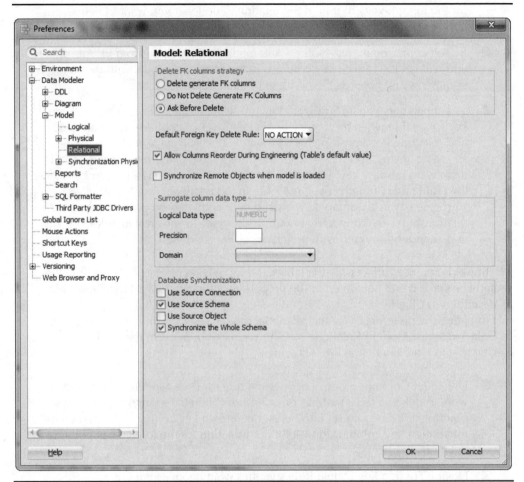

FIGURE 5-1. *Preferences for the relational model*

Columns Reorder During Engineering), and the property can be changed for an individual table. If you reorder the columns manually, the property will be automatically cleared.

■ Synchronize Remote Objects When Model Is Loaded defines whether the model where the shared object is will be automatically updated if the original object has been changed in its original location. You can synchronize your model with the database and vice versa. The Database Synchronization preferences define whether the source connection (Use Source Connection), source schema (Use Source Schema), or source objects (Use Source Object) are used in this synchronization. You can read more about synchronizing in Chapter 12.The default data type for the surrogate key is logical data type Numeric without precision. The surrogate key setting can be changed in Surrogate Column Data Type. You cannot change the logical data type (surrogate keys are always numeric), but you can define the precision for your surrogate keys, or you can select a domain to be used as the column data type for a surrogate key.

Chapter 2 discusses design-level properties. Make sure you have set them the way you want.

A relational model also has properties. In the Model Properties dialog, you can rename the model, make it visible or invisible, and define the default relational database management system (RDMS) type and site for the model. You can define the naming options for a logical model on the Naming Options tab. You can also define the naming options for the relational model by right-clicking the name of the relational model and selecting Properties. You can define naming options for a table, column, view, index, and constraint the same way as you did for the elements in the logical model. I suggest you use the same Valid Characters setting for the relational model as the logical model to make engineering work more fluent. Engineering To Relational Model can do a transformation between uppercase and lowercase, but it cannot convert, for example, Scandinavian letters. If you have characters allowed in the logical model that are not allowed in the relational model, Data Modeler will not check these during the engineering to the relational model but only when you try to open the properties that has a conflict, for instance, the table properties.

Transforming from a Logical Model to a Relational Model

When the logical model is complete (for now), it is time to transform it to a relational model. Before the transformation, it would be good to check the logical model one more time. Is your model solving all the needs and requirements for business data? Have the modeling and naming standards been followed? Are the primary keys correct and defined? Are there entities without a primary key? Do you want Data Modeler to define a surrogate key for them, or do you want to do something yourself? Are all the known attributes defined? Are their data types and compulsories defined correctly? This is a good time to run the design rules for the logical model. See Chapter 2 for more information about design rules.

If you have one-to-one relationships in your logical model, check one more time that they are correct. Sometimes there is a good reason for having a one-to-one relationship, for instance if the life cycle of the metadata and the rest of the data is different. An example could be an entity named Letter. There might be a business rule that the information about who the letter is for and when the letter was sent must be saved for 10 years but the content of the letter must be saved for only one month. From a maintenance perspective, two separate entities and a one-to-one relationship would be a good solution. If you make solutions that are purposeful but not obvious, remember to document them.

TIP
Document solutions that are justified but not so
obvious. You can use the Notes property for that.

Now make sure you have normalized the logical model as far as needed. Data Modeler supports normalized design, and it also allows you to document the level of normalization in each entity (and table) on the Volume Properties tab in the Normal Form property and to define whether it is normalized enough with the Adequate Normalized property. There are plenty of good books on relational theory that will explain normalization, among other things. In short, it means that the information has been saved and modeled just once. It is vital to make sure the data quality in your database is good; what is the point of having a database full of information you cannot trust? If the data is saved only once, it stays correct and good quality much easier than if it has been duplicated in the database in many places. When you are ready with your logical model, it is time to move on to transforming the relational model.

Setting Transformation Rules

The transformation from a logical model to a relational model is straightforward. An entity will become a table, an attribute will become a column, and a relationship will become a foreign key. For a one-to-many relationship, a new column for the foreign key will be added to the child table, and in a one-to-one relationship, it will be added to the table on the mandatory side of the relationship. In both cases, if the relationship is identifying, the new foreign key column will be also added to the primary key of the child table. If the Create Surrogate Key property is selected for the entity, a surrogate primary key is automatically generated for a table.

NOTE
If an entity does not have its own primary key and you want the primary key to be generated for the table based on the relationships and surrogate primary keys of the parent tables, make sure you create the primary key for the entity and select all the relationships for its columns before clicking Engineer To Relational. Otherwise, the child table will not have a primary key. See Chapter 8 for an example of generating data warehouse fact tables (Figures 8-1, 8-2, and 8-3).

If the relationship is on the cardinality of many-to-many (m:n), a new table will be created to resolve the m:n cardinality, and a new column based on the primary key attribute in each table in the relationship will be created. A primary key for the new table is created based on those columns. Also, new one-to-many relationships are created for both tables involved.

If a relationship has its own attributes, some tools will create a new table with all original relationships and attributes from the relationship. But Data Modeler does not do that unless the relationship is m:n. In one-to-many cases, Data Modeler adds the attribute as a column to the child table and creates a dependent column constraint for that (more about that in the next section). So, if you do not want the column to be added to the child table, do not create an attribute for the relationship but to the entity you want it to belong to. It might mean that you need to create a new entity.

If an attribute is multivalued such as a phone number (home number, office number, cell phone), there are a couple of choices. You can create a user-defined data type (collection) and use that for the data type for the attribute (see Chapter 4 for more information), or you can split the attribute into several attributes for the entity or create a new entity for the multivalued attribute. Usually a new entity is recommended because it is more flexible, but sometimes you need to limit the values to a certain number (maybe a Person is allowed to have no more than three phone numbers), and then it is better to use that number of attributes in the original entity. The solution really depends on the requirements and how far the model needs to be normalized.

If an attribute is composite (structured) such as an address (StreetName, Number, City, ZIP, Country), there are again a couple of choices. You can create a user-defined data type (structured) and use that for the data type for the attribute (see Chapter 4 for more information), or you can split the attribute for several attributes into the entity or create a new entity (or entities) for the composite attribute. Usually a new entity is recommended because it is more flexible, and you might find other attributes for that entity (AddressType, AddressValidUntil, and so on), but sometimes you need to denormalize to avoid joins and end up adding the attributes to the original entity (in this case, make sure your solution meets all the requirements). The solution really depends on the requirements and how far the model needs to be normalized.

NOTE
If you want to see the structured column expanded in a diagram, just right-click the relational diagram and choose View Details | Expand Complex Types.

The transformation rules just explained are shown in Table 5-1 in a more complex form.

Heading Element in Logical Model	Heading Element in Relational Model
Entity	Turns into a table.
Attribute	Turns into a column.
Relationship	Turns into a foreign key constraint.
Unique identifier	Turns into a primary key.
One-to-many relationship	Columns for the foreign key will be added to the child table; if the relationship is identifying, these new foreign key columns will be added also to the primary key.
One-to-one relationship	Columns for the foreign key will be added to the table on the mandatory side of the relationship; if the relationship is identifying, these new foreign key columns will be added also to the primary key.
Many-to-many relationship	A new table will be created (with the name of the relationship). Columns based on the primary key attributes on each table in the relationship will be added. A primary key for the new table is created based on those columns. Also, new one-to-many relationships are created for both tables involved.
Relationship with attributes, relationship one-to-many	Data Modeler adds the attribute as a column to the child table and creates a dependent column constraint.
Relationship with attributes, relationship many-to-many	A new table will be created (with the name of the relationship). Columns based on primary key attributes on each table in the relationship will be added. A primary key for the new table is created based on those columns. Also, new one-to-many relationships are created for both tables involved. A column for the relationship attribute is created for the new table.
Multivalued attribute	There are two choices: ■ Create a user-defined data type (collection) and use that for the data type for the attribute. ■ Split the attribute into separate attributes/entities before engineering to the relational model.

TABLE 5-1. *Transformation Rules for Engineering to a Relational Model (continued)*

Heading Element in Logical Model	Heading Element in Relational Model
Composite (structured) attribute	There are two choices: ■ Create a user-defined data type (structured) and use that for the data type for the attribute. ■ Split the attribute either for several attributes into the entity or create a new entity/entities for the composite attribute.

TABLE 5-1.   *Transformation Rules for Engineering to a Relational Model*

Sometimes, for example, a circular structure in an ER diagram can cause a situation where one or more of the candidate keys are overlapping. That means they have one or more attributes in common. Figure 5-2 shows a Faculty that has Students and Courses. When a Student passes a Course, it will be marked in StudentRecord. In Figure 5-2 you can see that both foreign key candidates in

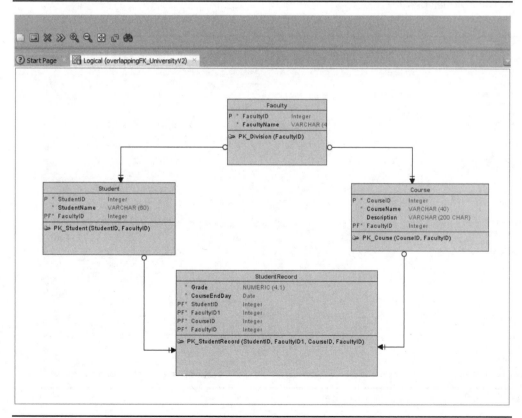

FIGURE 5-2.   *Overlapping keys (Bachman notation)*

StudentRecord (the one from Student and the one from Course) have the attribute FacultyID in it. This situation is fine if a Student can also take Courses from other Faculties than the one signed up for; this means that those two FacultyIDs can be different. But if a Student can take Courses only from their own Faculty, it might be confusing to bring the FacultyID from two different routes. You can see the same thing also in the Entity Properties dialog on the Overlapping Attributes tab, shown in Figure 5-3.

On this tab you can also specify that the attribute will be folded (not engineered as a column) by selecting the box without a heading (highlighted in Figure 5-3). The attribute with the actual attribute name (FacultyID) will be engineered, but the attribute with a name that contains a version number (FacultyID1) will be folded. You can define this with the creation order of relationships. Later in this chapter you will see how folding affects the process of engineering to the relational model.

Chapter 4 discussed the concept of inheritance. Before starting the transformation, check that your settings are correct for the transformation you want for the inheritance. In the next section, you will see, for instance, how the inheritance will be transformed in Data Modeler.

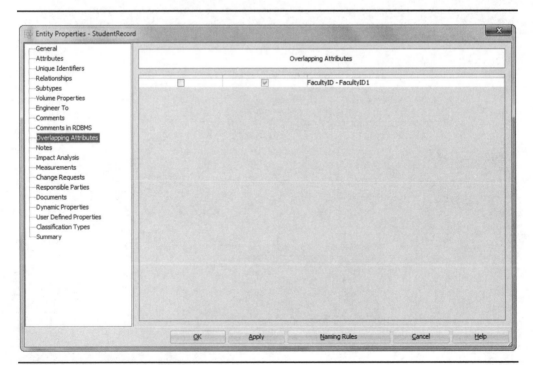

FIGURE 5-3. *An overlapping attribute*

Engineer to Relational Model

In Data Modeler the transformation functionality is called Engineer To Relational Model. You start the transformation either by right-clicking the logical model in the Browser pane and selecting Engineer To Relational Model or by clicking the double arrow pointing right (Figure 5-2). Figure 5-4 shows the Engineer To Relational Model screen. This is the tree view for selecting what will be transformed. It is also possible to use the tabular view, shown in Figure 5-5. This screen is for seeing and selecting what elements to transform. The green check in front of the element name indicates

FIGURE 5-4.   *Engineer To Relational Model screen, the tree view*

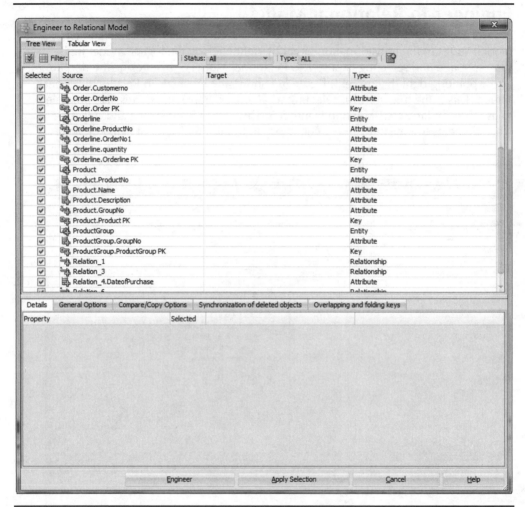

FIGURE 5-5. *Engineer To Relational Model screen, the tabular view*

that this element will be engineered. If you want to leave an element out of the engineering process, just deselect it.

In the tree view, you can select the scope of the objects: the logical model or one of the subviews in that logical model. You can also narrow down the number of objects with a filter (Figure 5-4) to show only new, deleted, or modified objects or a combination of those. If you have several relational models, you should select which one is the one to transform to the logical model; you do that with the list in the top-right corner. If you have selected a logical subview (not the whole model), you can also select As SubView, which will create a relational subview and engineer your elements also there (Chapter 4 covered subviews).

A green plus sign on the screen means that this element is new and will be added to the relational model (see Figure 5-6, which shows a new attribute called HelisNewAttribute), and a red X button indicates that this element has been deleted. A yellow triangle with the exclamation mark in front of the element name indicates that there are some changes in that element in the logical model compared to the relational model. Drill down to the level where the change is (in Figure 5-6 it is the attribute Name), and on the Details tab you can see what the difference actually is (in Figure 5-6 it is the comment). The difference is highlighted.

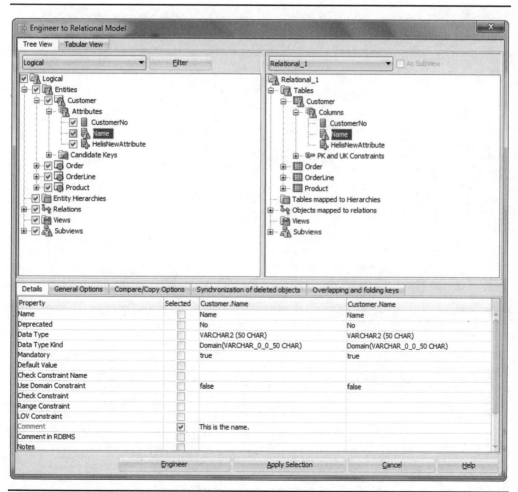

FIGURE 5-6. *Engineer To Relational Model screen, Details tab*

Options on the Engineer To Relational Model Screen

There are plenty of options for generating the relational model. If you click Engineer, the changes will be committed to the relational model, and the engineering is completed. If you click Cancel, no engineering will be done. If you click Apply Selection, your selections will be saved, and the Engineer To Relational Model screen will close.

At the bottom of the Engineer To Relational Model screen, you will find a tab called General Options (Figure 5-7). On the General Options tab you can specify general rules for the transformation. Engineer Coordinates defines whether the

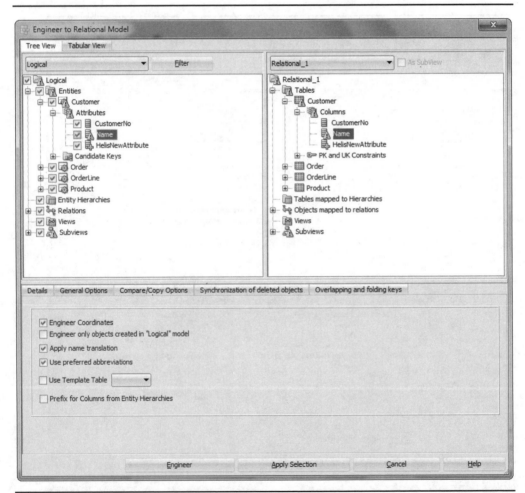

FIGURE 5-7. *Engineer To Relational Model screen, General Options tab*

objects will be positioned at the same way as their source objects. Engineer Only Objects Created In "Logical" Model limits the object to be engineered only to those objects explicitly created in the logical model.

If you attached a glossary to a design on the Naming Standards tab of the Design Properties dialog (see Chapter 2), you can use the glossary words to replace the names used for entities and attributes with other names defined in a glossary when engineering to tables and columns. You can do that by selecting Apply Name Translation. If you have defined a plural in the glossary for a table, that will be used for name translation; otherwise, the Abbreviation setting is used. If you do not have a plural or an abbreviation defined for a table, then the Alternative Abbreviation setting will be used. For a column, the order is Abbreviation, Plural, and Alternative Abbreviation, depending on which of them has been defined for a column. If the glossary has no definition for the word, the entity/attribute name is used.

During the name translation, also the model-level properties set on the Naming Options tab are followed. First the name is translated using the glossary. If the new name doesn't obey the Max Name Length restriction, then the Alternative Abbreviations settings are used for translating the name. If the Character Case option is set to Mixed, no case transformation is performed. If it is set to Upper Case or Lower Case, the possible transformation for cases is done. So, if you select Apply Name Translation, the tables and columns might not be called the same as the related entity and its attributes, but the names will be translated according to the glossary. The same applies also for reverse engineering (Engineer From Relational To Logical). If you have the Apply Name Translation option selected when engineering, you should also have it enabled when reverse engineering because if you do not, the names will be changed for entities and attributes like they are for tables and columns.

NOTE

If you select Apply Name Translation, it is wise to keep it selected all the time for engineering and for reverse engineering to guarantee correct naming for all your objects.

It is also possible to translate the names of the entities and attributes to the ones defined in the Preferred Abbreviation setting for the tables and columns by selecting both Apply Name Translation and Use Preferred Abbreviations. In this case, all your tables and columns will be called whatever was defined as the Preferred Abbreviation property for the entity and the attribute. If you have Preferred Abbreviation selected when engineering, you should also have it selected when reverse engineering because if you do not, the names will be changed for entities and attributes like they are for tables and columns. If you select the Preferred Abbreviation option, it is wise to keep it selected all the time for engineering and for reverse engineering to guarantee correct naming for all your objects.

TIP
*For the Preferred Abbreviation property, you do not actually need to define an abbreviation. You can also use it, for instance, if you want to have singular words in entity names and plurals in table names. For example, you can type **STUDENT** for the entity Name and type **STUDENTS** for the Preferred Abbreviation property for the entity. Then select both Apply Name Translation and Use Preferred Abbreviations when engineering. Now your tables will have plural names, while your entities still have singular names. Make sure to leave the Preferred Abbreviation property empty for those entities and attributes you do not want to use abbreviations for naming as relational objects.*

TIP
You can also use the Name Abbreviations utility on the Tools menu to convert abbreviations to names, and vice versa. You will learn more about that in Chapter 8.

If you select Prefix For Columns From Entity Hierarchies, the column names for tables in hierarchies will have the table name as a prefix for a foreign key or a primary key column even though you might have defined Apply Name Translation and Use Preferred Abbreviations for all other column names. If Prefix For Columns From Entity Hierarchies is not selected, the same rules as defined for other tables will be followed.

Sometimes there are some technical columns you would like to add to your tables, but there is no need to have those on your entities. These columns could be, for instance, CreatedDate, Creator, ModifiedDate, and Modifier. There is a simple way of adding those columns to every table or a set of tables with Data Modeler during the Engineer To Relational Model transformation. All you need is a table called table_template that will include only the columns you want to add to other tables. In this example, that table would be table_template (CreatedDate, Creator, ModifiedDate, Modifier). On the Engineer To Relational Model screen, first select all the tables where you want to add those columns and then select Use Template Table. Then select the table table_template from the Use Template Table list and click Engineer. You do not need to worry if you have already created the columns before because the functionality will add the columns only if they have not been added before.

TIP
If you want to add technical columns to your tables without adding them to entities, use the Use Template Table functionality when engineering to the relational model.

On the Compare/Copy Options tab (Figure 5-8), you can select a pair of objects (entity/table, attribute/column, unique identifier/index, relation/foreign key, relation/

FIGURE 5-8. *Engineer To Relational Model screen, Compare/Copy Options tabs*

table, entity view/view) and define which properties will be compared when checking what has changed and which changes to engineer to the relational model. So, you can decide which changes are worth mentioning and engineering and which are not. You can narrow down the properties shown on the Details tab by selecting the Show Selected Properties Only property to show only the properties that have been selected. In other words, if you uncheck a property from the list on the Compare/Copy Options tab, it will not be shown to you on the Details tab, it will not be shown as a change to you in the Engineer To Relational Model screen, and it will not be engineered to the relational model. If you select Don't Apply For New Objects, all changes (and changes to those unchecked properties) will be engineered to the relational model for all *new* objects but not those created before setting this property.

For instance, if you disable the property Comment From Entity/Table and select Show Selected Properties Only and Don't Apply for New Objects, the property Comment of an entity/table will not be shown on the Details tab, and any changes to it will not be shown with a triangle on the Engineer screen. Changes in comment will not be engineered to the relational model either except for new entities if you have checked Don't Apply For New Objects.

If you select the Exclude Unchecked Objects From Tree option, the unchecked objects on the Engineer To Relational Model screen will not be shown at all (and because they are unchecked, they will not be engineered either). When you make changes to Exclude Unchecked Objects From Tree, remember to always click the Update Tree button to get your changes updated to the Engineer To Relational Model screen.

If you uncheck, let's say, the entity Customer on the Engineer To Relational Model screen and select Exclude Unchecked Objects From Tree, you will not see the entity Customer on the Engineer To Relational Model screen at all, and it will not be engineered to the relational model.

In Figure 5-9 you can see that there is an attribute (HelisNewAttribute) deleted from the logical model, but it still exists in the relational model where it was engineered to earlier. If you want to delete that column from the relational model, you must select Select on the Synchronization Of Deleted Objects tab. If you do not select this, no deletion will be done during the engineering.

On the Overlapping And Folding Keys tab (Figure 5-10) you can see whether there are keys that are overlapping (see "Setting Transformation Rules" earlier in this chapter for more information about overlapping candidate keys), and you can decide what to do with them.

If you do not select Fold (Figure 5-10), the engineering is done as usual. If you select Fold, the engineering will not generate the FacultyID column for the Student foreign key. It will not generate the column and does not have that in the foreign or primary key in StudentRecord. In Figure 5-11 you can see on the left the engineering without folding and on the right the engineering with folding enabled.

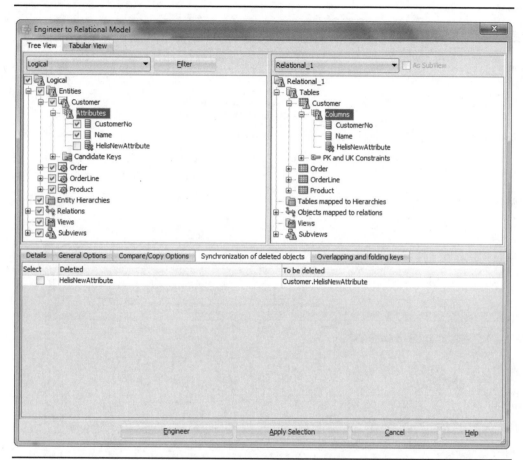

FIGURE 5-9.   *Engineer To Relational Model screen, synchronization of deleted objects*

In the tabular view (Figure 5-12), you can select/deselect all with the buttons in the upper-left corner. You can filter the element in the list with the Filter field by typing a name or part of the name. You can also filter the list of elements with the Status list, depending on the status of the element, with these values: All, Unchanged, Modified, New, and Deleted. Or you can filter with the Type list with these values: ALL, Attribute, Entity, Key, Relationship, Subview. On the Tabular View tab, there is a button in the upper right for generating a report (Figure 5-12) of what the engineering will be doing. Figure 5-13 shows the report properties. You can set Output Format to HTML, PDF, or RTF. You can give a title and a name for the report. If you select Separate Objects By Status, your report will show separately categorized modified, new, and deleted objects. Click Generate Report to generate the report.

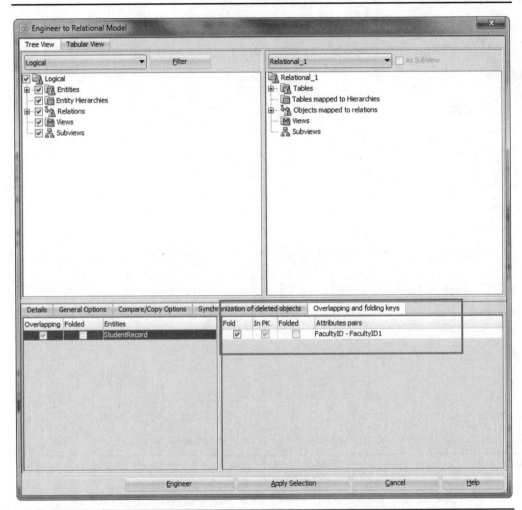

FIGURE 5-10. *Engineer To Relational Model screen, Overlapping And Folding Keys tab*

Examples for Engineering to the Relational Model

There are general rules for transforming to the relational model, as discussed earlier in this chapter. During the transformation, also the names of elements in the relational model are defined. Here are some guidelines about that:

■ If you do not interfere with the naming while transforming, an entity will become a table with the same Name setting as the entity, with a long name of the entity, and with an abbreviation of an entity's short name. A column will be named after the attribute Name, and the Abbreviation field for a column will be empty by default.

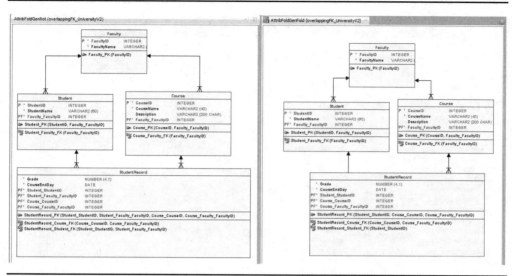

FIGURE 5-11.   *Overlapping key, no fold or fold*

- If you select Apply Name Translation and Use Preferred Abbreviations during the engineering, the table name and the long name will be the Preferred Abbreviation setting of an entity, the name for a column will be the Preferred Abbreviation setting of the attribute, and the abbreviation for the column will be empty.

- If you select Apply Translation and have a glossary assigned to the design, the glossary will be followed in the translation as described earlier in this chapter.

You can also define the Abbreviation property for a table and a column. These abbreviations can be used in templates on the Naming Standards tab for a relational model, as explained in Chapter 2. You can also exclude transforming properties from the engineering process using the Compare/Copy Options tab in the Engineer To Relational Model screen, as explained earlier in this chapter.

Chapter 4 discussed different ways of transforming an inheritance. Figure 5-14 shows an example of an arc solution (described in Chapter 4) and shows how it is transformed to a relational model. There are three tables (on the right). A foreign key column has been created for both child tables (marked with *PF*), and because the child entities are weak entities, the primary key of the parent entity is taken along to the primary key of both child tables. A foreign key has been created for both child tables. The arc in the relational model shows that a Customer can be either Person or Company, not both.

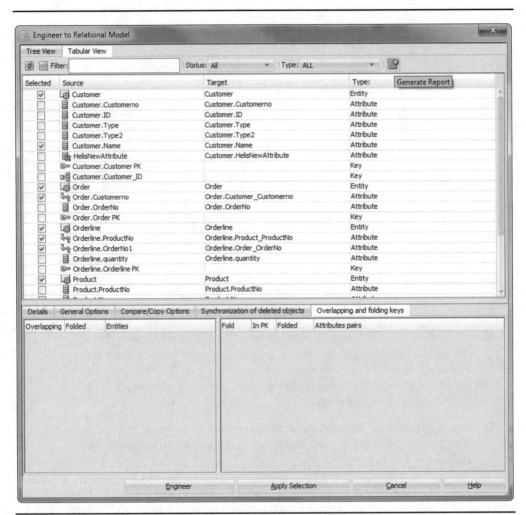

FIGURE 5-12. *Engineer To Relational Model screen, tabular view and Generate Report button*

Figure 5-15 shows an example of a single-table solution (described in Chapter 4) and shows how it is transformed to a relational model. There is only one table (on the right) including a column for each attribute in the entities on the left. Any mandatory attributes in the child entities are transformed to the obligatory columns in the table. No foreign keys are needed, and the primary key is the one for the parent entity.

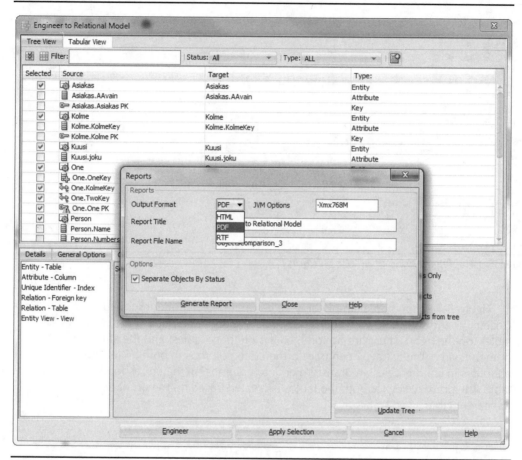

FIGURE 5-13. *Engineer To Relational Model screen, Reports dialog*

There is also a new column (Customer_TYPE), which is the discriminator column (see Chapter 4) for the table to divide the rows of the table to be either Companies or Persons. Data Modeler creates that automatically as well as the Existence Dependency Constraint shown in Figure 5-16. This constraint is a check constraint that verifies that if Customer_TYPE is C, the Company_ID cannot be NULL; however, SSN and PersonInfo must be null, and if Customer_TYPE is P, then CompanyID and CompanyInfo must be NULL, and both SSN and PersonInfo cannot be NULL. So, Data Modeler automatically creates the logic for the existence of either a Person or a Company. In Figure 5-17, you can see the check constraint with a list of allowable values created by Data Modeler to check for the discriminator column.

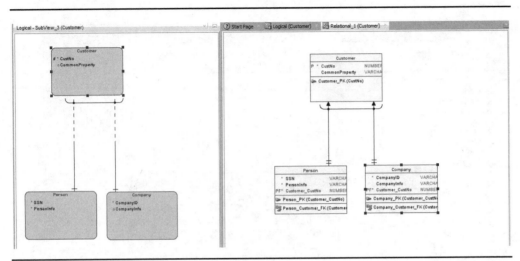

FIGURE 5-14. *Engineering of an arc solution*

Figure 5-18 shows an example of a table-per-child solution (described in Chapter 4) and shows how it is transformed to a relational model. There are two tables (on the right). There are no foreign keys on these tables, and the attributes from the parent entity have been transformed into columns in both table. The attributes in child entities are transformed into columns on the corresponding table. The primary key for both the tables is created based on the primary key of the parent table.

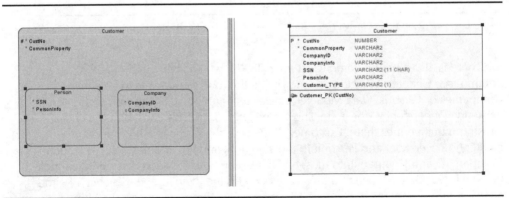

FIGURE 5-15. *Engineering of a single-table solution*

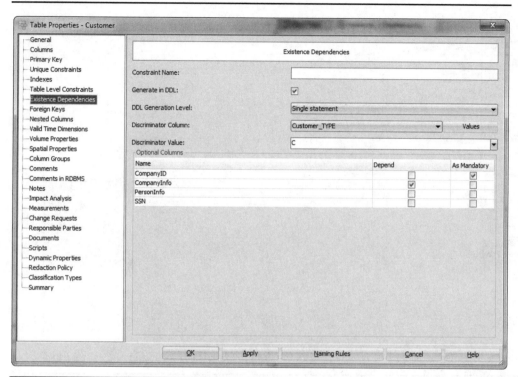

FIGURE 5-16. *Existence dependency for a single-table solution*

Figure 5-19 shows an example of a table-for-each-entity solution described in Chapter 4 and shows how it is transformed to a relational model. There are three tables (on the right). A foreign key column has been created for both child tables (marked with *PF*), and because the child entities are weak entities, the primary key of the parent entity is taken along to the primary key of both child tables. A foreign key has been created for both child tables. The arc in a relational model shows that a Customer can be either a Person or a Company, not both. You can also ask Data Modeler to create the discriminator column. It also creates the list of allowable values and triggers to watch that the Company_TYPE is correct compared to the row inserted or updated to a child table. So, if a row is inserted or updated in the Company table, the trigger checks that the value in Company_TYPE is C. If it is not, it raises an error.

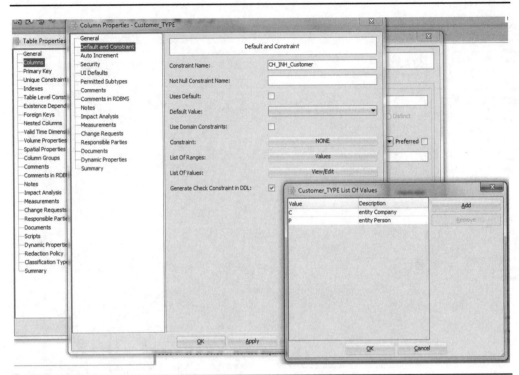

FIGURE 5-17. *A check constraint for a single-table solution*

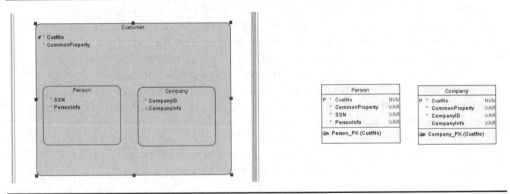

FIGURE 5-18. *Engineering of a table per child*

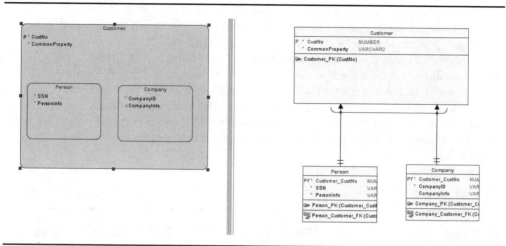

FIGURE 5-19.   *Engineering of table-for-each-entity solution*

Chapter 4 also discussed a case of a one-to-many relationship with its own attributes. In Figure 5-20 you can see how that is transformed. The relationship attribute (OrderDate) has been created as a column for the child table, and since it was not originally mandatory, it is not mandatory as a column either. A dependent

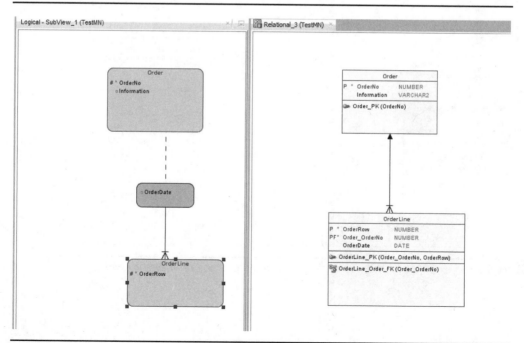

FIGURE 5-20.   *Example of an engineering of a one-to-many relationship with an attribute*

column constraint is created, a foreign key and its column (OrderNo) have been created for the child table, and since the child entity did not have a primary key, a surrogate primary key has been created for the child table.

In Figure 5-21 you will find an example of a many-to-many relationship with its own attribute. On the right you can see that a new table was created (Relation_1) with a mandatory column (OrderDate) like the attribute was. The Product entity did not have a primary key, so that has been created as a surrogate primary key, and the foreign key and its columns have been added to the child table (Relation_1). The primary key for the child table is created based on the primary keys in the parent tables.

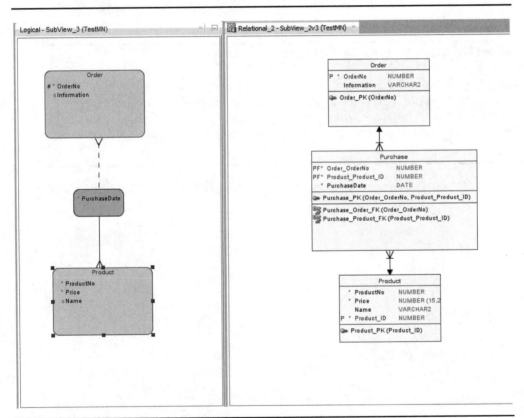

FIGURE 5-21. *Example of an engineering of a many-to-many relationship with an attribute*

TIP
*When engineering to a relational model, if the keys
or constraints are not named as you want, go to the
Browser pane, right-click the name of the relational
model, and select Apply Naming Standards To Keys
And Constraints.*

Introducing the Relational Model

The first relational model (Relational_1) is created automatically when the design
is saved the first time. You can add relational models by right-clicking the
relational model in the Browser pane and selecting New Relational Model. A
relational model (including Relational_1) can be renamed in the Properties dialog.
A relational model *diagram* can be closed by right-clicking in the Browser pane
and selecting Hide or opened again by selecting Show. A relational *model* can be
opened or closed, which means that the objects of a model either will be shown
in the Browser pane or not. In a relational model, you can create subviews and
displays the same way as described in Chapter 4.

In Figure 5-22 you can see an example of a relational model diagram. In a
relational model, the primary key column is marked with *P*, a unique key column

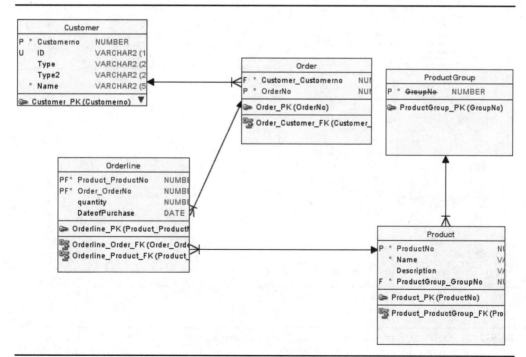

FIGURE 5-22.   *Example of a relational model diagram*

with *U*, a foreign key column with *F*, and a primary key column that has been created based on an identifying relationship with *PF*. A mandatory column is marked with an asterisk (*). A deprecated element is shown with strikethrough. If the table name has ":1" in the end of the name, it means you have created graphical synonyms for that table. If you right-click a relational model or a subview canvas, you can decide what details will be shown on the diagram by selecting View Details, as shown in Figure 5-23.

The main concepts in the relational model are tables, columns, and foreign keys. In a relational model you can share tables officially with other relational models in a same design but in practice also with other designs. If you drag a table to another design, the tool shows it is not possible, but it still creates a shared table between the two designs. Sharing between designs has some limitations: You cannot have design-level domains and definitions from the data types model because they cannot be used in table definitions. Sharing a table means that you will have a

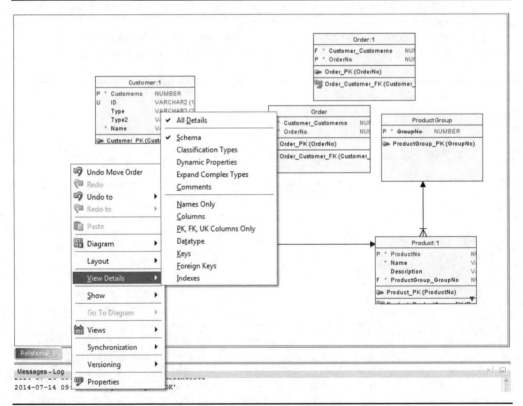

FIGURE 5-23. *Right-click menu for relational model canvas, with details options*

pointer to a table in another diagram, not a copy of it. If you want to create a shared table with another design/relational model, you must first open both the designs/ relational models. Then you go to the Browser pane and simply drag the shareable table to the relational model canvas of the other design or the other relational model. In the upper-left corner of the table, you can see a symbol that shows the table has been shared (Figure 5-24).

All the properties of this table will be grayed out on the shared end, and the table can be edited only at the original location. If the table has been changed in the original location, it is useful to transfer the updates to the shared to design. There are two ways of doing this: automatic or manual. For the automatic synchronization, set the property Synchronize Remote Objects When Model Is Loaded as explained earlier in this chapter, and in that case the table will be updated (when changed) whenever the relational model of the design where the table has been shared to is opened or activated. In practice, this means the table will always be up to date. If you have not set the property, you can synchronize manually by right-clicking the relational model in the Browser pane and selecting Synchronize Remote Objects or by right-clicking the relational diagram and selecting Synchronization and then Synchronize Remote Objects.

From the table's Properties Summary tab, you can see where the table has been shared from in the properties Remote Design and Remote Model. If you decide to share a table with another design, bear in mind that there are some limitations, as

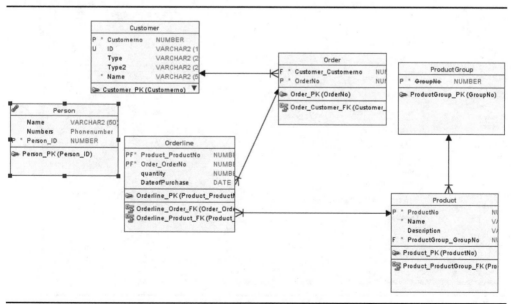

FIGURE 5-24. *Table (Person) shared from another design*

mentioned earlier: no design-level domains and no definitions from the data types model. I also suggest selecting the automatic synchronization in this case.

NOTE
Remember to save the original design before sharing tables to any other design.

Tables

Tables have many properties. The ones that also exist for an entity will be transformed from the entity during the engineering process, and those that are table specific can be edited in the Table Properties dialog, as shown in Figure 5-25. The first thing to do after the engineering would probably be to run the naming rules for a relational model. This can be easily done by clicking the Naming Rules button on the General pane of the Table Properties dialog.

Table Properties - Customer	

General
- General
- Columns
- Primary Key
- Unique Constraints
- Indexes
- Table Level Constraints
- Existence Dependencies
- Foreign Keys
- Nested Columns
- Valid Time Dimensions
- Volume Properties
- Spatial Properties
- Column Groups
- Comments
- Comments in RDBMS
- Notes
- Impact Analysis
- Measurements
- Change Requests
- Responsible Parties
- Documents
- Scripts
- Dynamic Properties
- Redaction Policy
- Classification Types
- Summary

General

Name: Customer

Long Name: Customer

Abbreviation:

Engineer: ☑

PK Name: Customer_PK

Based on Structured Type:

Schema:

Register as Spatial Table: ☐

Object Identifier is PK ☐

Allow Type Substitution: ☑

Generate in DDL: ☑

Engineer as relationship ☐

Allow Columns Reorder During Engineering ☑

Deprecated ☐

OK   Apply   Naming Rules   Cancel   Help

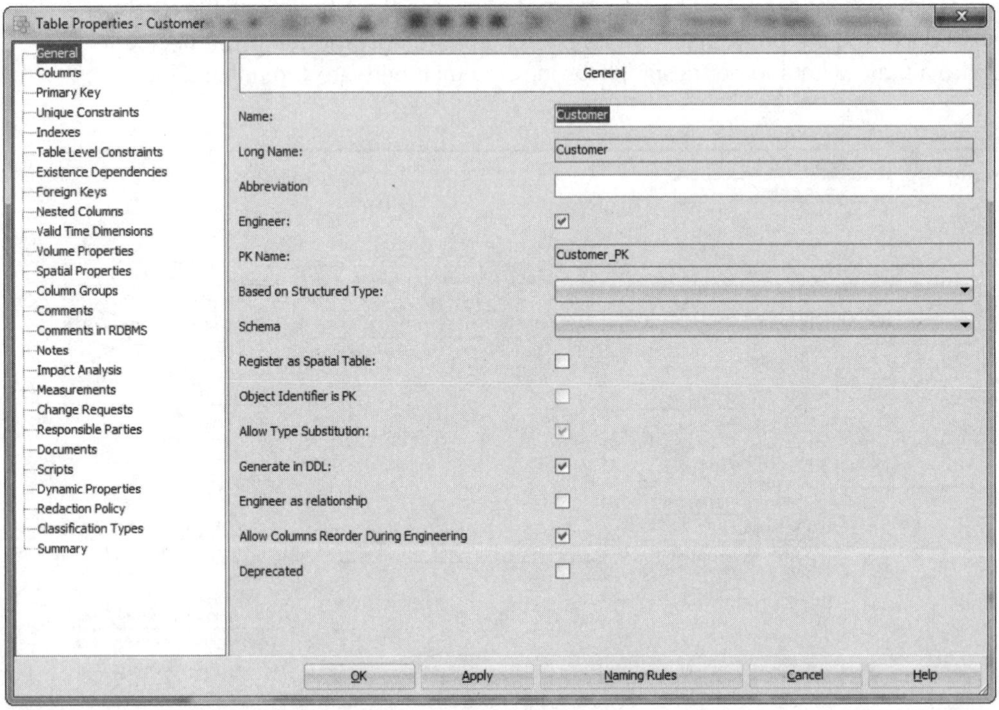

FIGURE 5-25. *Table Properties, General tab*

The General tab has properties for controlling engineering, reverse engineering, and DDL generation. Engineer defines whether the table and its properties will be included when engineering to the logical model (reverse engineering), and Allow Columns Reorder During Engineering lets Data Modeler reorder the attributes of the associated entity in the same order as their associated columns in the table definition. This property is copied from the preferences (Allow Columns Reorder During Engineering) introduced earlier in this chapter but can be changed if needed for an individual table. Generate In DDL defines whether the table is included when the DDLs are generated.

Engineer As Relationship defines whether relationship attributes are created during backward engineering. In other words, if the table is an intersection table, selecting this option will let the table be backward engineered as a many-to-many (m:n) relationship in which columns that are not in the foreign key become attributes of the relationship. This is the opposite behavior for the transformation as when the logical model has a many-to-many relationship with possible attributes. If you want to associate a schema name with a table, you can do that in the table properties by selecting the schema from the drop-down list. If you have not added the schema yet, you can do it in the Browser pane under Relational Model by right-clicking the schema, selecting New Schema, and giving a name to the schema. You can add tables, views, and indexes to a schema either on table/view/index properties or by selecting them in the schema properties. If you associate a schema to your relational model object, the schema name will appear in diagrams, and the schema name is also used during DDL generation. You can read more about DDL generation in Chapter 7. Usually schemas are added in the physical design, as shown in Chapter 6.

TIP
If you have created schemas and associated them with objects, you can create relational models based on that. In the Browser pane, go to the relational model, right-click, and select Create New Models Based On Schema Names. Data Modeler will create a new relational model for each schema you have specified and name it with the same name as the schema.

There are also other properties for a table. You can tell the tool that a table is a spatial table by selecting Register As Spatial Table. For a structured type, you can allow type substitution for DDL generation by selecting Allow Type Substitution. You can define that the table will have an object identifier primary key (OID) by selecting Object Identifier Is PK, and in DDL generation for Oracle the OBJECT IDENTIFIER IS PRIMARY KEY clause is generated.

TIP
To see the DDL for a table or a view, right-click the object on the canvas and select DDL Preview. When the previewer is open, you can select another object in the relational model, and the previewer is updated accordingly.

In the table properties there are also a list of columns and their properties. There are three tabs: Details, Overview, and Security. By double-clicking (or clicking the Property icon), you can see more column properties. On the Security tab, you can find a list of columns and their security properties (you can find the same properties also from the attribute Properties under Security). It is possible to define a sensitive type for an attribute, as explained in Chapter 4, but there are many other options for a column to be defined. For a column, you can define whether it contains personally identifiable information (PII) or sensitive information, and you can define the masking type (FULL, NO, PARTIAL, RANDOM, REGEXP). If you select either PARTIAL or REGEXP, you can also select Mask Template (see Chapter 4 for creating a mask template). A mask template must be of same data type as the column it will be attached to. If you mark a column as Sensitive Info, the name of the column will be shown in red on any diagram. If you know you will create an Oracle database (Oracle Enterprise Edition 11.2.0.4 or newer version, licensed with the Advanced Security option), you might also want to define a redaction policy for your table. The redaction policy can be defined in the table properties under Redaction Policy. You can define the name for the policy, define that the policy is Enabled and taken into account when generating DDLs (Generate In DDL), and define whether the real data will be presented to end users or not by setting the expression. If you leave Expression empty, it defaults to true and shows all data not defined to be masked to the users. Each redaction policy is for only one table providing a masking definition and condition when it's applied for one or more columns belonging to that table. So, after defining the redaction policy, you go to the column properties and define the Contains PII, Sensitive Info, Masking Type, and Mask Template properties for the columns you want to be marked sensitive and maybe even masked. These security features were introduced in Data Modeler version 4.0.

If a column is based on a structured type, for instance PersonName (FirstName, LastName), you can see that on the Nested Columns tab. Each name (Name .FirstName, Name.LastName), data type, and information about whether that column is a primary key (PK), foreign key (FK), or mandatory field (M) is shown, and you can go and see other properties either by clicking the Properties button (pencil icon) or by double-clicking the column name.

If you decided to split your structured type into regular attributes and columns, you might want to use the Column Groups properties to keep those columns together when generating a user interface or showing those columns on a screen (probably this will not be automatic but just documentation for the programmers). For example, a column group named PersonName might include columns FirstName and LastName. On the Column Groups tab, you can create, edit, and remove column groups and document them with the Note property.

On the Primary Key or Unique Constraints tab, you can see, add, modify, and delete primary key/unique constraints. You can also define them as Generate to get the element for the DDL generation, Engineer to let Data Modeler take the element in the reverse engineering process, and Deprecated to let people know this is an unsupported object. And you can see and modify the fields Notes, Comments, and Comments In RDBMS. By clicking the Properties icon (pencil icon) or double-clicking the constraint name, you can also edit other properties for that constraint. On the Foreign Keys tab, you can see a list of foreign keys defined for the table and all the details of each foreign key. You can add and remove foreign keys and edit their properties. For instance, if you did not decide the delete rules for your relationships in the conceptual design, you can now set them for foreign keys or go to the relationship and change it there and engineer to the relational model again. You might also want to check that the Transferable property is set correctly. It controls whether the foreign key relationship is updatable. For example, if a Student is a member of a Faculty and later wants to change to another Faculty, the foreign key value for FacultyID in the Student table should be able to be changed, and it can be changed if the relationship is transferable. In a nontransferable relationship, a foreign key value cannot be changed. For example, if an OrderLine has a nontransferable relationship to an Order, an OrderLine cannot be reassigned later to another Order. If the foreign key relationship is nontransferable, a white diamond appears on the line in the diagram. You might also want to check that the Generate In DDL property is the way you want it to be.

TIP
If you want to see the foreign key names in a diagram, right-click the diagram and choose Show | Labels.

TIP
If you want to be sure you have specified all the foreign keys (or did not accidentally define foreign key attributes for the child entity), you might want to run Discovered Foreign Keys, which can be found in the Browser pane by right-clicking the relational model name. You can use a template for foreign key columns defined on the Naming Standards tab (design-level properties) to verify. You can read more about this utility in Chapter 10.

In the logical database design, you can start thinking about indexes, but you may continue that part in the physical design when you know what relational database management system (RDBMS) you're using and what index types it supports. You can create a new index or edit an existing one in the Table Properties dialog on the Indexes tab. Just click the green plus sign and insert the index data. For an index you define the name, whether it is unique, whether it will be generated on DDL, and whether it will be engineered when reverse engineering. You can also specify an index to be a spatial index. You can either select the columns for the index or mark it as an expression (Index Expression) and write the expression clause for the index to get a function-based index. In Index Properties (either double-click the index name or click the Properties icon), you can define many other properties for the index. You can define whether it is a plain index, a unique plain index, a primary constraint, or a unique constraint. Or you can attach an index to a schema or define spatial properties for a spatial index. You can also see and modify the Notes, Comments, and Comments In RDBMS fields.

On the Table Level Constraints tab, you can specify table-level constraints and define them with a validation rule and whether they will be set with Generated In DDL. On the Existence Dependencies tab, you can create existence dependency constraints. You will find more information about the option Existence Dependency Constraints later in this chapter.

You can also define Valid Time Dimensions with a name and Start Time Column and End Time Column, and you can define Spatial Properties with a name and Spatial Column/Function Expression. You can double-click Spatial Property Name or click the Properties button (pencil icon) to display and edit the Spatial Definition properties.

If you defined the volume properties for an entity, you will see them in the table properties under Volume Properties. You can see, for instance, whether the model is (in your opinion) adequately normalized and which normal form it is in. Unfortunately, these properties are not used in estimating the space needed for your objects in an Oracle database. This information is used only for DB2 databases.

Classification types are useful for multidimensional models, but they can be used for operational databases as well, such as if you want to highlight all lookup tables (code tables) with a certain color to see them easily in a big diagram. You can set classification types for an individual entity or table in their properties, or you can use a Set Classification Type operation on the logical or relational model in the Browser pane. Or you can set it to a set of entities/tables by selecting Set Classification Type in the Browser pane by right-clicking the logical/relational model. You can find more information about this in Chapter 8.

TIP
You might want to create a new classification type of Lookup for your lookup tables (code tables) and assign that to all entities that are of that type. Reading the diagram is easier when the colors tell important things.

On the Scripts tab, you can define SQL statements to be run automatically at specified times: before a drop/rename of this table, before a create operation on this table, after a create operation on this table, or at the end of the script specified for this table. You can include these scripts in the DDLs by selecting Include Into DDL Script. You can also create your own dynamic properties for a table (and many other objects). Chapter 8 talks about dynamic properties.

NOTE
Scripts associated with a table or a view will not be shown in the DDL preview.

Views

On the logical model (see Chapter 4), you might have created some entity views. If you did, those entity views will be transformed to views on the relational model during the engineering process. On the logical model the entity views were shown in orange, but the views on the relational model are shown in green. In a relational model diagram, a view might have an icon next to its name indicating its status. A yellow triangle with an exclamation mark means it is an older-style view created with an earlier Data Modeler version or imported but not yet parsed. To parse a view, right-click the view in the diagram and select Parse Older Style Views. A red triangle with an exclamation mark means that this view is an invalid view. This might mean that something has changed after parsing or the view contains incorrect syntax. To validate the view, right-click the view in the diagram and select Validate Selected Views. You can validate or parse all views at the same time by right-clicking the relational model canvas, choosing Views, and choosing either Validate All Views or Parse Older Style Views.

You can also create views on the relational model. In the relational diagram, click the New View icon and click the canvas. A view has properties, as shown in Figure 5-26. First you should give the view a name, and second you should build the view. A view is basically a saved query that can have information from several tables. A query is built in Query Builder, which can be found by clicking the Query Builder field named Query (Figure 5-26). If you select the Auto Join On FKs property, the joins for tables in Query Builder will be created automatically based on foreign keys. And if you select a certain relational model or subview for the Use Object Only From property, only objects in that diagram will be shown in Query Builder. You can also define whether the DDL for the view will be generated by selecting Generate In DDL, and you can mark the view deprecated by selecting Deprecated. You can base the query on a structured type, define OID columns for it, and allow type substitution. You can also specify a schema for the query (the schema name will be shown on relational model diagrams) or select Include

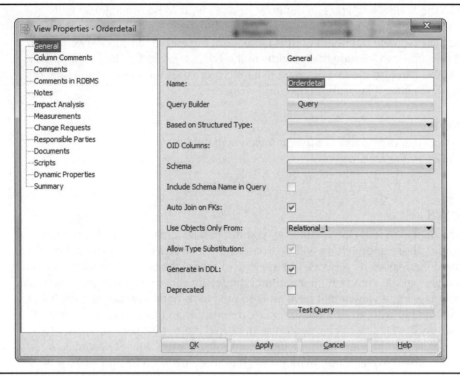

FIGURE 5-26. *General properties for a view*

Schema Name In Query to let Query Builder show the possible schema names of the elements in the query.

Query Builder, shown in Figure 5-27, helps you create a query for a view easily. The Query Builder consists of an element filter on the right and three screens for fine-tuning the query on the left: the main canvas, output criteria, and SQL preview. If you do not select Show Criteria List on the top of the screen, you will not see this output criteria screen in the middle. From the filter on the right, you can drag tables to the query canvas (Main) to be included in the query. You can limit the table list to tables in a certain relational model or a subview (Filter Metadata Objects By Diagram). On the canvas you can select the columns you want to be included and deselect the ones you do not want. In the window below Main, the output criteria screen, you can select which columns will be shown in the result of the query and also specify aggregates, aliases, sort types, sort order, grouping, and criteria for columns to be evaluated on. You can also specify the column order in the query. All these settings will affect the SQL query. On the bottom of the screen you can see the actual query

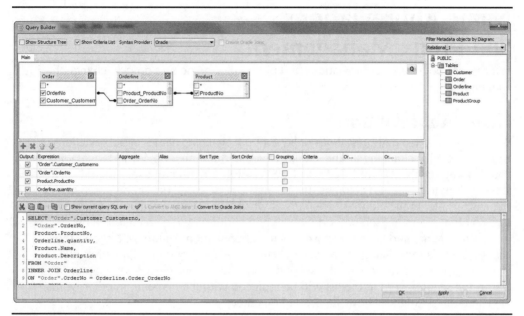

FIGURE 5-27. *Query Builder for creating views*

in SQL. You can also edit the SQL clause if needed, run a test query (the Test Query icon), and change the join syntax either to ANSI joins or to Oracle joins. If you edit the query manually, remember to click the Update Diagram icon to synchronize the diagram with the SQL query. You can also see the query in a structured tree format by selecting Show Structure Tree in the upper-left corner. It is possible to select the syntax from many different providers (in the Syntax Provider list) including Oracle, DB2, Informix, MSSQL, MySQL, PostgreSQL, SQLite, Sybase, and Firebird. You can also test your query by clicking Test Query in the View Properties dialog (shown earlier in Figure 5-26). In the upper-right corner of the Main window of Query Builder, you can see an icon with a capital Q. That is the Update Query button, and if you click it, the query in Main will be updated. Clicking Apply updates changes made in one of the Query Builder elements to all the other elements. Clicking OK saves the query and closes Query Builder, and clicking Cancel cancels the changes and closes Query Builder.

In the View Properties dialog you can add column comments to columns in queries or in comments, comments in RDBMS, and notes for the view. You can also specify scripts to be run before/after creation, before a drop/rename, or at the end of script just like you saw earlier in this chapter for tables. You can set these scripts to be created with the DDLs by selecting Include Into DDL Script.

Name Abbreviations and Prefix Management

You can use both name abbreviations and prefix management to quickly change the naming of objects to meet your needs.

Name Abbreviation

You can use the Name Abbreviations utility for bulk changing names or abbreviations. You can use it for changing all the similar words to the same one; for instance, you could change both CUS and CUST to CUSTOMER. Or you can use it to add abbreviations to tables and columns. The change is done based on a comma-separated value (CSV) file. In the file there are pairs of words, and those words are separated by a comma or another separator defined when performing the change. The first word is the name, and the second word is the abbreviation. Figure 5-28 shows the Name Abbreviations dialog. If you select Name To Abbreviation for Direction, the first word will be replaced with the second word. But if you select Abbreviation To Name, the second word in the list will be replaced with the first one. In other words, the Direction setting tells how the list will be read.

You can perform a name abbreviation either for names or for abbreviations by selecting All Objects or Abbreviations for the Scope setting. A name abbreviation for names can be done to names of tables, views, foreign key constraints, primary and unique key constraints, columns, and indexes. A name abbreviation for abbreviations

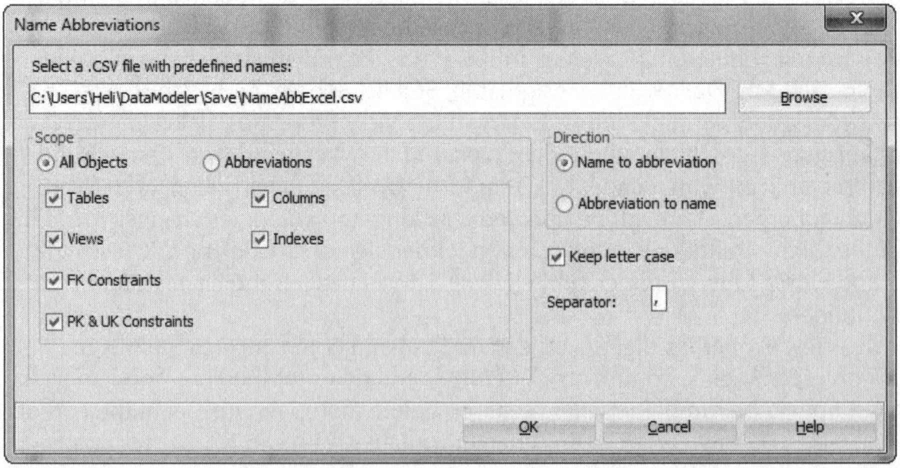

FIGURE 5-28. *Name Abbreviations dialog*

can be done to table and column abbreviations. The comparison is case sensitive, and only whole words or words with the underscore (_) separator are replaced. For example, these rows in the CSV file would have a different result:

Customer, CUST
CUSTOMER, CUST

The first one would replace, for instance, Customer_ID with CUST_ID, but the latter one would not find the word Customer at all because of the case sensitivity. And neither of them would replace CUSTOMERID with CUSTID because CUSTOMER in that word is not a single word or part of a word separated with an underscore. CUSTOMER_ID would be replaced with CUST_ID by the latter row in the CSV file.

You start a name abbreviation by selecting the CSV file; click the Browse button in the Name Abbreviations dialog and find the correct file. For the separator, you can define a comma or almost any other separator if wanted. If you select a separator that does not exist in the file, you will get an error message. After you select the file, you should select the scope and the direction for the transformation. If you want to keep the original letter case when changing part of the name, select Keep Letter Case. If you want to use the letter case defined in the CSV file, disable this property. For instance, say you have a file containing a row: customer, CUST. If you have a column named customer_name and you disable the Keep Letter Case property, the name will be changed to CUST_name. If the property is selected, the column name will be changed to cust_name. When you have selected the right setting, click OK. If you have several designs open, select the design you want to perform the name abbreviations on from the list. If you have several relational models, select the correct one from the list. Then click OK. The changes are made, and the log will show all the changes, as shown in Figure 5-29. You can save the log if you want.

 NOTE
If you perform name abbreviations in both directions with the same file and settings, names and abbreviations should be the same as they were when you started. In this case, the name/abbreviations combinations must be unique.

In datamodeler/datamodeler/templates, you can find two example files for name abbreviations: ABBREVS_SAMPLE.csv and plurals.csv. The plurals.csv file is an example of a use case of this utility. If you decide in the middle of the project that the table names should actually be plurals/singulars instead of singulars/plurals, you can use this utility to change the naming quite easily. But remember that name

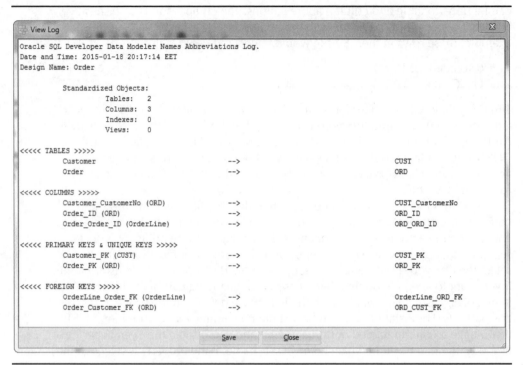

FIGURE 5-29. *The log for the name abbreviations*

abbreviations do not work for entities and attributes, so if you use the utility, remember to click Engineer To Logical Model to make the changes in the logical model as well.

Prefix Management

Prefix management is also quite useful when designing a database. Prefixes can be used to separate and categorize different kinds of objects for management purposes when you do not want to use different schemas. You might want to use prefix management for objects that have different life cycles, for instance history tables (HIST_) or summary tables (MONTH_, WEEK_, DAY_). You might want to use prefix management to categorize them based on the application or part of the application, for instance CUST_ for all customer information, tables, packages, and so on. The Oracle data dictionary views are an example of this: USER_, ALL_, and DBA_. Or you might want to use prefixes to describe the usage of the object, such as using TEMP_ for temporary objects or IDX_ for tablespaces that have only indexes in them. The prefix can be permanent or temporary for DDL generation.

You can add the prefix to the object name manually when creating the object or changing its properties. For example, instead of naming it ADDRESS, you can name it CUST_ADDRESS. But you can also do it automatically using the utility Data Modeler offers. You can do it for tables, views, foreign key constraints, primary and unique key constraints, columns, and indexes that are in a relational model or in a specific subview. In the Browser pane, go to the relational model wanted, right-click, and choose Change Object Names Prefix. You might have your objects divided into subviews exactly based on the criteria you are using for the prefix naming. In that case, select the subview from the Browser pane, right-click, and choose Change Subview Object Names Prefix. Or you might have the classification type attached to the object, which allows you to change the prefix for all the objects of that classification type, as described in Chapter 8. Depending on your needs, any of these can be used, and they all lead to the same Change Object Names Prefix dialog, as shown in Figure 5-30.

In the Change Object Names Prefix dialog, you can select either Prefix Replacement or Add Classification Prefix. Add Classification Prefix is explained in Chapter 8. Now you will see what you can do with Prefix Replacement. If you select Prefix Replacement, you can either replace an existing prefix or add a new one. If you want to replace an existing prefix, just set the current prefix to Current Prefix and the new prefix to New Prefix. You can spell the prefix either with the _ sign or

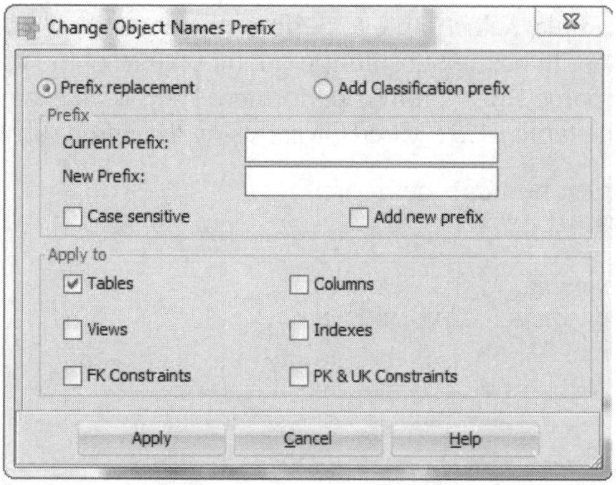

FIGURE 5-30. *Change Object Names Prefix dialog*

without it; it makes no difference if you already have a prefix with an underscore (_). For example, CUST and CUST_ are the same. It makes no difference either if the current prefix has been added manually or by using the Data Modeler Change Object Names Prefix utility. Then select whether you want to have the search for current prefixes case sensitive by selecting Case Sensitive. If this is selected and you have typed CUST for Current Prefix, those objects with a prefix of "cust" are not selected. Select the object types you want to select for the search in the Apply To section of the dialog. The Change Object Names Prefix operation will affect the object set that is in the relational model/subview selected and the object types specified here. Then click Apply.

If you want to add a new prefix for the objects, select Add New Prefix and type the prefix wanted in the New Prefix field; remember to also type the _ at the end of it. If you already had a prefix in the object name, this will be added in front of it, so make sure to use the replace functionality if you want to replace the existing prefix and use only the Add New Prefix functionality if you want to add a new one.

You can also change the prefix temporarily when generating the DDLs. Choose File | Export | DDL File as explained in Chapter 7. If you have several designs open, select the one you want to generate the DDLs for and select the relational model you want to use for the DDL generation. Select the RDBMS site wanted, and if you want a subview from the selected relational model, select that. Click Generate. Select the Name Substitution tab in the DDL Generation Options dialog. Type the prefix you want to replace in the Old field and the prefix you want to use in the New field. For example, type **CUST_** in Old and **TEST_** in New. Then select Selected to have this name substitution rule be included in the DDL generation process. Select the Object Types tab and enable the object types you want to be included in the change. For example, select Table to perform the change only on table prefixes. Then select Apply Name Substitution on the bottom of the screen. If you do not select this, no name substitution is performed. Here is an example of a DDL script generated for the table CUST_CUSTOMER using the name substitution:

```
PROMPT CREATING TABLE 'CUST_CUSTOMER';
CREATE TABLE "TEST_CUSTOMER"
    (
      "Cust No"  NUMBER (16)  NOT NULL ,
      "CustName" VARCHAR2 (30)  NOT NULL
    ) …
```

NOTE
Using name substitution affects only the DDL generated; no changes are performed on the objects in Data Modeler.

Tuning and Refactoring Your Model

Sooner or later you need to make changes to your model. Especially when the system development methodology is agile, there will be many changes in the logical model after the first version; the design work is very iterative. The more you check the models in every phase, the better the outcome will be.

Problems with refactoring are not usually with the database and its objects but everything on top of that: test cases, programs, data classes, migrations, and so on. It is good to find the main concepts and their relationships as early as possible and to understand them correctly. Splitting an entity or fixing a problem in later phases of the process usually causes a lot of work. In the sense of database objects, refactoring is easy, especially if you have a tool like Data Modeler. You just make your changes to the logical model and engineer them to the relational model. Your changes will go to your physical model, and you will produce the new DDL scripts easily. My opinion is that you should always follow the procedures no matter how busy you are: make a change in the logical model and then forward engineer to the relational model. Never make the changes first in the relational model or database. With a tool you can of course do that, but it is not wise. Why? First, processes are made to get work done systematically, and if you break them, you take a risk that some of the work is not actually done (for instance, documentation for an entity or an attribute). Second, even though the tool provides all possible comparisons between different models and databases, I do not see it as a full-time job for anybody trying to find differences. And if there are differences, how do you know how things actually should be if the processes are not followed? It is the same thing as with the same data in many databases: One of the sources must be the master, and all the rest are copies of the master. If they are not the same, the master is correct. The entity is the master in database design.

During the logical database design process, you can make decisions about denormalization to get better performance, but make sure each decision is made wisely and documented. A typical optimization strategy in logical database design is splitting or merging tables. Splitting a table means that a table is vertically divided into two (or more) tables. Merging means that two (or more) tables are merged as one to avoid joins and that way get better performance. These operations are usually done for the relational model, and they have no effect on the logical model. Data Modeler supports both operations.

To split a table, select the table in the relational model diagram and click the Split Table icon in the relational model toolbar to start the Split Table Wizard. Enter the name for the new table (in Table Name), type any comments needed for the Add Comments For The New Table property, and click Next. Then select the foreign keys to be added to the new table from a list and click Next. Select other columns to be added to the new table from a list and click Finish. To merge tables, click the Merge Tables icon in the toolbar and then select tables you want to merge from the diagram. To the question "Are you sure you want to merge the selected tables?" click Yes. Then reply to the next questions, and your tables will be merged into one.

Summary

Logical database design starts with the logical model from the conceptual design. With Data Modeler, the logical model will be transformed into a relational model using the Engineer To Relational Model functionality. The results of this phase of database design is the relational database schema: a set of relational objects and their constraints. The Engineer To Relational Model functionality is an easy and quick process, and it should be done whenever you have change requests to the conceptual model.

Designing a database is an iterative process. To have an efficient and reliable process, it is valuable to always follow the same procedures and in the same order: Change the logical model and forward engineer the changes to relational model using the Engineer To Relational Model functionality. It is also possible to reverse engineer a database. You can read more about that in Chapter 10. You can use both name abbreviations and prefix management to quickly change the naming of objects to meet your needs.

CHAPTER
6

Introducing Physical
Database Design

The physical database design continues from the relational model created in the logical design. One relational model can have no physical models or as many as needed, and the physical model will be defined by its relational database model system (RDBMS) site. An RDBMS site is an alias associated with an RDBMS type (Oracle 12c, Oracle 11g, SQL Server 2008, and so on) supported by Oracle SQL Developer Data Modeler. To be able to design the physical model, you need a good understanding of the RDBMS site selected to be able to make the right decisions.

In physical database design, you design the physical database elements related to the selected technology (tablespaces, data files, and so on) and add physical properties to elements from the relational model. You estimate the space needed for the database, plan disks and disk groups, and figure out which database objects to put in which disk. You must plan the backup and recovery strategies and decide how to document the database changes, including changes in objects and changes in the RDBMS (which patch was run when, and so on). You also need to agree on who will create the documentation, what they will document, and where they will do it. You also design the database schemas, which are logical subsets of the database based on namespaces defined by schema names. You define users, roles, and privileges. You define indexes needed, other than just indexes for primary keys and foreign keys. You design the physical database so that you will be able to create the database as designed. The data definition language (DDL) script generation will be mainly based on a physical model. Physical models do not have graphical presentations or diagrams, only a browser to create, edit, and remove elements. The outcomes from the physical database design process are the DDLs needed to create the database designed. In Chapter 7, you will learn how to get the database generation files after all the objects and their properties have been defined in the physical model.

TIP
Agree on naming standards for creating physical objects such as tablespaces and data files. These cannot be documented as part of the naming standards in Data Modeler, but for the consistency it is valuable to have a standard naming convention.

This chapter will not go through all the tasks in the physical design process. You will read about only those tasks that can be done with Data Modeler to design a physical model for Oracle 12c. All technologies have their own physical objects that need to be designed. There is a lot of designing work in physical database design, and some of the decisions must be made with the end users (such as user and role definitions) and even with the company board (such as backup strategy and definitions for sensitive data).

Setting Preferences and Properties

Data Modeler has some preferences that will affect the physical model. In the Preferences dialog, on the Model tab, you can define the default RDBMS type and site. You can also define some default values for physical models in DB2, Oracle, SQL Server, and universal database (UDB). The predefined default values depend on the RDBMS you are using. For Oracle and DB2, the list is bigger, but for SQL Server you can define the Default Database setting and for UDB the Default Owner setting.

In Figure 6-1, you can see the defaults that can be defined for an Oracle physical model. You can define the default user and default tablespace. The default user and tablespace take effect only after you have created this user and tablespace in your physical model and closed and reopened the design. If you have changed a user or a tablespace property for any element before that, it is not overwritten. You can

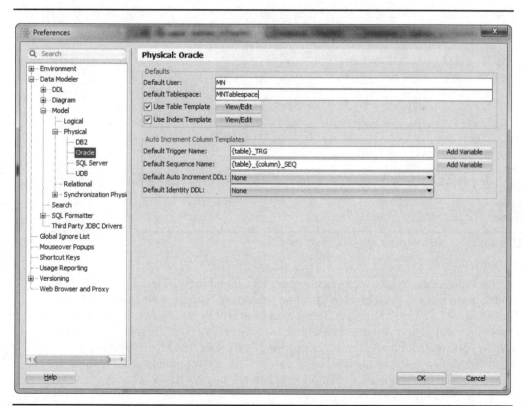

FIGURE 6-1.   *Defaults for an Oracle physical model*

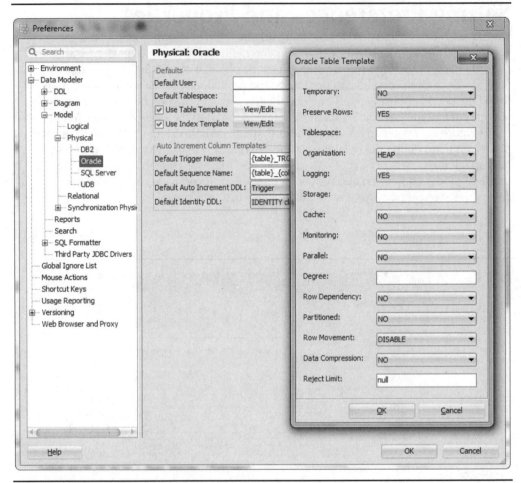

FIGURE 6-2. *Table template specification for Oracle*

predefine a template for the physical properties of a table (see Figure 6-2) and of an index (see Figure 6-3). To be able to define a template, you must first select Use Table Template or Use Index Template. These templates will be used when a physical model is created and when a new table or index is created on the relational model. When you create a physical model using templates, save and close the design before doing anything so Data Modeler can save all the modified data. If you view the physical model right after creation, you will not be able to see what the templates actually have done.

You can also define Auto Increment Column Templates settings. For a trigger or sequence, you can use the variables (as you did in Chapter 2 for many elements) to define a template for naming new, automatically created objects. This means that if

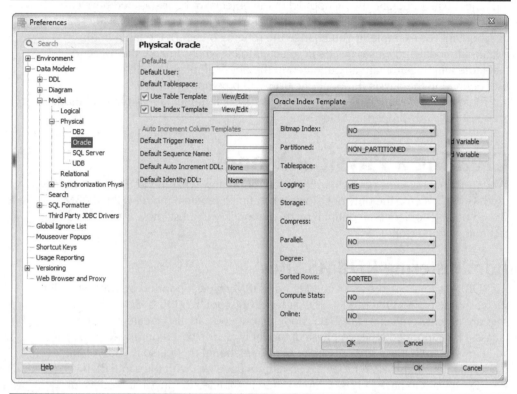

FIGURE 6-3. *Index template specification for Oracle*

Auto Increment in the Properties column for a column has been selected, a sequence and a trigger for that will be created automatically following the rules defined in Auto Increment Column Templates, unless you have defined them explicitly in the column properties on the Auto Increment tab. You can define a name for a sequence and a trigger in the column properties. The sequence and the related trigger are not created as objects in the physical model, but if these objects have been defined to be generated, they will be included in the DDL script when generating.

You can define a default value for an auto-increment DDL (Default Auto Increment DDL): None, Trigger, or DEFAULT Clause. You can also define a default for an identity DDL (Default Identity DDL): None, Trigger, DEFAULT Clause, or IDENTITY Clause.

There are also preferences for synchronizing the physical model. You can find these settings under Data Modeler | Model | Synchronization Physical, and they are related to the RDBMS type. For each listed type of object, you can specify whether to synchronize it with changes in the relational model or not. Synchronization means that if an object type is changed in the relational model, the change on the object will automatically be applied to the objects in the associated physical models. For Oracle, those object types are, for example, a user, cluster, tablespace, or synonym. For example, if you change the schema owner of the table in the relational model and a user has been selected to be synchronized, the owner of that table will be automatically updated in the physical model. If there is no such user defined in the physical model, the user will be emptied for the table.

There are no design-level properties for a physical model, and a physical model does not have any properties of its own.

Creating a Physical Model

When you create a new physical model, you must know what the RDBMS technology used will be because the only decision for creating a physical model is the RDBMS site. To be able to design an optimal physical model, you must know the selected technology quite well.

Administering RDBMS Sites

An RDBMS site is a name associated to an RDBMS type supported by Data Modeler, such as Oracle 12c, Oracle 11g, SQL Server 2008, or DB2/390 8. Several RDBMS sites are already predefined in Data Modeler, but you can also create new sites (aliases) for supported types. A physical model is always based on one RDBMS site. You can use an RDBMS site only once in one relational model, so if your relational model has several physical models, you cannot have two with the same RDBMS site. If you want to have, let's say, three different Oracle 12c physical models for a relational model (for test, education, and production environments), you must define your own RDBMS sites. Your test environment might be very simple, your education environment might be different from the other environments, and production might be using features such as encryption/compression/redaction. Or maybe you are selling your own software and want to have support for both SQL Server and Oracle and therefore need a physical model for both SQL Server and Oracle along with different versions of those products and different setups (small environment versus large environment). All this can be done by defining your own RDBMS sites.

The RDBMS sites are administered with the RDBMS Site Editor (see Figure 6-4), which you open by choosing Tools | RDBMS Site Administration. You can add RDBMS sites to the current design or to an external file. If you add them to an external file, you can share the sites with other users and other designs. A file called defaultRDBMSSites .xml is the default file for RDBMS sites, and it is kept in the directory defined as the default system types directory. Each design has its own file for RDBMS sites in its own directory, but when you open the design, the new sites are copied from the default file to the file of this design. So, when opening a design, you will have available all the sites defined for that design and those defined in the default file.

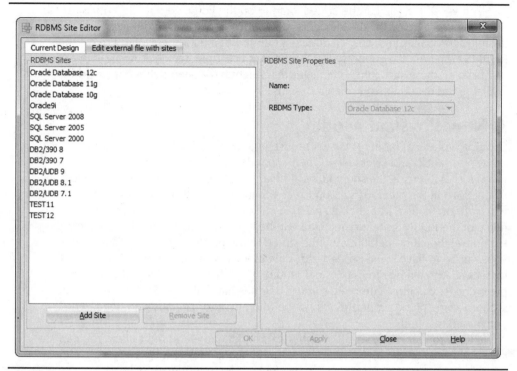

FIGURE 6-4. *RDBMS Site Editor*

TIP
*If you want to have the same RDBMS sites
for all users, it would be wise to save the file
defaultRDBMSSites.xml in version control. Always
copy it to your default system types directory when
you have added a new site.*

You can add a new RDBMS site to a current design by clicking the Add Site
button, entering the name for the site, and selecting the RDBMS type from the
supported RDBMS types list. Then just click Apply.

NOTE
*Changes to the default file are not applied to open
designs. You need to close the designs or restart Data
Modeler to copy the new sites to the site file of the
design.*

A new RDBMS site can be added to a file on the Edit External File With Sites tab. Click Select, navigate to your default system types directory, and select defaultRDBMSSites.xml. Click Add Site. Enter the name for the site and select the RDBMS type from the supported RDBMS types list. Then just click Apply. Now you will have all these sites (plus other sites that might have been defined for a design) available the next time you open a design.

A New Physical Model

Creating a physical model is easy. You just go to the physical model in the Browser pane, right-click, and select New. Then you will see a list of available RDBMS sites. If you forgot to create the site you would like to use, just click Cancel and follow the instructions in the previous section for creating an RDBMS site. If you see the one you want on the list, just click it and then click OK. A physical model with the same name of the RDBMS site just selected will be created. When you add new elements to your relational model, they will be stored in the physical model automatically. If you wanted to have some properties for the elements set by default, you can do that by setting a preference for a physical model. If you have not set templates in the preferences, you must complete some properties manually, as described in the next section. Some of the properties cannot be filled in automatically and need to be completed manually.

In the Browser pane, select the physical model name and right-click. You can save a physical model if you select Save, and you can delete it by selecting Delete.

You can open or close a physical model by selecting Open or Close.

When you open a design, the physical models are not opened automatically. The reason for this is performance because you might have several physical models in your design with plenty of objects. So, when you want to see or edit the physical model, go to the name of the model in the Browser pane, right-click, and select Open.

TIP
When you start Data Modeler, in the Select Relational Models pane you can tell Data Modeler to open selected relational models when opening Data Modeler. You can also select the first physical model for a relational model to be opened automatically when starting Data Modeler. So, not all physical models are opened (and suggested to be opened) except the first one in the Browser pane.

In Data Modeler it is possible to clone physical models. This means all the elements that are not in the physical model where you are cloning to will be added. And all the properties for objects that already were in that physical model but have been changed in the model you are cloning from will be updated. All objects that exist only in the model you are cloning to remained as they are. You start cloning by selecting the physical model name where you want to clone to and right-click. Choose Clone From, and from the Database Sites list select the physical model you want to clone from; then click OK.

You can clone a physical model only on the database site of the same release or earlier. For Oracle 12c, you can clone from Oracle 12c or earlier, and for Oracle 11g, you can clone from Oracle 11g or earlier, not from Oracle 12c.

TIP
When cloning the physical details from one physical model to another, make sure you have saved the physical model you want to clone from.

Defining Physical Model Properties

In the physical model, there are elements linked to the relational model, but these elements do not have all the properties set yet for the DDL creation because these properties depend on the selected RDBMS type. One step in the physical database design is to set those properties. There are also new elements that did not exist in the relational model at all, and those elements are totally dependent on the selected RDBMS type. Another step in the physical database design is to define those elements and while doing that design the physical database. The elements and properties in the physical model depend on the RDBMS type selected; these are the elements and properties for getting a database created on the selected RDBMS. In this chapter, you will see the elements and properties for Oracle 12c since you probably have at least one Oracle database and the number of elements and properties is the largest for Oracle. I will not go deep into the details of these properties but discuss them at a general level.

Some of the objects were already created in previous phases of the design, and in the physical database design phase, you cannot create new ones; you only need to add some physical properties for the existing ones. If you need to create new ones, you do it in either the logical or relational model.

Some properties you cannot complete without creating a new physical model object. For instance, to be able to complete the table properties, you must define at least users and roles to be able to grant privileges. You also must define tablespaces, storage templates, rollback segments, temporary tablespaces, undo tablespaces, and so on, to be able to define storage settings. Then there are elements such as the actual database and maybe directories, disk groups, external tables, materialized views, clusters, contexts, and so on.

TIP
*You might want to close a physical model if you are
not using it to free memory for other purposes.*

Defining Users and Roles

To be able to define and grant privileges, you need to define users and roles. And to be able to define users and roles, you need to know what kind of users you will have for the system so you can design the roles and name them accordingly. And of course then create the users and name them accordingly. An important question when designing the roles and users is what kind of privileges they will need for the database. The same needs can be grouped together for a role, and a user can be granted all the roles needed. It is also important to create a naming standard for the users and roles. Naming standards for users and roles cannot be documented in Data Modeler, but they still must exist. If the naming standard is clear, creating and maintaining roles, users, and database object privileges is much easier.

TIP
Agree on naming standards for users and roles.

There are two kind of users: object owners (schema owner) and individual users who will be granted privileges. You might want to have a different naming standard for these two kinds of users to know which one is which. Every Oracle physical model has the users MDSYS and PUBLIC by default. You can create additional users in the Browser pane by right-clicking Users and selecting New. You will see several tabs in the User Properties dialog that opens: General, Roles, System Privileges, Clusters, Tables, Indexes, Materialized Views, Triggers, Views, Dimensions, Sequences, Synonyms, Procedures, Functions, Packages, and Comments. In the General properties, you define the name for the user, the authentication method (by password, externally, or globally), and the password (identifier). You can also define the default tablespace, temporary tablespace, profile, and other properties used when generating the DDL for a CREATE USER clause for Oracle 12c. On the Roles tab, you can grant roles to this user, and on the System Privileges tab you can grant system privileges to this user. On the Comments tab you can type comments on this user. If a user is a schema user and has objects on its schema, those objects are listed on the other tabs in the User Properties dialog.

NOTE
*If you defined schemas in the logical model, they
are completely different than these users and are not
copied to the physical model.*

If you want to grant privileges to the user, click the button Permissions in the User Properties dialog. In the Permissions dialog that opens, you can grant privileges to this user for all objects in the physical model (see Figure 6-5). In the upper-left corner you can select the object type (Available Objects) and can select the object type for which you want to grant privileges. If you select Tables, you can grant privileges either to the whole table or to some of the columns in that table. To grant privileges, select the object in the Available Objects box and click the arrow pointing to the right. Now the object name appears in the box in the upper-right corner (Objects). Select the object, and in the lower-right corner (Available Privileges) you can see the list of possible privileges on that object. Select the privilege you want to grant and click the arrow pointing right; you can see it on the box on the right (Granted Privileges). Select the privilege by clicking Grant.

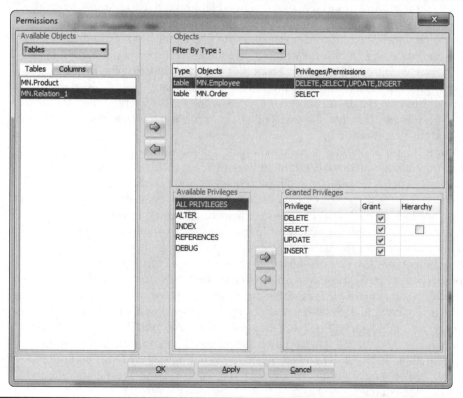

FIGURE 6-5.   *Permissions dialog*

NOTE
*All passwords set in the physical model are
encrypted when saving a design in the file system.*

If you want to revoke privileges, select the privilege or object you want to revoke from the list on the right and click the arrow pointing left. If you have many privileges in the Objects box, you can filter them by object type by selecting the type from the Filter By Type list.

NOTE
*You can see the privileges granted to an object only
if you select the object name in the Objects box.*

If needed, you can define quotas for users. A quota means that a user can use only a certain amount of the space of a defined tablespace. This is a way to ensure that a single user will not use all the space in a tablespace. This might be useful, for instance, in a test environment to make sure every user has equal resources. To define a quota, go to Quotas under the username in the Browser pane, right-click, and choose New. In the QuotaItem Properties dialog, you define the tablespace (select from the list of tablespaces) and the amount of space (Size). This space is not allocated from the database, but it is watched by the RDBMS, and if the user tries to use more space than this, the user will get an error. You can also document the quota on the Comments tab.

A role is a set of privileges that can be granted to a user or to another role, and when you grant it, you actually grant all the privileges the role has. You can use roles to more easily administer database privileges. You could, for instance, have a role called SystemAReportUser that has only Select privileges on selected tables, a SystemAMainUser role that has Select privileges and some Insert and Update privileges, and a SystemASuperUser role that has Delete privileges. You could also have similar roles for SystemB: SystemBReportUser, SystemBMainUser, and SystemBSuperUser. Maybe you have a user named Mark who need to see all the reports in both systems (these systems are in the same database, probably two different schemas); you can grant him two roles: SystemAReportUser and SystemBReportUser. If there is a new table in SystemA, you do not need to worry about Mark's privileges since the new privilege will be granted to role SystemAReportUser and Mark gets it automatically. And maybe you have two superusers, Lisa and Tom, who can do almost anything in the system (even delete rows) but only in SystemA and not in SystemB, where they are not even allowed to see any data. You can grant Lisa and Tom the role SystemASuperUser.

You can create roles in the Browser pane by right-clicking Role and choosing New. In the dialog that opens there are four tabs: General, Roles, System Privileges, and Comments. In the General properties, you define the name for the role, whether the role will be identified (NO/YES), the identification type (by password, externally, globally, or using package), and the password. If you choose identification by using a package, you can define the schema of the package (Schema) and the package name (Package). On the Roles tab, you can grant/revoke other roles (and their privileges) to this role, and on the System Privileges tab you can grant system privileges to this role. On the Comments tab you can type comments on this role. In General properties you can click the Permissions button and grant and revoke the same privileges as described earlier (Figure 6-5).

TIP
Use roles to make maintaining the database object privileges easier.

Storage Templates and LOB Storages

A storage template is a template for properties of physical_attributes_clause in DDLs for tables, indexes, materialized views, or clusters. The clause physical_attributes_ clause lets you specify how Oracle Database should store a permanent database object, and the storage parameters are important not only because they affect the amount of space needed in the database but also because of the time it takes to access data stored in the database. It is good practice to define storage templates both to make physical designing easier and to make the database definitions more standardized. Before you can define storage templates, you must design them and how you will use them.

To create a new storage template, select Storage Templates in the Browser pane, right-click it, and choose New. On the General tab of the properties, you can define the values for the parameters in the clause physical_attributes_clause: PCTFREE (PCT Free), PCTUSED (PCT Used), INITRANS (Initrans), INITIAL (SC Initial Extent), NEXT (SC Next Extent), MINEXTENTS (SC Min. Extents), MAXEXTENTS (SC Max. Extents), maxsize_clause, PCTINCREASE (SC PCT Increase), FREELIST (SC Free Lists), FREELIST GROUPS (SC Free List Groups), and BUFFER_POOL (SC Buffer Pool). The physical_ attributes_clause parameters OPTIMAL, FLASH_CACHE, and ENCRYPT cannot be specified for the storage template. In the storage template General tab, the Currently Used property is automatically selected when this storage template is used.

On the Clusters, Tables, Indexes, and Materialized Views tabs, you can set objects to be using the specified storage template. Click the green plus sign, select from the list all the objects that you want to use the storage template, and click OK. You can also specify in, for instance, table properties that a table will be using this storage template.

You can also specify LOB storage for columns in a table or a materialized view. Go to the Browser pane and select Lob Storages under the table or materialized view where you want to create it, right-click it, and select New. In the Lob Storage Properties dialog on the General tab, you define all the parameters needed for a LOB clause, and in Storage Properties you define the storage clause parameters for it. After that, you assign it to the column that these parameters are attached to during the DDL generation by typing the name of the column in the Lob Column property. You must design the LOB storage before implementing them in Data Modeler.

Tablespaces

Before entering tablespaces in Data Modeler, you must design them and plan how you will use them. A database object is saved on a tablespace, which is a logical set of data files in a database. These tablespaces are categorized as permanent tablespaces because they save the data permanently. There are also two other kinds of tablespaces: temporary and undo. A temporary tablespace is used, for instance, to manage space for database sort operations and to store global temporary tables. A temporary tablespace contains schema objects only for the duration of a session. Objects in temporary tablespaces are stored in tempfiles. An undo tablespace is for managing undo data. Undo records are used to roll back transactions when a ROLLBACK statement is issued, to recover the database, to provide read consistency, and by using Oracle Flashback Query features to analyze data as of an earlier point in time or to recover logical corruptions. Oracle Database versions before Oracle 9*i* used rollback segments for most of that. Data Modeler supports also rollback segments even though Oracle strongly recommends using undo tablespace rather than rollback segments.

One object must be saved in one tablespace, but several objects can be saved on the same tablespace. Usually the objects saved on the same tablespace are similar in the way of stability and size. Usually just one kind of object is saved in one tablespace (this is not a rule, but it usually makes life easier): tables to one, indexes to another, and so on. Whatever your preference is when designing the tablespace use, remember to design them and know why you did it the way you did.

A tablespace is created in the Browser pane by selecting the tablespace, right-clicking, and selecting New. The tablespace properties have eight tabs: General, Default Storage, Storage, Tables, Clusters, Indexes, Materialized View, and Comments. On the General tab, you define the name and other properties for the DDL clause of a tablespace. On the Default Storage tab, you can specify the default storage values for the tablespace. If the object that will be created on this tablespace has no storage settings, the default storage settings for the tablespace are used. On the Storage, Tables, Clusters, Indexes, and Materialized View tabs, you can see whether a tablespace is used on that type of an object, and on the Comments tab you can document the tablespace.

When you have created the tablespace in the physical model, you can see in the Browser pane that under the tablespace name there is a new branch called Data Files. If you right-click that and select New, you can define the data files for the tablespace. For a data file you can define the properties needed for generating the DDL and comments.

You create a temporary tablespace in the Browser pane by selecting Temp Tablespaces, right-clicking, and choosing New. Temporary tablespace properties have only two tabs: General and Comments. On the General tab, you define the name and other properties for the DDL clause of a temporary tablespace. On the Comments tab, you can document the temporary tablespace. Just like for the tablespace when you created the temporary tablespace in the physical model, you can see in the Browser pane that under the temporary tablespace name there is a new branch called Data Files. If you right-click that and choose New, you can define the data files the same way as for a tablespace.

An undo tablespace is created in the Browser pane by selecting Undo Tablespaces, right-clicking, and choosing New. Undo properties consist only of two tabs: General and Comments. On the General tab, you define the name and other properties for the DDL clause of an undo tablespace. On the Comments tab, you can document the undo tablespace. Just like for the tablespace when you created the undo tablespace in the physical model, you can see in the Browser pane that under the undo tablespace name there is a new branch called Data Files. If you right-click that and choose New, you can define the data files the same way as for a tablespace.

Synonyms

You might have defined synonyms in previous phases of your designing process. Those synonyms are completely different synonyms than the ones Oracle Database has as objects. The first time and place to define the Oracle synonyms is in the physical database design and physical model. A synonym is an object in the database that provides an alternative name for another database object (table, view, sequence, procedure, stored function, package, user-defined object type, and so on). Synonyms provide both data independence and location transparency, meaning that you do not need to know which user is the owner of the object or in which database the object is located; all this information is hidden in the synonym details. A synonym does not replace privileges. If you do not have privileges to the object behind the synonym, you cannot access the object.

To create a new synonym, go to the Browser pane, select Synonyms, right-click, and choose New. For a synonym, you must create a name, the owner of this synonym (User), and whether the synonym is public (YES/NO). If a synonym is public, it is available to all database users. If it is private, then only the database user who owns the synonym can actually use it. Next you define the Object Owner and Object Name settings for the object this synonym is created for. The owner can be selected from the list, but unfortunately the name must be written manually. I hope in future releases of Data Modeler there will be a list of values here since there is a big risk you might misspell the object name. You can also specify the database link (DB Link) for the synonym to tell Oracle where the object is located. Of course, you can document the synonym using the Comments and Notes fields.

Tables

In previous phases you have defined tables, but you might not have defined external tables. This is probably better because an external table is really dependent on the RDBMS type and therefore is an element that should be defined in the physical database design. The idea of an external table is that you can access data outside the database as if it were in a table in a database. The presentation and processing for external tables have changed in Data Modeler version 4.0.2. The External Tables branch in the physical model is not used anymore, and older-style external tables are transformed to new definitions when the physical model is open. In the logical/relational model, you could have defined an entity or a table and set its classification type as External. External tables defined like this are shown under Tables in the physical model, but they are not actually external tables. You can define the real external tables in the physical model by setting the Organization property for the table to External. The table will automatically show up in the relational model defined as an external table.

TIP
You can also design and create hive tables with Data Modeler. In the physical model, define the table as external by setting the Organization property for a table to External and setting the Access Driver property in External Table Properties to ORACLE_HIVE. You can also set dynamic properties named hiveName and hiveSchema for the table in the relational model, and these will be taken into account during the DDL generation. Note that you can find the table on the External Tables tab in DDL Generation Options.

The tables you created in previous phases are automatically brought to the physical model under Tables in the Browser pane. And all the properties and elements defined under them in the relational model's Browser pane will be brought to the physical model under Tables. In the physical model, you add the properties needed for the DDL generation for the selected RDBMS type for a table and for all the elements under it. In this example, you define the parameters needed in the create_table clause to create a table for Oracle 12c on the General tab: Schema Owner (User); Name; Temporary (NO/Yes (Preserve Rows)/Yes(Delete Rows)); Organization (HEAP/INDEX/EXTERNAL); Cluster (select the cluster name from the list); Logging; Storage (select the storage template from the list); Cache (NO/YES); Parallel (NO/YES); if YES, then Degree; Row Dependency (NO/YES); Partitioned (NO/YES); Row Movement (DISABLE/ENABLE); Data Compression (NO/YES); if YES, Compression Type (select the compression type from the list); Structures Type (if it is based on one), and Implement As Materialized View (select a view name from the list). If you have defined a cluster for the table (selected a cluster name for the cluster), you can select the columns involved in that cluster on the Cluster Columns tab. If you have set Partitioned to YES, you can define on the Partitioning tab the parameters for the partitioning clause. If you have set Organization to INDEX, on the IOT Properties tab you can define the parameters for the index-organized table clause. If you have set Organization to EXTERNAL, on the External Table Properties tab you can define the parameters for the external table clause. On the Supplemental Log tab, you can define the parameters for enabling the supplemental logging at the table level. Supplemental logging is used for having additional columns logged into redo log files.

If the table is not a relational table, it can be either an object table or an XML-type table. If the table is an object table, you can define the parameters needed for the object_table clause on the OID Properties tab, and if it is an XML-type table, you can define the parameters needed for the XMLType_table clause on the XMLType Properties tab. Of course, an important thing is to define privileges for the table, which can be done, for instance, in the Permissions dialog that opens when you click the Permissions button.

In previous phases of the design process, you also defined columns for the tables. Those columns can be found under Tables in the physical model's Browser pane. All the logical properties for the column have been defined in the relational model and can be changed only there (if you change any, the changed values will be immediately shown in the physical model), but in the physical model you define the physical properties for a column. On the General tab, you can define a default value for it and the Max Size As String setting. If you set Encrypt to YES, you can define the encryption parameters on the Encryption tab.

NOTE
If you change a logical property of a column in the relational model (data type, length, and so on), you can see the change in the physical model immediately.

On the Column Not Null Constraints tab, you can change the parameters for a possible Not Null constraint for this column or create a new one if there is no constraint. First you define the name for the constraint: Initially (Immediate, Deferred), Deferrable (yes/no), Enable (yes/no), Validate (yes/no). Then you select a table name from a list as an exceptions table. On the Column Check Options tab, you can change the parameters for a possible check constraint for this column: Initially (Immediate, Deferred), Deferrable (yes/no), Enable (yes/no), or Validate (yes/no); then select a table name from the list as an exceptions table. If the column is an auto-increment column, you can define the parameters on the Auto Increment tab. Data Modeler also supports the native identity column in Oracle 12c.

You can also specify special parameters for XML types, nested table collections, and Varray collections on these tabs: XMLType Options, XMLType Storage, Varray, and Nested Table. You can see and edit the Comments and Comments In RDBMS fields on the Comments tab, but remember that if you change them in the physical model, then changes in the logical model (for these comments) will not be shown in the physical model anymore.

NOTE
If you change the Comment or Comment In RDBMS setting for a column in the physical model, you will not get changes made to those properties in the relational model brought to the physical model anymore. Changing them in the physical model cuts the link to the relational model. This flexibility is for dealing with different physical model implementations that might require separate comments per install.

Under a table name in the Browser pane, you can find a primary keys branch and a unique keys branch. Primary keys/unique keys and their properties defined in the relational model can be found here. You are not able to create new primary keys/unique keys in the physical model, but you are able to add physical properties for existing ones. If a primary key/unique key is missing or needs to be changed, go to the logical model and change it (remember to engineer the change to the relational model). On the General tab for a primary key/unique key property, you can define the following properties: Initially (immediate/deferred), Deferrable (NO/YES), Enable (YES/NO), Validate (YES/NO), Using Index (NO/YES), and Exceptions Table (select the table name from the list). If you selected No for Validate, you can also define Rely (NO/YES). You can check the meaning of each parameter from the Oracle manuals. For instance, Using Index means the index is created automatically when the primary key/unique key is generated and definitions for a separate index are not needed. The default value is No, which is probably good because every index in the database must be thought about carefully and named wisely. On the Columns tab, you can see columns associated with this primary key/unique key, and on the Comments tab you can see the Comments and Comments In RDBMS fields edited for the primary key/unique in the relational model. On the Global Partitioning and Global Hash Partitions By Quantity tabs, you can define partitioning parameters.

NOTE
If you change the Comment or Comment In RDBMS field for a primary key/unique key in the physical model, you will not get changes made to those properties in the relational model brought to the physical model. Changing them in the physical model cuts the link to the relational model. This applies to other elements too.

Under a table name in the Browser pane you can find a foreign keys branch. Foreign keys and their properties defined in the relational model can be found here. You are not able to create new foreign keys in the physical model, but you are able to add physical properties for existing ones. If a foreign key is missing or needs to be changed, go to the logical model and change it (remember to engineer the change to the relational model). On the General tab for a foreign key property, you can define the following properties: Initially (immediate/deferred), Deferrable (NO/YES), Enable (YES/NO), Validate (YES/NO), and Exceptions Table (select table name from the list). If you selected No for Validate, you can also define Rely (NO/YES). You can check the meaning of each parameter in the Oracle manuals. On the Columns And Referenced Columns tab, you can see columns associated with this foreign key, and on the Comments tab, you can see the comments edited for the primary key/unique key in the relational model.

In the relational model you might have created some table-level constraints in the Table Properties dialog under Table Level Constraints. You can find those constraints from the physical model under that particular table in Table Check Constraints where you can define the physical properties for the constraint and see the comments from the relational model. The physical properties for a table check constraint are as follows: Initially (Immediate, Deferred), Deferrable (NO/YES), Enable (YES/NO), Validate (YES/NO), and Exceptions Table (select from the list of tables).

TIP
If you want to create general scripts for generating database objects (DDLs) without physical parameters, do not open a physical model.

Sequences

A sequence is a database object for generating unique integers that multiple users can use. You can, for instance, use a sequence to automatically generate primary key values, and usually that is combined with a trigger in the table to get the next value from a sequence and add it to the primary key column. A sequence is not guaranteed to be gapless since the sequence is always incremented after a sequence number is generated, no matter whether the transaction was committed or rolled back. You can also use the CACHE option with sequences. The sequence numbers will be reserved—those numbers are defined in that cache—and none of them will be returned. If CACHE is set to 20 and the next value of sequence A is 1, this next value operation takes values 1 to 20 from the sequence, and when you ask for the next value again, you will get 21. The CACHE option is usually used with bulk loading. A sequence number is unique in that two users cannot get the same sequence number (unless the sequence is altered or re-created), but a user can use the sequence number generated as many times as needed (Oracle does not stop that). One sequence can be used for multiple tables, but that is not usually recommended. Usually it is recommended to create one sequence per table.

In the physical model you define a sequence by right-clicking Sequence in the Browser pane and choosing New. For a sequence you define the name, the owner (User), the first number for the sequence (Start With), how much the sequence is incremented each time (Incremented By), the smallest and largest values for the sequence (Min Value, Max Value), whether the sequence can start from the first value again when the last value has been reached (Cycle, NO/YES), whether the cache will be disabled (Disable Cache, NO/YES), the cache size (Cache), whether the order of sequences generated in a Real Application Cluster (RAC) environment is guaranteed to be the order of requests (Order, NO/YES), and whether the sequence is only session wide (Session Only, NO/YES). You can also enter comment and notes and add privileges by clicking the Permissions button.

In Oracle 12c you can also use an identity column. In a CREATE TABLE clause, you simply tell that the column is an identity column, and the value is automatically incremented as you have defined it; no trigger is needed. Data Modeler supports this, and it is defined for a column in the relational model in Column Properties by selecting Identity Column.

Views

If you created views in the relational model, you will see them in the physical model automatically. You cannot create new views in the physical model, but you can add the schema and other physical properties related to the selected RDBMS site and grant privileges.

Materialized Views

A materialized view is a database object that contains the result of a query at a certain moment, and you can define how and when the result is updated. A materialized view can be based on tables, views, or other materialized views. In replication terms, the term for these objects that the materialized view is based on is *master tables*; in data warehouse terms, they are called *detail tables*. In previous versions of Oracle, some of the functionalities of materialized views were called *snapshots*.

You can create a materialized view in the physical model by selecting Materialized Views in the Browser pane, right-clicking, and choosing New. For a materialized view's properties there are seven tabs: General, Body, Cluster Columns, Partitioning, Refresh Clause, Comments, and Notes. On the General tab you can define the name and the owner schema (User) from the materialized view. Then you can define whether it will be partitioned, part of a cluster, the tablespace where it will be saved, storage settings, and other physical properties for the DDL clause. You can also define whether it will be updated (Build) immediately or deferred, whether it will be updatable (For Update), and if it is query rewrite enabled. On the Body tab, you can edit the logic for the materialized view. On the Refresh Clause tab, you can specify the refresh part of the DDL. In Comments and Notes, you can document the materialized view. And with the Permission button, you can grant privileges for the materialized view.

Stored Procedures, Functions, and Packages

In Oracle Database there are objects that are actually PL/SQL programs such as stored procedures, functions, and packages; you can also create these with Data Modeler. In the Browser pane, go to the object type you want to create (Stored Procedures, Functions, or Packages), right-click, and choose New. Then define the name and the owner for this object (User). You can also add comments and notes and grant privileges (Permissions). When you save the object (OK), you will be taken to an editor to edit the code. You can also copy and paste the code if you would rather edit it somewhere else. After you have finished editing, you can save it by clicking the Save icon. You can edit these objects if you select the object name in the Browser pane, right-click, and choose Edit, and you can delete an object by choosing Delete.

Although you can create these types of objects with Data Modeler, the editor is not that great, so probably it would be wiser to create them with Oracle SQL Developer. You can either just document the names and privileges to Data Modeler or copy and paste the code from Oracle SQL Developer to Data Modeler.

Triggers

In Data Modeler you can create triggers for tables and views. In Oracle you can also assign them to a schema or a database, but those features are not supported in the current version of Data Modeler, and probably there is no need for that functionality either. A trigger is much like a stored procedure except you cannot explicitly invoke it; the database does it automatically based on a triggering event. If a trigger is disabled, it will not be invoked at all. Maybe this is the reason not everybody likes triggers. There can be a lot of traffic in the database without anybody actually calling a program, and a trigger can be disabled without anyone realizing it. So, having triggers in a database means you need to have processes to control, maintain, and watch them in order to know what is happening and to be able to be prepared.

To create a new trigger, go to the physical model's Browser pane and select the table or view name you want to add the trigger for, go to Triggers, right-click, and choose New. For a trigger you define properties on four tabs: General, Trigger Body, Update Columns, and Comments. On the General tab, you define the name for the trigger and the schema owner (User) and the action that will invoke it (Insert and/or Update and/or Delete). You also specify the triggering time (Before/After), the scope (for each row, for each statement), and the state (enable/disable). You can also define the names for old parameters (Ref OLD as), new parameters (Ref NEW as), and parent parameters (Ref PARENT as) and the condition. On the Trigger Body tab, you can write the actual PL/SQL code for the trigger action, and on the Update Columns tab, you can select or remove columns to be updated if the action for the trigger is Update. On the Comments tab, you can document the trigger.

User-Defined Data Types

You are not able to create data types in the physical model, but the collection types and structured types you might have defined earlier in the data types model will be automatically brought to the physical model.

You are able to change the name of a collection type and define the settings Owner, Force Replace (NO/YES), OID (Object Identifier), and Comments for it. You can also define privileges by clicking the Permissions button.

You can also rename a structured type and define the settings Owner, Force replace (NO/YES), Global OID, Invoker Rights (empty, Current_user, Definer), Map Order Functions, Map To Java Class (NO/YES), and Comments for it. You can also define privileges by clicking the Permissions button.

Other Elements

If you want to have the whole database designed and documented in Data Modeler, you can do that. You can add a database with its properties to the physical model to get the DDLs for it. In Database Properties, you can define properties on the General, Logging, and Tablespaces tabs, and you can write comments. After defining the database for the physical model, you can see in the Browser pane new branches for adding data files, redo log groups, and SYSAUX files to that database.

You can define directories and disk groups, and you can define *contexts,* which are sets of application-defined attributes that validate and secure an application. You can also create clusters. A cluster is a schema object that contains data from one or more tables. The idea of a cluster is that the data that are often retrieved together are saved close to each other to enable fast performance. All the tables in a cluster must have at least one column in common. An index cluster stores together all the rows from all the tables that share the same cluster key, and a hash cluster stores rows that have the same hash key value together. In the physical model, you can create a cluster and attach tables or materialized views in it on the Table/Materialized View Properties tabs of the Cluster Properties dialog.

Propagating Properties

In most of the properties dialogs you will see a Propagate Properties button. This is useful functionality when you have defined the properties for one kind of object and want to have the same property copied to other objects of the same type. For instance, you might have defined the properties for a table such as User, Tablespace, Logging, Storage, Row Dependency, Row Movement, and Permissions, and you want to have the same settings for another 25 tables. Instead of manually entering all this information for your 25 tables, you can use the Propagate Properties utility. After setting the properties wanted on one table, just click Propagate Properties. The Properties Propagation dialog opens where you can first select which properties to propagate and then to which objects these properties will be propagated. This tool will probably be your or your DBA's favorite tool in the physical database design process.

TIP
You can use the Propagate Properties button for copying privileges. You can define privileges to one table and click Propagate Properties to copy the same set of privileges to other tables.

Indexing

Defining the indexes so that the database can perform as well as possible is one of the most important tasks in physical database design. To be able to do that, you must know what users are going to do with the database, and you must understand what kind of index types your RDBMS site supports. There are plenty of books on indexing theory as well as indexing on a particular RDBMS. Please study those for more information on indexing, especially indexing for your RDBMS. In this book, I will talk about the topic briefly.

An index is a database object that provides a quick lookup of the data in a database. There are different types of indexes for different kinds of searches. Usually an index need is justified by its usage: the amount of data, how the data is mainly used (select/update/insert/delete), and the frequency of selects. If the amount of data is small, there is probably no need for an index. If the data is mostly inserted, updated, and deleted, it might not be a good idea to add an index because indexes make only selects faster while making other operations slower. If you have a query that is run only once a year, it might not be a good idea to have an index supporting it in the database for 12 months a year. An index is defined for a column or columns in a table, and it supports select queries only with those columns in the WHERE clause of the query. An index does not support all the queries, and it is not a silver bullet for performance.

There are different kinds of indexes. The most common is a B-tree index (B-tree, B+-tree, B*-tree); for spatial data there is the R-tree index (R-tree, R+-tree, R*-tree), and there are the following types: bitmap index, context index, multilevel index, hash index, function-based index, bitmap join, reverse key index, and so on. A primary key has a special index called a *primary index*, and a table can have only one of those. Many times indexes for foreign keys are created to support the joins and to avoid locking problems. But to be able to decide about other possible indexes, you should research the most common queries and their frequency. If the query retrieves only a small part of the data in a table, an index might be useful; if it retrieves a major part of the data, an index is not useful because a full table scan will be more efficient.

When defining the index, it is vital to set the index columns in the right order, with the most selective ones in front. Also, having the columns used in "equals to" evaluations would be better to set in front of the index and the ones used in range evaluation at the end. When using an index in performing a query, usually the biggest cost comes if you need to go to the table to get something. For this reason, sometimes columns in the WHERE, JOIN, ORDER BY, or SELECT part of a query are added to the index to avoid the need to access the table. Make sure you do not have too many indexes in a table and that they are not too similar. Remember that updating a column that is in an index costs two to three times more than a column not in an index. Be careful when selecting the columns for the index, make sure they are in right order, and remember you can also use temporary indexes in some cases.

TIP
Using the wrong data type in a query can prevent using index because a data type conversion must be done. Make sure you know what data type the column is in order to query correctly. For instance, WHERE ProductID = 123 would not perform well since ProductID is numeric and it is compared to a character set.

An index is created in the relational model, and it will be immediately visible in the physical model's Browser pane under the table it is attached to. In the physical model, you can add all the physical properties for the index in nine tabs: General, Columns, Column Sort Order, Indextype Parameters, Global Partitioning, Hash/Composite By Hash Tablespaces, Global Hash Partitions By Quantity, Spatial Index, and Comments. On the General tab, you define Bitmap Index (NO/YES); Indextype (you can type whatever you want, and that will be in the DDL for the index type); Tablespace; Logging (YES/NO); Storage (select a storage template from a list); Compress; Parallel (NO/YES); if you set Parallel to YES, then you can also define

Degree for parallelism; Sorted Rows (Sorted, Reverse, No); Compute Stats (NO/YES); Online (NO/YES); Invisible (NO/YES); and Partitioned (Non-partitioned, Local, Global by Range, Global Hash Partitioned By Quantity, Global Hash Partitioned By List). If the index is partitioned, you can define the global partitioning columns on the Global Partitioning tab. If Partitioned is set to Global Hash Partitioned By Quantity, you can define the parameters needed on the Global Hash Partitioned By Quantity tab. On the Column Sort Order tab, you can define the sort order for the columns. If it is a spatial index, select Spatial Index on the General tab.

Bitmap join indexes are created in the physical model. They are an index type supporting joins of two or more tables. In the physical model, you can create bitmap join indexes by selecting the table you want to assign it and going to Bitmap Join Indexes, right-clicking, and choosing New. You can insert all parameters needed for generating a bitmap join index.

NOTE
You can also define an index for a cluster.

Partitioning

If a table, index, or materialized view is big, it is possible to partition it. Partitioning in Oracle requires the partitioning option that is available for Enterprise Edition databases. Partitioning makes maintaining easier and sometimes improves the performance. In my opinion, the main advantage of partitioning is the maintenance, and secondary is the improvement on performance. For instance, partitioning makes deleting data fast; you can just drop a partition. If you decide to use partitioning, study carefully the possibilities your RDBMS has for it and design partitioning carefully.

Partitioning operation affects only the physical schema. That means that usually the logical model (and relational model) stay untouched, and no programs need to be changed. Sometimes partitioning may need some extra columns for tables to get a working partition key, and then the logical model and programs must be changed.

You can create a new partition in the physical model in the Browser pane; under the table you want to create it, right-click, and choose New. There are five tabs: General, Subpartition Order, Subpartition Tablespaces, Local Index, and Comments. On the General tab you can specify the following settings: Name, Value List (free text edit), Tablespace (select from the list of tablespaces), Logging (null, YES, NO), Storage (select from the list of storage templates), and Data Compression (null, YES, NO). For a table in Table Properties, you set the Partitioned property to YES, and on the Partitioning tab you specify the partition type and if needed the subpartition type. After selecting the subpartition type for the table, you can create a new subpartition of the selected type (Hash, List, Range) under the partition name in the Browser pane (under the table) and specify the parameters needed for the DDL. You can also define a storage template and LOB storage for a subpartition.

Summary

In physical database design, you design and define physical elements related to the selected RDBMS site and add the physical properties to elements created in the logical design. The outcomes from the physical database design process are the DDL scripts for creating the database. To be able to design the physical model, you need a good understanding of the RDBMS site selected to be able to make the right decisions. During the physical database design you must also design other things, such as backup and recovery strategies.

CHAPTER
7

Generating DDL Scripts for Creating Database Objects

A data definition language (DDL) is for creating database objects. Generating DDL scripts with Oracle SQL Developer Data Modeler is quite simple, and it can be done over and over again to find the right settings to get the right kinds of scripts. The difficult task is to decide what kind of DDL files you want. Do you want a version of a whole database at a certain time in just one file, or do you want a file per object or something else? Where do you plan to keep the files, and who will have access to them? What are you going to do with these files? Do you need a file for creating a whole test database of a particular version? Maybe you also need a file for creating the latest version of the Customer table for production? Before creating the DDL files, you must decide what they are for so you know what you need. Do you need different versions of DDLs for production and test? How are they different? Where do you keep the DDLs? Chapter 12 talks about comparing models to a database and generating DDL scripts for altering the database objects. Before the DDLs are run in the database, they must be reviewed, and there should be a documented process for that. There should also be clear understanding of who runs the DDLs on the database and when and how this person documents what has been run.

The DDLs are based on the relational model and one of its physical models. If you do not have any physical models open, only the relational model is used, and the DDLs will be basic without physical parameters. You might want to use this, for instance, when creating objects for your test database where you have defined the defaults for tablespaces and users and creating an object does not need physical parameters of its own.

Setting Preferences and Properties

Certain preferences affect how the generation of DDLs will be performed and how the generated DDLs will look. In every new version of Data Modeler there are new preferences to make the generation more tunable. The DDL preferences should be studied carefully since setting them correctly will help you get the kind of DDLs you want from the tool without any manual work.

Figure 7-1 shows the Preferences dialog open to the Data Modeler | DDL tab. With Statement Termination Character For DB2 And UDB, you can define the termination character for DDL clauses for IBM DB2 and UDB databases. You type the character wanted as a terminator into the box.

On this tab there are several parameters for defining the trigger generation.

- The Create Type Substitution Triggers For Oracle And UDB setting defines whether type substitution triggers are generated in Oracle and IBM UDB.

- Create Arc Constraints defines whether the triggers for foreign key arc constraints are generated in the DDL scripts.

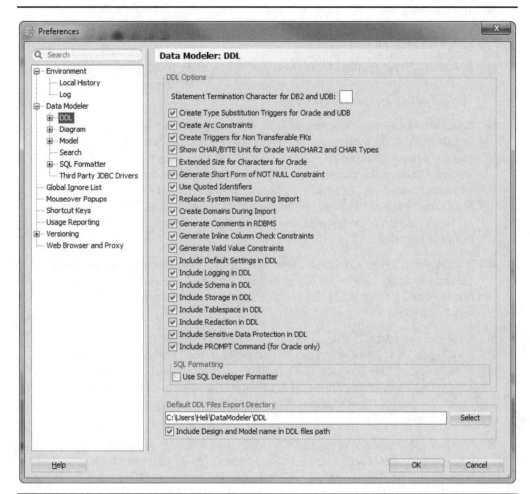

FIGURE 7-1. *DDL options*

■ Create Triggers For Non Transferable FKs defines whether triggers for nontransferable foreign key relationships are generated in the DDL scripts.

Then there are some preferences for the generation.

■ The Show CHAR/BYTE Unit For Oracle VARCHAR2 And CHAR Types preference defines whether the unit (CHAR or BYTE) associated with the attribute length for Oracle types CHAR and VARCHAR2 are included in the generated CREATE TABLE statements.

- The Generate Short Form Of NOT NULL Constraint preference defines whether the NOT NULL constraint name is used in the CREATE TABLE statement for column definitions.

- By selecting Use Quoted Identifiers, you define that object names will be enclosed in double quotes in the generated DDL statements (for example, "CUSTOMER" instead of CUSTOMER).

- If you select Generate Comments In RDBMS, the text in the field Comment In RDBMS will be included in the generated DDL statements. Remember that if you have changed the Comment In RDBMS field in the physical model, the link between the comments has been cut, and the text written in the relational model will be used if the physical model is not open. If it is open, the Comment In RDBMS text in the physical model is used. The same logic applies to other properties that can be changed in both the relational and physical models.

- If you select Generate Inline Column Check Constraints, the Column Check Constraint clause will be included in the CREATE TABLE statement. If this is not selected, a separate ALTER TABLE statement for the constraint definition will be created.

- If the Generate Valid Value Constraints setting is selected, the List Of Values and Range Of Values constraints are included in the generated DDL; if it is not selected, the generated DDL will be without the List Of Values and Range Of Values constraints. This is useful if you want to only define the constraints in your model but do not actually want to implement them in the database.

- The Include Default Settings In DDL preference will add all possible DDL keywords for the object created in the generated DDL statements. This option is useful if you want to see the syntax for an object DDL.

- Include Logging In DDL, Include Schema In DDL, Include Storage In DDL, Include Tablespace In DDL, Include Redaction In DDL, and Include Sensitive Data Protection In DDL define whether the mentioned parameter is included in the generated DDL. If a schema is not included in the DDL, the object will be created for the schema of the username that has been used to log in to the database for running the DDL. If the tablespace is not included in the DDL, in Oracle the default tablespace of the username who has logged in will be used. If the storage is not included, in Oracle the storage setting of the tablespace where the object is saved is used.

- The Include PROMPT Command (For Oracle Only) preference is valid only when generating DDL statements for Oracle; it defines whether the

PROMPT command is added before each DDL statement in the generated DDL statements. The PROMPT command is used for viewing the progress of a script execution.

■ If the Use SQL Developer Formatter preference is selected under SQL Formatting, the SQL formatting uses the SQL Developer defaults; if it is not selected, the formatting follows the traditional Data Modeler defaults.

■ In Default DDL Files Export Directory, you can specify the directory where the DDL files will be saved by default.

■ The preference Extended Size For Characters For Oracle was introduced in version 4.0.3. It defines whether the MAX_STRING_SIZE = EXTENDED initialization parameter is available when generating the DDL.

■ A new preference called Include Design And Model Name In DDL Files Path was introduced in version 4.0.3. By selecting this preference, you will have the design and model names for the DDL file paths, which makes finding the right DDLs easier. I recommend selecting this preference.

Here is an example of a DDL script for a table called Order with all the preferences introduced earlier selected:

```
PROMPT CREATING TABLE 'Order';
CREATE TABLE "Order"
    (    "OrderNo"      NUMBER NOT NULL ,
      "Information" VARCHAR2 (100 CHAR) NULL
    )
    ORGANIZATION HEAP NOCOMPRESS NOCACHE NOPARALLEL NOROWDEPENDENCIES
DISABLE ROW MOVEMENT ;
COMMENT ON TABLE "Order"
IS
'This is the table for Orders.' ;
    PROMPT CREATING PRIMARY KEY ON 'Order';
    ALTER TABLE "Order" ADD CONSTRAINT "Order_PK" PRIMARY KEY ( "OrderNo"
) NOT DEFERRABLE ENABLE VALIDATE ;
```

If the Use SQL Developer Formatter preference under SQL Formatting is not selected, the same DDL would look like this:

```
PROMPT CREATING TABLE 'Order';
CREATE TABLE "Order"
      (
        "OrderNo"      NUMBER  NOT NULL ,
        "Information" VARCHAR2 (100 CHAR)   NULL
```

```
     )
     ORGANIZATION HEAP
     NOCOMPRESS
     NOCACHE
     NOPARALLEL
     NOROWDEPENDENCIES
     DISABLE ROW MOVEMENT
;
COMMENT ON TABLE "Order" IS 'This is the table for Orders.'
;
PROMPT CREATING PRIMARY KEY ON 'Order';
ALTER TABLE "Order"
    ADD CONSTRAINT "Order_PK" PRIMARY KEY ( "OrderNo" ) NOT DEFERRABLE
ENABLE VALIDATE ;
```

You can also use the preferences to set formatting. In the Preferences dialog, under Data Modeler | SQL Formatter there is a parameter called Autoformat Visible SQL And PL/SQL. If you select it, the SQL Formatter options are applied automatically in the generated PL/SQL code for procedures, packages, views, and triggers. If you do not select it, the SQL Formatter options are applied only when you so request. There are also product-specific formatting options and the Export/Import functionality to share the formatting with other users.

TIP
Define the Default DDL Files Export Directory setting and you will always know where your DDL files are saved.

NOTE
Chapter 10 will cover the DDL preferences that affect importing (Replace System Names During Import, Create Domains During Import).

Figure 7-2 shows the Preferences dialog open to the Data Modeler | DDL | DDL/ Storage tab. The options under DDL Storage Options For Import And Export allow you to define whether the storage options will be included in the DDLs for import and export operations. You can either include or exclude these parameters from the storage clause in DDL: PCTFREE, PCTUSED, INITRANS and MAXTRANS, INITIAL, NEXT, MINEXTENTS, MAXEXTENTS, PCTINCREASE, BUFFER_POOL, FREELIST, FREELIST GROUPS, OPTIMAL, and Encryption. The default behavior is that all these keywords are selected, and the values defined in the physical model are included for them in the generated DDL.

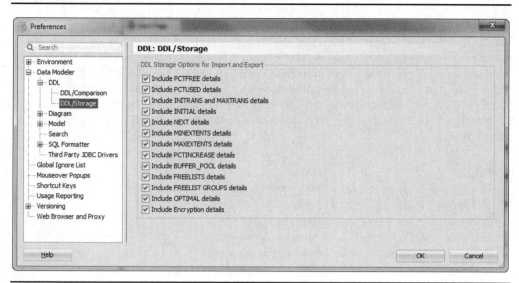

FIGURE 7-2. *DDL storage options for import and export*

There are also two *design properties* that will affect the DDL generation. In the DDL Properties dialog (which you open by choosing Design Properties | Settings | DDL), you can decide whether you want automatic index generation for primary, unique, and foreign key constraints. If you enable the automatic index generation, the index will be generated automatically, and you do not need to define it in the physical model. I suggest you disable these design properties (the functionality is also a default value in the tool) and specify each index in your database. Sometimes there are two similar index candidates, and maybe it is the foreign key index you decide not to create because the other candidate has all the foreign key columns and some extra columns at the end of the index. It is important to manually see all the indexes and decide whether the index will be created. The other property is Preserve DDL Generation Options, which controls whether to restore the original DDL generation options after a current DDL generation operation.

TIP

Remember that in the design-level properties you can also define a template for the naming standard for automatically generated indexes.

In DDL Migration Properties (Design Properties | Settings | DDL | Migration) on the Name Substitution tab, you can define old strings to be replaced with new strings in object names when the DDL statements are generated. This will take effect only if you also select Apply Name Substitution in the DDL Generation Options dialog. This is useful in many cases. For instance, if your test database has a schema named TEST and your production database has a schema named XYZ, you do not need to have two separate physical models; you can use name substitution to replace the name XYZ when generating the DDLs for the test database. If you specify the Name Substitution rules in Design Properties, you can see them on the Name Substitution tab in the DDL generation, and they can be used for name substitution.

TIP
The quickest way to test how these preferences and properties affect things is to use DDL Preview. Select a table in the relational diagram, right-click, and choose DDL Preview. Now that the previewer is open, you can select another object in the diagram, and the DDL script will be updated accordingly. You can also change preferences or design properties and see how the change will affect the DDL generation.

Exporting a DDL File

You can start the DDL generation either by choosing File | Export | DDL File or by clicking the Generate DDL icon on the toolbar in the relational model. First you select the RDBMS site and the relational model you want to use for the DDL generation, and then you click Generate (Figure 7-3). If you have several physical models for a relational model, Data Modeler will suggest the RDBMS site that has been changed most recently by default; you can of course select another one if you want. This same screen is also shown after the DDL has been generated, which is the reason for the buttons Clear, Save, and Find. Clear clears the screen, and Save saves the content to a file. You can use Find to search for some particular text in the SQL generated. The example in Figure 7-3 is after generation. You can also see the generated DDL on the screen.

NOTE
If you select an RDBMS site that does not exist for this relational model or is not opened, the DDL generated will include information only from the relational model and will show syntax from the selected RDBMS site.

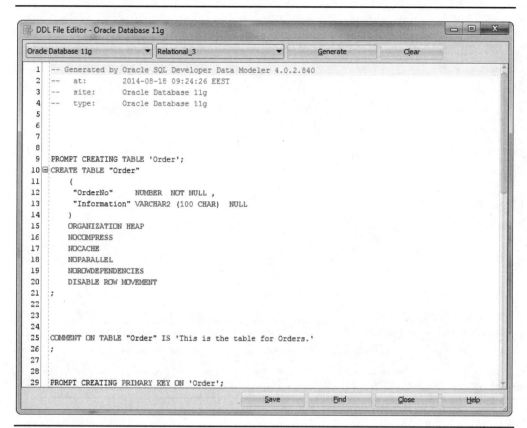

FIGURE 7-3. *DDL File Editor*

Exploring DDL Generation Options

Figure 7-4 shows the tree view for the DDL generation options. These options control the content to be included in the generated DDL script. In the tree you can see all the elements in the selected physical model, and the name of the selected physical model appears at the top of the list. You can select and unselect elements from the list to get only the DDLs generated you want.

On the bottom of the tree you can see these tabs: Tables, PK And UK Constraints, Indexes, Foreign Keys, Views, Clusters, Dimensions, Materialized Views, Synonyms, Sequences, Bitmap Join Indexes, External Tables, Collection Types, Triggers, Packages, Package Bodies, Stored Procedures, Functions, and Structured Types. On these tabs you can select and deselect objects by the object type. For instance, on the Tables tab

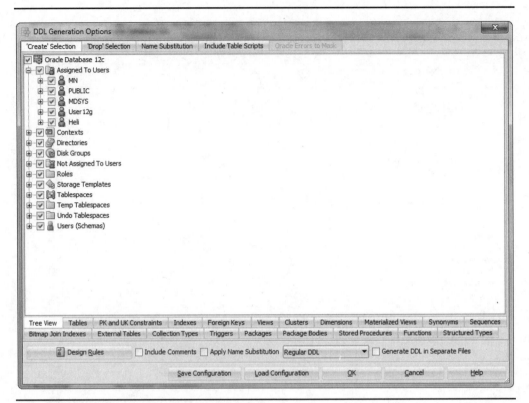

FIGURE 7-4. *DDL Generation Options dialog*

you can select some tables and deselect others, and only the ones you have selected will be included in the DDL generation.

Below those tabs there is a Design Rules button. This button enables you to run a check for the predefined design rules on the current design for any violations. It would probably be wise to run this and fix any violations before generating the DDLs. If the Include Comments option is selected, the DDLs will include the comments defined in the relational model. There is also a list of supported DDL types: Regular DDL, Advanced Interactive DDL, and Advanced CL DDL. Regular DDL generates regular DDL, while Advanced Interactive DDL and Advanced CL DDL support interactive DDLs. At the beginning of the generated DDL script (in the comments), you can see what kind of interactive support this script type has and what privileges are needed for that functionality. The regular DDLs look like the example you saw earlier in this chapter when creating a table called Order.

A piece of a DDL script defined as Advanced Interactive DDL for creating a table Order would look something like this:

```
...declare
    statement varchar2(32000);
    comments varchar2(200);
begin
statement :=
    'PROMPT CREATING TABLE ''Order'';
CREATE TABLE "Order"
    (     "OrderNo"     NUMBER  NOT NULL ,
     "Information" VARCHAR2 (100 CHAR)  NULL
    )
    ORGANIZATION HEAP NOCOMPRESS NOCACHE NOPARALLEL NOROWDEPENDENCIES
DISABLE ROW MOVEMENT ';
comments := 'PROMPT CREATING TABLE ''Order'';
CREATE TABLE "Order" ';
adv_scripting.EXEC_STATEMENT(10,statement,comments);
end;
/
-- end Step10
-- Step20
declare
    statement varchar2(32000);
    comments varchar2(200);
begin
statement :=    'COMMENT ON TABLE "Order" IS ''This is the table for
Orders.''';
comments := 'COMMENT ON TABLE "Order" ';
adv_scripting.EXEC_STATEMENT(20,statement,comments);
end;
/
-- end Step20
-- Step30
declare
    statement varchar2(32000);
    comments varchar2(200);
begin
statement :=    'PROMPT CREATING PRIMARY KEY ON ''Order'';
ALTER TABLE "Order"
    ADD CONSTRAINT "Order_PK" PRIMARY KEY ( "OrderNo" ) NOT DEFERRABLE
ENABLE VALIDATE ';
comments := 'PROMPT CREATING PRIMARY KEY ON ''Order'';
ALTER TABLE "Order"
    ADD CONSTRAIN';
adv_scripting.EXEC_STATEMENT(30,statement,comments);
end;
/
```

And here's the code for the same example when selecting Advanced CL DDL:

```
-- Step10
declare
    statement varchar2(32000);
    comments varchar2(200);
begin
statement :='PROMPT CREATING TABLE ''Order'';
CREATE TABLE "Order"
    ( "OrderNo"      NUMBER   NOT NULL ,
     "Information" VARCHAR2 (100 CHAR)   NULL
    )
    ORGANIZATION HEAP
    NOCOMPRESS
    NOCACHE
    NOPARALLEL
    NOROWDEPENDENCIES
    DISABLE ROW MOVEMENT
    ';
comments := 'PROMPT CREATING TABLE ''Order'';
CREATE TABLE "Order" ';
adv_scripting.EXEC_STATEMENT(10,statement,comments);
end;
/
-- end Step10
-- Step20
declare
    statement varchar2(32000);
    comments varchar2(200);
begin
statement :='COMMENT ON TABLE "Order" IS ''This is the table for
Orders.''';
comments := 'COMMENT ON TABLE "Order" ';
adv_scripting.EXEC_STATEMENT(20,statement,comments);
end;
/
-- end Step20
-- Step30
declare
    statement varchar2(32000);
    comments varchar2(200);
begin
statement :='PROMPT CREATING PRIMARY KEY ON ''Order'';
ALTER TABLE "Order"
    ADD CONSTRAINT "Order_PK" PRIMARY KEY ( "OrderNo" ) NOT DEFERRABLE
ENABLE VALIDATE ';
comments := 'PROMPT CREATING PRIMARY KEY ON ''Order'';
ALTER TABLE "Order"
```

```
    ADD CONSTRAIN';
adv_scripting.EXEC_STATEMENT(30,statement,comments);
end;
/
-- end Step30
spool off
exit ;
```

If you want to have a separate DDL file for each object, select Generate DDL In Separate Files. Otherwise, all the DDLs will be generated in a single file. This option has been available since version 4.0.2. It was added to the tool because many users wanted to have one DDL file per object, and before that, it was possible only by generating one at a time. Now you can generate them at once by selecting Generate DDL In Separate Files. The files will be generated either to the directory you specify during the generation or to the one you have defined in Preferences. Data Modeler will create a directory with the design name and under that a subdirectory for the relational model and under that a subdirectory for the physical model. Under the physical model directory, you can find DDLs for creating redaction policies if you have defined them and a directory called DataObjects. Under DataObjects you can find directories for all object types, and under them you will find all the DDLs for each object type. In my opinion, this is the best way of handling DDLs for production since in production you usually create objects one by one and carefully plan and test them. For a test environment, you might want to create the whole database of a certain version, in which case you would want to have all DDLs in one file. If you have selected any other DDL type besides the Regular DDL option, the option to have DDLs in separate files is not available.

On the top of the same tree view, you can see tabs for different kinds of DDL operations. On the 'Create' Selection tab (shown earlier in Figure 7-4), either you can select the elements you want to include in the DDL generation or you can use the tabs on the bottom to select and deselect them by object type. On the 'Drop' Selection tab (Figure 7-5), you can specify which object types will have DDLs with the DROP clause included before the CREATE clause. You can also decide whether the DROP clause is generated for all the objects selected or only for the ones generated (Drop Generated Objects Only) and whether the CASCADE option will be added to all the DROP clauses. CASCADE means that the child tables will be included in the DROP operation.

On the Name Substitution tab (Figure 7-6), you can define old strings to be replaced with new strings in object names when the DDL statements are generated. This will take effect only if you also select Apply Name Substitution at the bottom of the screen. You can also define name substitutions in the design properties as explained earlier in this chapter. Name substitutions defined in the design properties

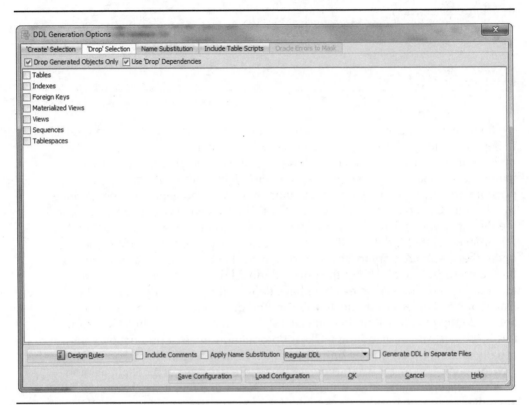

FIGURE 7-5. *'Drop' Selection tab*

will appear on this screen automatically. On the Object Types tab, you can specify the object types for the name substitution: Index, Role, Table, Tablespace, and User.

If you have table scripts (see Chapter 5) defined for your tables, you can see them on the Include Table Scripts tab (Figure 7-7). On this tab you can define whether these scripts will be included in the generated DDLs. This does not affect the scripts defined for views; they can be controlled only by Include Into DDL Script on the Scripts tab for View Properties in the relational model. If you disable the script generation for a table in DDL Generation Options, the property Include Into DDL Script for the table on the Scripts tab for table properties in the relational model will automatically be disabled.

NOTE
You cannot see the table scripts in DDL Preview.

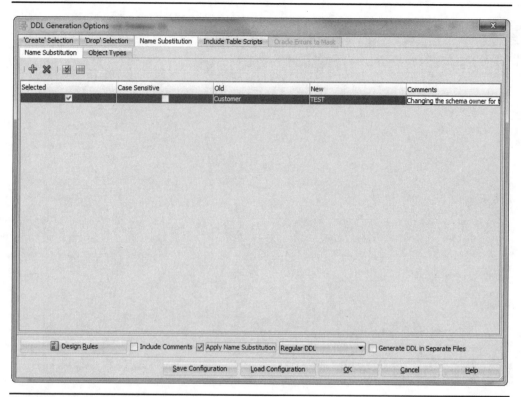

FIGURE 7-6. *Name Substitution tab*

If you have selected either Advanced DDL or Advanced CL DDL instead of Regular DDL on the Oracle Errors To Mask tab, you can specify any Oracle errors to be ignored during script execution. Specify only the error number with a hyphen and significant digits in the Type field. For example, for ORA-00942, specify -942. You can also specify the error description, but that is informational only and does not affect the script execution.

You can save the configuration with the Save Configuration button on the bottom of the DDL Generation Options dialog, and the current configurations will be saved in an XML file. You can later get those settings by clicking the Load Configuration button. This functionality is useful; for instance, when you have found the right combination of settings for your test databases, just save the configuration and use it the next time you need to create a test database. Remember to name the configuration files so you know which is which.

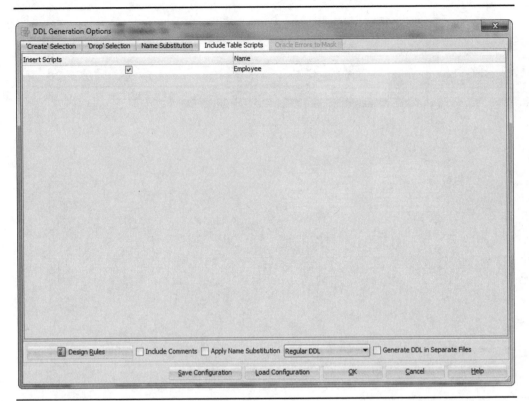

FIGURE 7-7. *Include Table Scripts tab*

If you want to generate the DDLs, just click OK. If you want to cancel, click Cancel.

When you have clicked OK, you will be taken back to the DDL File Editor screen, but this time it is not empty. You will see all the DDL clauses for objects you selected with the parameters you defined. The design rules are also checked automatically, so you might also see a message telling you that there are errors, and you should check the design rules for more details. In the DDL File Editor, you can scroll up and down in the code, you can save the DDL file (remember that the preference Default DDL Files Export Directory defines the default value for this directory), you can click Find to search a string from the file, or you can click Clear to clear the screen of the code.

TIP
When saving the DDL file, remember to add the extension for the filename, for example Customer.sql.

Starting from version 4.1, you can customize the DDL generation using transformation scripts. With transformation scripts you can dynamically generate DDL to prefix/append your objects or to replace them entirely. For example, you can have journaling tables created immediately after the tables are generated in the DDLs.

Summary

Generating DDLs with Data Modeler is simple, and you can do the DDL generation over and over again. Remember to decide what kind of DDLs you need and how they will be used to be able to define the preferences, design properties, and generation options to support your needs. DLL Preview is a useful tool for testing different combinations of preferences and design properties.

CHAPTER
8

Designing a Data Warehouse Database

Designing a data warehouse (DW) database is usually different from designing an operational database, which is a database for online transaction processing (OLTP). A DW database can be designed like any other database using the principles of entity-relationship (ER) modeling, such as third normal form (3NF) and so on, but usually that is not an optimal solution because of the need for complex relationships, drill-downs, and so on. Therefore, you can use a logical design technique called *dimensional modeling* to design a data warehouse database. The biggest difference may be that designing a dimensional model is about business rules, while designing a traditional ER model is about data and data rules.

An operational database usually faces a lot of short and fast inserts, updates, and deletes and reasonably simple select queries for fundamental operational tasks, while a DW database is usually for bulk loading and complicated select queries on a large amount of data for planning, analyzing, and decision support purposes, called *online analytical processing* (OLAP). The data for a DW database usually comes from several other databases, and the data can be transformed or consolidated on loading to the database. There are several techniques for modeling a DW database: ER modeling (3NF), dimensional modeling (the most popular ones are star schema and snowflake), and Data Vault (a hybrid of ER and dimensional modeling). These techniques also include pattern solutions for known issues when designing a DW database. Quite often a DW database is constructed with data marts (or *information marts* as they are called in Data Vault 2.0) that include one or more dimensional models. The dimensional modeling is done with ER notation. If the database also supports OLAP features, multidimensional notation can be used on top of the dimensional modeling. Multidimensional modeling includes the concept of cubes.

When designing a DW database, your tool should support ER notation, classification types, dimensional modeling, reverse engineering of the sources, forward engineering for the DDLs, source to target mapping, a data dictionary/repository for the elements in design, reporting capabilities, and multidimensional modeling. Data Modeler supports all this.

This chapter does not go into all the details of designing a DW database, which would be a topic of a whole new book, but you will learn how Data Modeler can help you when designing a DW database.

Introducing Dimensional Modeling Techniques

In an OLAP environment, the queries to the database can be much more complex than the ones in OLTP. Here's an example of a typical two-dimensional query in OLTP: "How much of that product has been sold this month?" In an OLAP environment, the query is probably not two-dimensional but multidimensional;

it is probably something like this: "How much of each of our products was sold on a particular day, by a particular salesperson, in a particular city?" In a multidimensional model, each separate part of that query is called a *dimension*. In a database in an OLAP environment, many of the answers to the subqueries are not calculated but determined from the database.

Several techniques are available for modeling a DW database with a dimensional model. You will learn about three of them: star schema, snowflake, and Data Vault model. These techniques include the modeling techniques and predefined solutions for known issues in DW databases.

A star schema/star model is based on one central table (fact) and several tables that radiate from it (dimensions). Those tables are connected by primary and foreign keys. The snowflake schema is also based on a central table (fact) and a set of constituent dimension tables that are further normalized into subdimension tables. The Data Vault model consists of three basic parts: the architecture (systems architecture, three-tier architecture), the methodology (rules on how and why), and the model (standardized data model with strictly defined entities). The Data Vault model is a combination of the star schema and 3NF. The model is based on three key components: hubs, links, and satellites. A hub is a unique list of business keys for tracking and identifying key information, a link is an association to hook together multiple sets of information, and a satellite is a descriptor that provides context for hubs and links.

When building data warehouses using the agile methodology, the Data Vault method is the most flexible and probably the best for the purpose. But what is the difference between star schema and snowflake, and which one should you choose? Snowflake has less redundancy than star schema since the dimension tables are in normalized form. That means a snowflake model is easier to maintain, but queries on it might get quite complicated and therefore can sometimes perform badly. The snowflake model is good with dimension analysis, whereas star schema is better with metric analysis. Snowflake works better as the data warehouse core and when there are complex many-to-many relationships, and star schema is better for data marts and simple relationships (one-to-one and one-to-many). Snowflake modeling is a bottom-up approach, and star schema is a top-down approach to modeling.

Exploring Dimensional Design

The process of dimensional design is of course similar to designing any database, but there are some tricks and tools that will help when designing a DW database.

The requirements analysis is mainly about collecting requirements and documenting them as described in Chapter 3. The difference in a DW database is that you also must collect the source-driven requirements. They can be collected by investigating the ER models of the source databases and the business process documentation. If the source databases do not have documentation and ER models, you can easily generate the model as described in Chapter 10 if the source database system is supported in Data Modeler. Otherwise, dimensional requirements analysis is the same process as described in Chapter 3.

In conceptual and logical database design, the tools are ER models and data flow diagrams. The process is similar to the one described in Chapters 4 and 5. What is special in DW database design is that you should take advantage of the classification types and sometimes also transformations. There are already preset classification types in the Data Modeler tool, but you can create as many new ones as you want. Right-click the design and select Properties. In the Design Properties dialog, go to the Settings | Diagram | Classification Types tab. In Design Properties, you can see all classification types defined for this design. You can add new ones by clicking the green plus sign, or you can change the existing ones by selecting the one you want to change and changing the properties how you want. You can define the name for the classification type, define a prefix for it, and define the color used for that type of object in diagrams. Using classification types not only makes the diagrams easier to read but also gives you as a designer more tools when operating with different kinds of objects in your DW database. Classification types have been used in all the figures in this chapter.

What is also different from what you learned in Chapters 4 and 5 is that the relationship between an ER model for an operational database and a dimensional model (made with ER notation) is that a single ER diagram might be broken into multiple dimensional models based on the business processes. For instance, ordering might be one business process and invoicing another business process, but they both would be modeled in the same ER diagram. That is why the business processes must be understood and documented well to be able to understand them.

The process of loading data into the data warehouse database can be designed with data flow diagrams, and the transformations can be designed with transformation packages (introduced in Chapter 3). In data flow diagrams, you design the process of loading the data, and in transformation packages, you design all the transformations needed for the data before loading it into the data warehouse database.

Star Schema or Snowflake

There are already predefined classification types called Fact and Dimension for designing a star schema model or a snowflake model. You can edit those specifications if you want to define the prefixes for the classification types (on the Settings | Diagram | Classification Types tab of the Design Properties dialog). You could, for instance, define FACT_ for fact tables and DIM_ for dimensions. First you design the dimensional model using ER notation from the logical model as you would for a star schema/snowflake: You select the business process, declare the grain, identify the dimensions, and identify the facts. The grain of the model describes the central process of this dimensional model in a single sentence and helps you to define the dimensions and facts. Then you define the classification type for every entity in the diagram. You can do it in the Entity Properties dialog under Classification Types, or in the Browser pane you can right-click the logical model and select Set Classification Types. In the dialog that opens you can specify which entities are, for instance, of type Fact. You can define additional classification types for an entity by selecting Set Additional Classification Types in the Browser pane. On the diagram a capital D in the top-left corner of the entity shows that this entity is a type of dimension, and a capital F shows it is a fact table. If you want to see the classification type name or you have defined several classification types for an entity, right-click the diagram and choose View Details | Classification Types. Figure 8-1 shows a design for a star schema (left) and snowflake (right) in ER notation using Data Modeler with the classification types displayed.

When you are ready with the ER model, you can move to the relational model as described in Chapter 5 by running the Engineer To Relational Model command. This transformation is done automatically based on the logical model, preferences, and properties. If you want to have surrogate keys generated automatically (IDs) for your tables, as usually recommended for DW databases, remember to define the Create Surrogate Key property for your entities (usually dimensions). And if you want the fact table to have a primary key constructed only on foreign keys from parent tables, first define the relationships as identifying (see Chapter 4 for more information on the identifying relationship) for all the relationships you want for the primary key. Then go to the properties of the Fact entity and define a unique identifier for it on the Unique Key tab. Then go to the properties of this unique key (double-click or click the Properties icon) and set the unique identifier State to Primary Key.

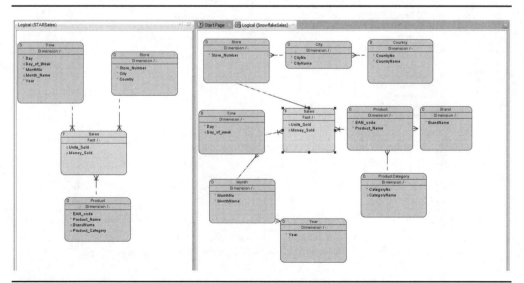

FIGURE 8-1. *Logical dimensional model for star schema and snowflake*

Then select the Attributes And Relations tab and select all the relationships for the primary key, as shown in Figure 8-2. Now the fact table will have a primary key.

If you are using the automatically generated IDs and want to use this dimensional model as a base for a multidimensional model, select Relational Model as the Bound Model setting when creating the multidimensional model (more about this later in this chapter). If you select Logical Model, you will not see the IDs (because they are created only for the relational model) to be able to link the dimensional model entities and multidimensional model objects. If you want to base the multidimensional model on the logical model, define the IDs for the logical model manually. Any other IDs except the primary key surrogate key you must add manually (such as possible IDs for elements inside the entity you might want to use when mapping to the multidimensional model). And remember that in the Design Properties dialog on the Setting | Naming Standards | Templates tab you can define the name for the automatically generated surrogate key

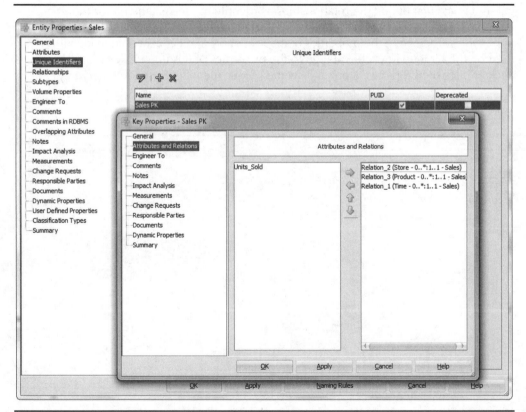

FIGURE 8-2. *Defining a primary key for a fact entity*

(Surrogate Key) and its column (Surrogate Key Column). After engineering, there are two things to do: You must set the constraint names correctly if they are not automatically set and associate the prefixes to the tables according to their classification type. If you do not want to have table prefixes on the constraint names, go to your relational model in the Browser pane, right-click, and choose Apply Naming Standards For Keys And Constraints; then right-click the relational model again and choose Change Object Names Prefix. In the Change Object Names Prefix dialog, select Add Classification Prefix. Figure 8-3 shows the snowflake example on the right; you can see that the classification prefixes are not in key and constraint names. If you want to have the prefixes in constraint names, then run Change Object Names Prefix and only after that run Apply Naming Standards For Keys And Constraints. Figure 8-3 shows the star schema example on the left so you can see that classification prefixes are also in key and constraint names.

Because the dimensional model is a standard framework, it includes templates or patterns for common modeling situations for business needs, such as slowly changing dimensions (SCDs), fact table structure, heterogeneous products, pay-in-advance databases, event-handling databases (factless fact tables), periodic snapshot fact tables, accumulating snapshot fact tables, dimension table structure, dimension surrogate keys, degenerate dimensions, denormalized flattened dimensions, multiple hierarchies in dimensions, flags and indicators as textual dimension attributes, calendar date dimensions, role-playing dimensions, junk dimensions, snowflaked

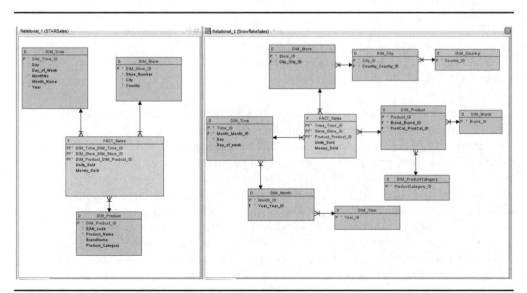

FIGURE 8-3. *A relational dimensional model for star schema and snowflake*

dimensions, outrigger dimensions, and many more. In this book I do not go through these, but I encourage you to find more information about them and use the ones you find useful.

You can find a lot of literature about these solutions and best practices for designing data warehouses. For instance, www.kimballgroup.com is a good place to start.

Data Vault

Data Vault is an emerging method for modeling a data warehouse. It was created by Dan Linstedt. Data Vault is a hybrid of third normal form and star schema. There are excellent books on Data Vault by Dan Linstedt and Kent Graziano available. You can also find more about Data Vault from LearnDataVault.com or http://danlinstedt.com/about/data-vault-basics/.

When starting to model your data warehouse as a Data Vault model, you must first define the classification types for hubs, links, and satellites. As mentioned earlier, you can do this in the Design Properties dialog. You can also define the prefixes for them, such as HUB_ for Hubs and SAT_ for Satellites. To define a Data Vault model, you must first define the hubs and associated satellites and define the classification types for them. Then create the many-to-many relationships between the hubs. Name the relationship as you would like the resulting link table to be named. If you want to use prefixes for Link tables too, name the relationships with the prefix, for example LNK_SalesProduct. Also remember on the hubs to select Create Surrogate Key in the Entity Properties dialog on the General tab because all tables in Data Vault should have a hash key as a surrogate key, for example an MD5 hash.

TIP
In Preferences (on the Data Modeler | Model | Relational tab), you can define the length of the surrogate key or select a domain for it.

When the logical model is completed, select Engineer To Relational Model. Figure 8-4 shows an example of a logical Data Vault model.

After running the Engineering To Relational Model command, you should define the classification type to the link tables just created. In the Browser pane, select your relational model, right-click, and choose Set Classification Types. From the Classification Types list, select Link, and in Find type **LNK**. Select the tables and click the arrow pointing to the right. Click Apply or OK. Then it's time to do the same two things you saw earlier for star and snowflake; in other words, set the constraint names correct if they are not automatically set and associate the prefixes to the tables according to their classification type. If you do not want to have table prefixes on the constraint names, go to your relational model in the Browser pane, right-click, and choose Apply Naming Standards For Keys And Constraints; then

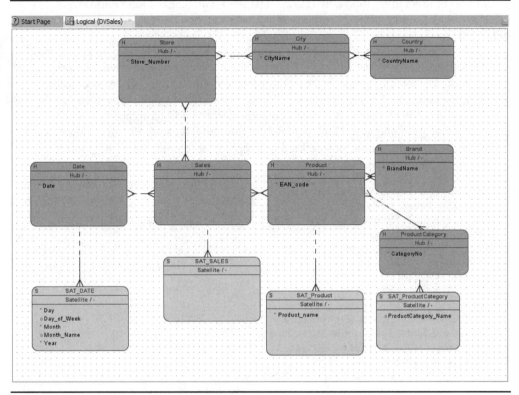

FIGURE 8-4. *A logical model for Data Vault*

right-click the relational model again and choose Change Object Names Prefix. In the Change Object Names Prefix dialog, select Add Classification Prefix. If you want to have the prefixes also in the constraint names, then run Change Object Names Prefix and Apply Naming Standards For Keys And Constraints only after that.

In a Data Vault model, each table must have some predefined columns. You can, of course, define them on the entity and engineer to the table if you want, but you can also use a transformation script to add the columns to the engineered tables or apply a table template during forward engineering. A hub should have the business keys needed (a business key is a key for which the business has some kind of meaning), a surrogate key (SQN or hash key), last seen date (LSDT), load date (LDTS), and record source (RSRC). A link should have a surrogate key (SQN or hash key), last seen date (LSDT), load date (LDTS), record source (RSRC), and the hub keys. A satellite should have a surrogate key (SQN or hash key inherited from the parent hub or link table), load date (LDTS), last seen date (LSDT), load end DTS (LEDTS), record source (RSRC), and possibly load sequence ID (LSQNID) and hash diff (HDIFF).

I defined three template tables: table_template_Hub, table_template_Lnk, and table_template_Sat. In table_template_Hub I defined the columns needed for hub tables, in the table table_template_Lnk I defined the columns needed for link tables, and in table_template_Sat I defined the columns needed for satellite tables. Then I asked my son Patrik to modify the transformation script "Table template – uses column name" (predefined in Data Modeler) to find the tables whose names start with *hub* and to add the columns defined in template table table_template_Hub to them (if not added before). Here's the code:

```
// columns are found by column name
// allowing reuse of already existing columns
// dynamic property ctemplateID is set afterwards - will keep
connection to template
// column even if the name of column is changed
var t_name = "table_template_Hub";
var p_name = "ctemplateID";
template = model.getTableSet().getByName(t_name);
if(template!=null){
    tcolumns = template.getElements();
    tables = model.getTableSet().toArray();
   for (var t = 0; t<tables.length;t++){
     table = tables[t];
        // compare name ignoring the case
     if(!table.getName().equalsIgnoreCase(t_name)){
        if((table.getName().substring(0,3).equalsIgnoreCase("HUB"))) {
          for (var i = 0; i < tcolumns.length; i++) {
             column = tcolumns[i];
             col = table.getElementByName(column.getName());
             if(col==null){
              col =
table.getColumnByProperty(p_name,column.getObjectID());
             }
             if(col==null){
              col = table.createColumn();
             }
             column.copy(col);
             //set property after copy otherwise it'll be cleared
by copy
             col.setProperty(p_name,column.getObjectID());
             table.setDirty(true);
          }
        }
      }
    }
}
```

Then I asked him to create another script for tables whose names start with *lnk* and whose columns are specified in template table table_template_Lnk. That code is here:

```
// columns are found by column name
// allowing reuse of already existing columns
// dynamic property ctemplateID is set afterwards - will keep
connection to template
// column even if the name of column is changed
var t_name = "table_template_Lnk";
var p_name = "ctemplateID";
template = model.getTableSet().getByName(t_name);
if(template!=null){
    tcolumns = template.getElements();
    tables = model.getTableSet().toArray();
   for (var t = 0; t<tables.length;t++){
     table = tables[t];
         // compare name ignoring the case
     if(!table.getName().equalsIgnoreCase(t_name)){
       if((table.getName().substring(0,3).equalsIgnoreCase("LNK"))) {
         for (var i = 0; i < tcolumns.length; i++) {
             column = tcolumns[i];
             col = table.getElementByName(column.getName());
             if(col==null){
              col =
table.getColumnByProperty(p_name,column.getObjectID());
             }
             if(col==null){
              col = table.createColumn();
             }
             column.copy(col);
             //set property after copy otherwise it'll be cleared
by copy
             col.setProperty(p_name,column.getObjectID());
             table.setDirty(true);
         }
       }
     }
   }
}
```

Then I asked him to create one more script for tables whose names start with *sat* and whose columns are specified in template table table_template_Sat. That code is here:

```
// columns are found by column name
// allowing reuse of already existing columns
// dynamic property ctemplateID is set afterwards - will keep
connection to template
```

```
// column even if the name of column is changed
var t_name = "table_template_Sat";
var p_name = "ctemplateID";
template = model.getTableSet().getByName(t_name);
if(template!=null){
    tcolumns = template.getElements();
    tables = model.getTableSet().toArray();
   for (var t = 0; t<tables.length;t++){
     table = tables[t];
         // compare name ignoring the case
     if(!table.getName().equalsIgnoreCase(t_name)){
       if
(table.getName().substring(0,3).equalsIgnoreCase("SAT")) {
         for (var i = 0; i < tcolumns.length; i++) {
             column = tcolumns[i];
             col = table.getElementByName(column.getName());
             if(col==null){
              col =
table.getColumnByProperty(p_name,column.getObjectID());
             }
             if(col==null){
              col = table.createColumn();
             }
             column.copy(col);
             //set property after copy otherwise it'll be
//cleared by copy
             col.setProperty(p_name,column.getObjectID());
             table.setDirty(true);
         }
       }
     }
   }
}
```

You can add these transformation scripts by choosing Tools | Design Rules and Transformations | Transformations. Click the green plus sign, define a name for a script, and define the following: Set Object to Relational, Engine to Mozilla Rhino, and Variable to Model. Then write the code in the script editor. Save, and you are ready to run the script by clicking Apply. When writing transformation scripts, you can use dynamic properties to give you a lot of possibilities for adjusting Data Modeler to your demands. I will talk more about dynamic properties later in this chapter.

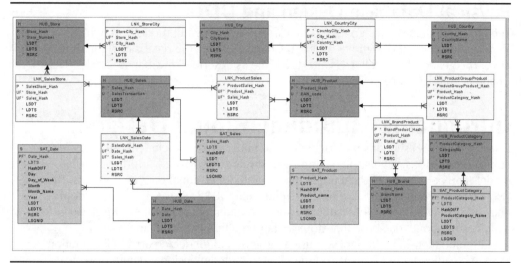

FIGURE 8-5. *A relational model for Data Vault*

The diagram in the Data Vault model is usually quite big, and you might want to keep the template tables separate from the actual Data Vault tables. Select the template tables and select Create Subview From Selected. Then select the main table of your Data Vault model (in this example Sales), and after you right-click, choose Select Neighbors and then Create Subview From Selected. Now you can define the layout as wanted. Figure 8-5 shows an example of a relational model for Data Vault based on the logical model shown in Figure 8-4 and after the operations described earlier. Also note the grid on the canvas. You can turn it on by right-clicking the canvas and choosing Show | Grid. The grid makes it easier to adjust the objects on canvas and actually to some people makes it easier to read the diagram.

TIP
If you want to straighten the foreign key lines in a relational model, do not try to move the line; move the table. When moving the table, if the line looks straight enough, release the mouse.

Use the relational model as the base for the multidimensional model since all the settings are not on the logical model. If you want to use the logical model as a base for a multidimensional model, you should define all the attributes, full names (with the prefix), and surrogates in the logical model manually.

Physical Database Design and DDLs

The physical database design for a dimensional or Data Vault model is much the same as the physical design described in Chapter 6 since the database objects are alike. The generation for DDLs is also the same as described in Chapter 7. See Chapters 6 and 7 for more information.

Introducing Multidimensional Design

Data Modeler also supports multidimensional models, which include these elements: cubes, dimensions, levels, links, and ragged hierarchy links. Multidimensional models can be used if the database supports multidimensional database objects. The two choices are ROLAP or MOLAP. A relational OLAP (ROLAP) is a relational database extended with OLAP support, and a multidimensional OLAP (MOLAP) is a multidimensional database that stores data in multidimensional arrays.

In multidimensional design, you use a dimensional model (created in ER notation as shown earlier in this chapter) and map that to multidimensional notation. Typical operations in multidimensional modeling are slicing, dicing, drilling down/up, rolling up, and pivoting/rotating. In a slice operation, you select a single value of one of the dimensions and create a new cube with one less dimension than the original one. For instance, you could have sales figures for only year 2013, with all other dimensions as they were in the original cube. In a dice operation, you or the end user can select specific values of each dimension on the original cube and create a subcube based on those. In a drill down/up operation, the user is able to navigate among levels from the most summarized (up) to the most detailed (down). A roll-up operation summarizes the data along a dimension. The summarization rule might be computing totals through a hierarchy or applying a set of formulas. A pivot operation allows the end user to rotate the cube to see different sides of the cube.

Creating a Multidimensional Model

Multidimensional models are an essential part of designing a data warehouse. A multidimensional model is designed to help business users retrieve data in a meaningful way, and it maps easily to real business queries. Oracle OLAP not only can access data stored in relational tables but also includes a special storage structure called an *analytic workspace* (AW) that manages multidimensional objects with Analytic Workspace Manager (AWM).

In Data Modeler you can create a new multidimensional model by right-clicking the multidimensional model in the Browser pane and choosing New Multidimensional Model. On the toolbar you will see icons for the types of elements used when designing a multidimensional model. When creating a multidimensional model, you can also define its properties. You can define the name for the model, whether it is visible (Visible), what model it will be based on (logical or relational and which one, such as Bound Model), comments, and notes.

NOTE
*You cannot change the bound model for the
multidimensional model after you have started
to create it. Make sure you set it correctly before
starting to design. The decision depends on how
you decided to create the dimensional model and
whether you have all the information needed in the
logical model or in the relational model.*

Start your multidimensional design by creating a *cube*. A cube is a database
object that stores data in a dimensional array. In the General properties, you can
define the name (Name) for the cube and some other properties. If you select
Virtual, the cube will be defined as a virtual cube. A virtual cube is a logical
combination of several cubes. Partitioning is a method for storing measures in a
cube and can be used to improve the performance of large measures. You turn
partitioning on by selecting Partitioned. If you have defined the cube to be partitioned,
you should also define the other partitioning properties, but of course you can do
them only after you have defined the whole model with dimensions, hierarchies,
and levels. In the Part. Dimension field, you specify the dimension for partitioning
the cube. The dimension must have at least one hierarchy based on a level to be
defined as a partitioning hierarchy in the Part. Hierarchy field and as a partitioning
level in the Part. Level field. If the dimension has multiple hierarchies, choose the
one that has the most members and define that as the default hierarchy.

A composite is an analytic workspace object that maintains a list of all the
nonempty, sparse dimension-value combinations. When data is added to a measure
dimensioned by a composite, the Oracle analytic workspace automatically maintains
the composite with new values. A global composite is a single composite for all data
in a cube. Depending on the compression and partitioning decisions you make,
the behavior of Oracle Analytic Workspace Manager will change. If you select
Global Composites, the cube will use one global composite; otherwise, it will use
several composites. This choice is valid only for uncompressed, partitioned cubes,
and since compression is usually more valuable for any cube, this option is not
used often. If a cube is not partitioned, it always has one composite for the cube,
and if it is partitioned, it always has a composite for each partition. If you select the
Compressed Composites property, it means that the cube will be compressed. That
is useful if the cube is very sparse. Use the Compression option (since Oracle OLAP
10g), which is excellent for aggregating sparse multidimensional data. It improves
aggregation performance. Query performance might be improved and disk storage
reduced with compression. This feature is for large volumes of sparse data but is not
suitable for dense cubes.

In Full Cube Materialization, the entire data cube is physically materialized in
Oracle; this affects the materialized view with all the materialized view capabilities

including prescheduled refreshment. You get the cube materialized by selecting Full Cube Materialization.

On the Entities tab, you can see the Available entities on the left and Selected entities on the right. On this tab you select entities that the cube will be based on. If you want the list of available entities only to show the fact entities, select List Fact Entities Only.

On the Joins tab, you can see the list of joins for the cube and add or remove joins for it. If you want to add a new join, click the green plus sign. Now you will be taken to the Join Properties screen. Define the name (Name) for the join object. Then define the left entity (Left Entity) and the right entity (Right Entity) in the join operation. For the Existing Relation property, select the relationship from the list that those entities have defined. The Cardinality property is not editable; it shows the cardinality of the selected relationship. If the entity is dominant, select Dominant Role.

On the Attribute Pairs tab, you define the attribute pairs that join the left and right entities. You can also define comments and notes.

The Dimensions tab is for viewing, adding, and removing dimensions for the cube; defining the order of the dimensions; and setting Set Oracle AW Presummarized Levels for a dimension. You can also edit the properties for a dimension. You will learn more about that later in this section.

On the Measures tab, you can add and remove measures for the cube. You can also edit the Measure properties (click the Properties icon or double-click the measure name). A measure in a dimensional model is typically a column in a fact table. On the General tab of the Measure Properties dialog, you can edit the name of the measure. If you select the Is Formula property, the formula in the Formula field is used for the measure, and the formula type (No, Base Formula, OLAP Formula, MS Computed) can also be specified. You can also define whether it is a custom formula. If you do not select the Is Formula property, the Aggregation Function property is used instead. You can also define a fact that it will be based on (Based On Fact). In both cases you can define the additivity (Fully-Additive, Semi-Additive, Non-Additive) and the WHERE clause limiting the aggregation (Where Clause). On the Aggregation Functions tab, you can view, add, and remove aggregation functions and measure aliases. If you want to set summary levels for a measure alias, select the item from the Functions list and click the Set Oracle AW Presummarized Levels icon. If you have selected the formula to be an OLAP formula on the General tab in Formula Type, then on the Oracle OLAP Measure tab you can specify the OLAP properties. On the Oracle Names tab, you can specify different names for the measure: Short Name, Long Name, and Plural Name. You can also specify comments, notes, and a description for the measure.

On the Precalculated Slices tab, you can edit, add, and remove slices that are precalculated and stored in the cube. On the Oracle Names tab, you can specify different names for the measure: Short Name, Long Name, and Plural Name. On the SQL Access To Oracle AW tab, you can edit, add, and remove SQL Access to Oracle Analytic Workspaces objects. You can define a name for the object (Name) and the analytic workspace where the data is stored (AW Name). If you select Include GIDs, a grouping ID is included. If you select Use Object Types, you can specify the name of the object type (Object Type Name) and the name of the table type (Table Type Name). If you select the Use Model Clause property, the Use Model Clause default statement will be included in the SQL statement, and if you select Include RowToCell, the Include RowToCell default statement will be included in the SQL statement. After clicking the SQL Statements button, you will be able to view and change the order of attributes (Attributes Order) and to view and edit the SQL statement that reflects the current settings (SQL Statements). By selecting Show Formatted Limit Map, you define that the dimension information can be divided over several lines. On the Dimensions And Attributes tab, you can view, edit, add, and remove dimensions associated with the object. For each dimension, you can specify predefined attributes and hierarchies. On the Measures tab you can view, edit, add, and remove measures. You can also specify comments, notes, and a description for a slice. Measures are, for example, the number of sales (SalesAmount) or the quantity of sales (SalesQty).

For a cube, you can also specify a description, comments, notes, and a description for the partitioning (Partitioning Description).

Then you create *levels*. Usually data is summarized by a level. For instance, you might have a base level called Day, and the sales data is summarized per day. You might also want it to be summarized by weekly, monthly, and yearly bases (levels). On the General tab for Level Properties, you define the level name (Name) and the entity associated with this level (Level Entity). If you enable Value Based Hierarchy, that means you have defined the hierarchy as value based; otherwise, it will be level based. Level based is more common and therefore the default in Data Modeler. The difference is that in a value-based hierarchy, the parent-child relationships do not have named levels like they do when using a level-based hierarchy. If you have selected the value-based hierarchy, you should also define the Root Identification (ParentIsBlankSelfOrMissing, ParentIsSelf, ParentIsMissing, ParentIsBlank, ParentHasValue) and Identification Value settings. In both cases, you can also select a default attribute from a list if needed.

On the Selection Criteria tab, you can specify the selection criteria for this level. On the Selection Criteria Description tab, you can write a description for it. On the Level Key tab, you can view all the attributes that are keys for the level. You can add and remove attributes to/from the key list, and you can edit some of the attribute properties. On the Descriptive Attributes tab, you can see, add, and remove descriptive attributes. For a new descriptive attribute, you define the name (Name) and select the attribute from the list (Attribute). You also define whether it will be indexed (Indexed) and whether it is a slowly changing attribute (Slow Changing, NONE, 1, 2, 3). If the level has been defined as a value-based hierarchy, you can see the list of attributes of the parent entity on the Parent Key tab to be selected as a parent key attribute. On the Calculated Attributes tab, you can define calculated attributes and their expressions. On the Oracle AW Attributes tab, you can define the properties needed for Oracle analytic workspaces, and on the MS

Olap tab, you set the ones needed for Microsoft OLAP. On the Oracle Names tab, you can define different names for the level (Short Name, Long Name, Plural Name). You can also write comments and notes, and on the Description tab you can write a description for a level.

Next you create *dimensions* for the cube. A cube dimension is a database object that can be seen as an edge of a cube or an index to the data stored in a cube. First you define the name for the dimension (Name) on the General tab. If you select Use Natural Keys, the source keys from the relational sources are used without modification; if you disable it, a level prefix is added to dimension members when loading them into the analytic workspace to ensure the uniqueness. If you select Time Dimension, this dimension is defined as a time dimension; otherwise, it will be defined as a user dimension. A time dimension must have at least one level that supports time-based analysis.

On the Hierarchies tab, you can view and edit the hierarchies associated with this dimension. To view or edit a hierarchy property, double-click the hierarchy name or select the Properties icon (pencil icon). In Hierarchy Properties, you can define a name for the hierarchy. If you select Value Based Hierarchy, the hierarchy will be defined as value based; otherwise, it will be defined as a level-based hierarchy. If you select Time Based Hierarchy, the hierarchy will be defined as time based. If you select Ragged Hierarchy, the hierarchy will be a ragged hierarchy, where leaf nodes can be located at different levels. You can find a ragged hierarchy later in Figure 8-6 indicated with the dotted line. By selecting Default Hierarchy, you define this hierarchy as the default hierarchy for the dimension. On the Levels tab, you can view or edit level definitions associated with this hierarchy, whereas on the Rollup Links tab you can view or edit rollup link definitions. On the Oracle Names tab, you can specify different names for the hierarchy: Short Name, Long Name, and Plural Name. And in Description, you can define the description for the hierarchy. You can also define comments and notes for a hierarchy.

On the Levels tab, you can view or edit a level definition associated with this dimension. On the Slow Changing Attributes tab, you can view and edit the slowly changing attributes associated with a slowly changing dimension (SCD). On the Calculated Members tab, you can view, add, and remove calculated members associated with this dimension. On the Oracle Names tab, you can specify different names for the dimension: Short Name, Long Name, and Plural Name. On the Description tab, you can define the description for the dimension. You can also define comments and notes for a dimension.

Finally, you should create *links* between the cube and dimensions and between dimensions and levels. Figure 8-6 shows an example of a simple logical dimensional model on the left and a multidimensional model based on that logical model on the right.

If you want to see the model more simplified, just go to the Browser pane, right-click, and choose Show Compact Model. Figure 8-7 shows a compact diagram. To see all the details again, choose Hide Compact Model.

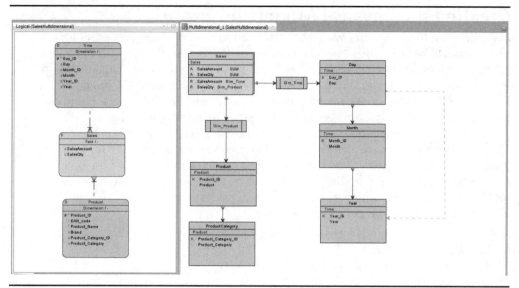

FIGURE 8-6. *A multidimensional model based on a logical dimensional model*

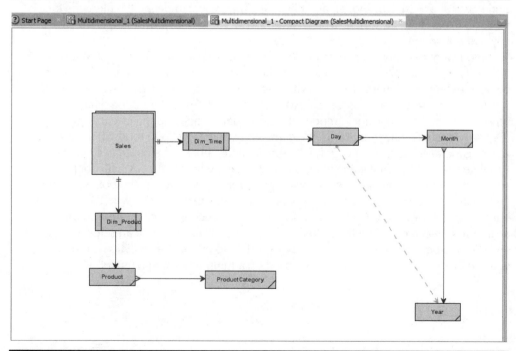

FIGURE 8-7. *A compact diagram*

Creating the Physical Model and Exports

In the physical model for an Oracle database, you can define some properties for dimensions. Otherwise, the physical model is defined as described in Chapter 6. To get your dimensions to the physical model, you go to the multidimensional model in the Browser pane, right-click, and choose Engineer To Oracle Model. If you choose Engineer From Oracle Model, the multidimensional model will be created based on the physical model and parameters given during the reverse engineering.

The DDLs for creating relational objects can be exported as described in Chapter 7. The multidimensional model can be exported to cube views metadata, to Microsoft XMLA, or to Oracle Analytic Workspace (Oracle AW). You can find all of these options in the File menu under Export. The DDLs for both cube views metadata and Microsoft XMLA can be generated without a connection to a database, but Oracle AWs can be generated only with a connection to a database.

NOTE
Multidimensional models can also be imported to Data Modeler.

If you want to export as a cube views metadata, choose File | Export | Cube Views Metadata. Insert the default schema, select Dimensional Model And Relational Model And Physical (DB2 UDB) Model, and click OK. Then you can define the filename for the XML file and the location it will be saved. Now you can deploy it in a UDB v8.1 physical environment.

If you want to export as a Microsoft XMLA (XML for Analysis) file, select Microsoft XMLA. Type the database name, select the dimensional model, and click OK. Then you can define the filename for the XMLA file and the location where it will be saved.

If you want to export it as Oracle AW, select Oracle AW. Define the default schema, select the dimensional model, the relational model, and the physical model (Oracle Model). Define the Oracle AW name and select the export mode (Recreate AW or Export Metadata To File Only). If you want the cubes to be populated, select Populate Created Cubes. Define the Output XML File, which is the XML file for the exported definition. You can specify the output directory by clicking the box with three dots (…). You can select a JDBC connection or create a new one with the Create button next to New JDBC Connection. To test the connection, click the Test button next to Test Selected Connection. On the Cubes And Slices tab, you can select cubes and slices to be included or excluded. By exporting to an Oracle analytic workspace, you can create the analytic workspace based on a multidimensional model.

NOTE
The fields Oracle AW Attributes Short Description and Long Description must be defined before exporting.

NOTE
When Exporting to Oracle AW, some validation rules are checked, and if you break the rules, an error message will be shown in the validation log. For example, if you do not have reference attributes defined for a dimension, you do not have a fact attribute defined for a measure or you have not defined a short description.

There are also import functionalities for cube views metadata, Microsoft XMLA, and Oracle AW. You can use these functionalities for reverse engineering and for documenting an existing multidimensional database.

Reporting

Chapter 11 will talk more about reporting, but in this chapter you will see the possibilities of getting reports of multidimensional model definitions. There are no standard reports in the main reporting functionality (File | Reports) for multidimensional models. But probably there is no need for that since you can easily define a custom report template in the search functionality (Chapter 11 will discuss more about search functionality).

Activate your multidimensional model (click the canvas) and select the Search button (binoculars icon) from the toolbar. Type, for instance, **Time** in the search. Select Dimension Multidimensional_1 (where Multidimensional_1 is the name of your multidimensional model) in the Filter field. Select from the results the line with "Property = All levels" and click Report. Click Manage in Custom Templates and create your own template that can be used every time you want to run a report. Save the template, and you can find it in the Custom Templates list when generating a report. You can read more about creating a report template in Chapter 11.

NOTE
The Report button is available only if you have selected an object type in Filter.

Using Dynamic Properties and User-Defined Properties

You can use dynamic properties to add your own functionality to Data Modeler. Dynamic properties are name-value pairs that can be created and used during scripting. One example is the Discover Foreign Keys utility described in Chapter 10 where Data Modeler creates a dynamic property named createdByFKDiscoverer and attaches that to all foreign keys created automatically during the Discover Foreign Keys process. You can create new dynamic properties on the property screen of most of the elements in Data Modeler on the Dynamic Properties tab. On that tab you define a property and a value for the property you want to create. On the same screen you can also remove dynamic properties. You can also create dynamic properties using transformation scripts and attach them to objects. Figure 8-8 shows a transformation script that adds a dynamic property called Heli to all the tables and sets it to the value of True. The last row in the script, table.setDirty(true); is

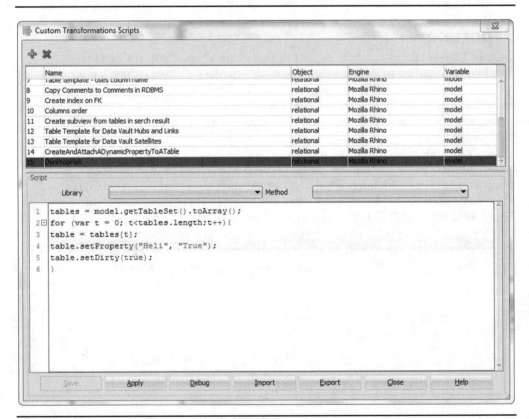

FIGURE 8-8. *Custom transformation script for adding a dynamic property for a table*

necessary because when saving in Data Modeler, only objects with a dirty status equal to True are saved. If the dirty status is not set to True, the change will not be persistent.

TIP
You can read more about scripting from
.../datamodeler/xmlmetadata/doc.

TIP
You can use transformation scripts for many things.
For instance, you can use them for creating an
Oracle Data Integrator (ODI) model based on a
Data Modeler relational model, as David Allan
explains in his blog post at https://blogs.oracle.com/
dataintegration/entry/odi_12c_building_models_in.

You can use the following methods that are related to dynamic properties during scripting:

- void setProperty(String key, String value);

- String getProperty(String key);

- boolean hasProperty(String key);

- boolean hasProperty(String key, String value);

- void removeProperty(String key);

- void clearProperties();

- Iterator getPropertyNames();

Since version 4.0.1, you can include dynamic properties in custom report templates and in generated reports. And since 4.0.2 there has been an option to show dynamic properties in relational and logical diagrams. You can set that in Design Properties (right-click the design name in the Browser pane and choose Properties or double-click the design name) on the Settings | Dynamic Properties tab by selecting the Visible property. You can define a different name to be shown in a diagram by typing that into the Presentation Name field. See Figure 8-9 for more information. Then go to the diagram canvas, right-click, and choose View Details | Dynamic Properties.

In Data Modeler 4.1 you can upgrade the existing dynamic properties to user-defined properties. User-defined properties are dynamic properties but with an additional metadata layer. User-defined properties can have a type (number, text,

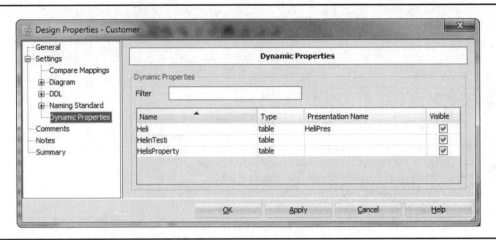

FIGURE 8-9. *Design Properties dialog, Dynamic Properties tab*

date, list of values) with related controls. They can have checks in the user interface, they can be visualized in a diagram, and in addition to dynamic properties, they can have a color set.

Summary

Designing a database for a data warehouse is a bit different than designing an operational database. The main difference is that you do not concentrate on the data but on the business processes, business rules, and requirements for reporting and analytics. A data warehouse database usually consists of the business processes described in a dimensional model.

The main tools in Data Modeler to assist in data warehouse design are data flow diagrams, transformation packages, dimensional modeling (the logical model and the relational model), and the multidimensional model. The process for data warehouse modeling is similar to the one described in Chapters 3 to 7 except that usually a data warehouse–specific modeling technique is used instead of 3NF. The most common techniques are star schema, snowflake, and Data Vault. The multidimensional model is created based on a dimensional model (star or snowflake) and can be implemented in a database that supports multidimensional arrays. Multidimensional objects are used by OLAP tools for analyzing the data.

Data Modeler has excellent support for many kinds of search and reporting operations. You can also create your own templates for reporting. Dynamic properties and user-defined properties can be used to add your own functionality to Data Modeler.

CHAPTER
9

Using Version Control and Working in a Multiuser Environment (Subversion)

U sually software development projects implement a version control tool and methods. Therefore, it makes sense to use version control for database design as well and maybe even use the same version-numbering system and logic as in application development. Often the development team asks for a specific version of a database. Without a version control tool integrated into the database design, this would be impossible to produce.

For database designers who usually are not familiar with version control tools and how they work, using version control might sound difficult. In fact, when I heard that Oracle SQL Developer Data Modeler would be based on files and version control instead of a real database, I disapproved because version control was not something I knew about. I decided to take a look at the version control capabilities first and then form my opinion. Now I think the decision Oracle made was correct because Data Modeler provides much better support for database design in the world we live in today than it would if it were built on top of a database. Believe me, I never thought I would say that.

Data Modeler has an integrated user interface to a version control tool called Subversion. Subversion is a free, open source version control tool. In the Preferences dialog (choose Tools | Preferences | Versioning | Subversion) on the Subversion tab, you can check which version of Subversion is supported by your version of Data Modeler.

All the content in Data Modeler consists of directories and files, so any version control product that supports versioning files could be used manually, but that would not be wise since there are so many files in each design and the filenames are based on object IDs that are not easy for humans to read and identify. Managing those files manually would not end well, so I do not advise you to use any other version control tool. Also, the integration to Subversion in Data Modeler has been implemented so that instead of showing the filename, Data Modeler shows the object name, such as in Pending Changes.

Before starting to use version control, you must make many decisions. First, you need to decide whether you will have only one Subversion repository or several repositories. Then, you need a directory for designs. If you already decided that earlier, as advised in Chapter 2 (the Default Designs Directory field in the Preferences dialog), you do not need to think about it any further. In this directory, you need to create a directory for each design. The reason for this is that each design is considered a project in Subversion, and each project must have its own working directory to be linked to Subversion as the working directory.

You should also decide how to name the designs in Subversion. If you have decided on the naming for designs already, you don't need to worry about it anymore. These are other questions to consider: What other files do you want to bring to Subversion? Will you share files with other users using version control? Will you use templates for commenting the changes? What kind of templates?

Will you use version numbers in comments? Are you going to use the same version numbers as in application development or other ones? How and who will install Subversion if it has not been installed? Who will manage it? How will you define the user privileges in Subversion? When using a version control tool, you must learn to communicate well with team members because communication is the key factor for successful version control usage. Subversion can be used for both version control and to select a multiuser environment.

Setting Preferences and Properties

Data Modeler doesn't have any properties that will affect version control, but there are some preferences that affect how Data Modeler behaves. In the Preferences dialog (choose Tools | Preferences), go to Versioning | Subversion.

In Comment Templates, you can define templates for comments when committing changes to Subversion. It would be wise to spend a little time thinking about what kind of templates would serve your users the best. You can always add new templates or edit existing templates. You can set one of the templates as a default template. You can also remove templates if needed. You can export the templates by clicking the Export button and then import them to another computer by clicking the Import button on that computer. A template could be something like this:

Version no.:
Specification description and ID:
Fix description:

On the General tab, you can define environmental settings and operation timeout, and you can edit the Subversion configuration file. These preferences are as follows:

- The state overlay properties (the icons and labels) indicate the state of version-controlled files in the folder versus in Subversion (for example, Up To Date, Unmodified); they exist only on folders under version control and can be seen only in the Files browser. State overlay icons are small symbols shown on top of the icon identifying the file type of a file in the Files browser. If you select Use Navigator State Overlay Icons, the state overlay icons appear. State overlay labels are labels associated with object names in the Files browser. If you select Use Navigator State Overlay Labels, state overlay labels are shown.

- The normal behavior with Subversion is that a commit commits only changes; if you have a new file to add to version control, you must use Add to get the file in version control. Data Modeler is smart and actually adds the Data Modeler element files automatically, so you only need to commit them to Subversion. The Automatically Add New Files On

Committing Working Copy preference is not needed because of the default behavior of Data Modeler.

- If you select Automatically Lock Files With Svn:needs-lock Property After Check Out, files you check out from the repository are automatically locked. This behavior is not recommended by Subversion, and I suggest you disable this preference. Locking makes using the tool more complicated, and the tool works perfectly well without locks. As a database person, I wanted to use locking, but after selecting it for a while and locking the files from myself, I decided not to use locking and found it more flexible but still a safe way of working. But if you decide to use the locking model of working, remember that when a strange locking occurs, there is a way to solve it: Choose Team | Cleanup Working Copy.

- When performing a merge operation, there are two choices: a dialog box or a wizard. If you select the Use Merge Wizard For Subversion Merging preference, the wizard is used. Otherwise, the Merge dialog box is opened for merge requests.

- If you select Show Log Messages In Subversion Console, the SVN Console – Log pane opens automatically when there are log messages to be shown. These messages are about operations between Data Modeler and Subversion when you commit changes. Here's an example:

```
commit -m "" -N C:/…/rel/62A6D118-081ABFB6E3EE/table/seg_0/
F5891AED-CA75-BB62-C06F-083F15171634.xml
Adding C:/Users/Heli/DMSubversionTestiMallit/User2/Design1/
rel/62A6D118-081ABFB6E3EE/table/seg_0/F5891AED-CA75-BB62-C06F-
083F15171634.xml
Transmitting file data ...
Committed revision 66.
```

Having this preference on all the time might get annoying since you will get a lot of information. You might want to disable it and select it only if you for some reason need to debug problems with Data Modeler and Subversion or if you are importing a design to version control. If you change this preference, you need to restart Data Modeler to put the new setting into action.

- In Operation Timeout, you specify the maximum number of seconds, minutes, or hours allowed for a Subversion operation to complete.

- If you want to edit the Subversion configuration file, you can do so by clicking the Edit "Server" button in Edit Subversion Configuration File. Lines beginning with # are comments. If you click Reset, your unsaved changes are removed from the file, and the editor stays open. If you click OK, the changes are saved, and the editor is closed. Cancel cancels all the changes and closes the editor. If your company has strict security settings, you might need to also edit the configuration file and add a proxy exception to be able to use version control. You just add the following line in the [global] section: http-proxy-exceptions = *.mycompany.com. Or you might want to edit the Web Browser And Proxy preferences.

On the Version Tools tab, you can define how the Pending Changes dialog and Merge Editor works. In the Pending Changes dialog, you can see the options Outgoing Changes (changes you have made and saved) and Incoming Changes (changes somebody else has made and committed to Subversion). For the Pending Changes Window option, you can specify whether the Outgoing Changes dialog will always be shown, shown when comments are hidden, or never shown (Use Outgoing Changes Commit Dialog). The Incoming Changes Timer Interval preference specifies the time interval for Data Modeler to check the status of files in Subversion for incoming changes. You can manually check the status at any time with the Refresh Incoming Changes preference on the Incoming Changes tab in Pending Changes. You can also define whether the merge will be done locally or at the server by setting the Merge Editor preference. My personal preference is locally so I always know that my local version is the one I want to commit to Subversion.

Introducing Subversion

Before you can start working with Subversion, you must install it. Check in the Preferences dialog to see which version of Subversion is supported by your version of Data Modeler. Download that version of Subversion, follow the instructions, and install it.

If you need Subversion only for version control purposes, not for a multiuser environment, the easiest way is probably to use Oracle SQL Developer to create a local repository. Then you do not need to download anything. In Oracle SQL Developer, choose Team | Subversion | Create Local Repository. Follow the instructions, and you will have a local repository that you can use for version control. If you also need the multiuser environment features, you need to create a real Subversion repository on a server.

When you are working with Subversion, you always have a working copy of your design on your own computer. When you save, you save the changes to that copy of the design. When you commit, you bring your changes from the local working copy to the copy in Subversion. Checking out from a Subversion repository creates a working copy of that directory on your computer and the .svn directory in it. Unless otherwise defined during the checkout, this copy contains the most recent versions of the directory and its tree found in the Subversion repository.

In the working copy directory, there is always a directory called .svn that includes files Subversion is using to manage your working copy and to control that everything works as it should. If you accidentally remove the .svn subdirectory or anything else happens to it, the easiest way to fix the problem is to remove all the files and directories from the design directory and check out the design from version control again to the same directory. The Subversion server does not know whether there are working copies on your computer, so deleting the working copy does not affect Subversion. But make sure you have committed all the changes before deleting the working copy. There is no need based on performance or any other reason to delete the working copies unless you know you will not be working with this design anymore.

The working model with Subversion is a copy-modify-merge solution. Copy (from the version control to your working directory), modify your copy in the working directory, and merge your changes to the copy in Subversion. Each time you commit, you create a new *revision* of your design to the Subversion repository. There is always a number identifying the revision. Each revision number has a whole file system tree attached to it, which is a snapshot from the moment it was saved. The revision number applies to the whole tree, not individual files.

In Subversion, a project is a solid unit of something like a design is in Data Modeler. It is a directory under which all the files are saved. In Subversion you can define user permissions per directory for user groups and add user accounts to the right groups to grant them permissions. But think first if you really need to do that because in that case somebody must create the projects/design directories in Subversion and grant privileges before anybody can insert the files. And somebody must maintain the hierarchies. The other possibility is to grant privileges to the Subversion repository or to the main directory for Data Modeler designs.

Subversion does not give the structure for your project layout, and it does not define for you whether you need one repository or several repositories. You can have one project per Subversion repository, all your projects in one repository, or something in the middle. If you decide to have just one repository, it means typically less administration, but revision numbers are global and cannot be used as meaningful version numbers. Large projects can cause problems to other projects in the same repository, for instance, by taking a lot of resources from the repository. Multiple repositories usually work best if the projects have nothing to do with each other and they need to be administered separately. In that case, the repository structure can be tailored to each project separately and user permissions can be defined easily, but there is a big limitation: Subversion does not support merging between different repositories. In general, usually the easiest solution is to have one repository for all the Data Modeler designs.

Subversion does not define the structure of a repository or the project layout. You might want to have three subdirectories in your Subversion repository either in the root or per design directory: trunk, branch, and tags. The trunk is the main line or root of the design, and the main development line should be saved in the trunk folder. You might want to create specific branches, and they should be saved in the branch directory. Tags are named, stable snapshots of a particular line of development and saved in the tags directory. For example, version 1.0 of the design could be saved as a tag to have a solid and easy way to find a version of it. In Subversion each repository revision is actually the same as a tag in general: a snapshot of the file system after each commit. In the sense of Subversion, there is no need for tags; you can find a specific revision of the design from version control anytime. But if people are used to creating tags, it is better to create a directory for them. So, creating a branch or a tag is a copy operation to Subversion, and only the selected location tells the user which kind of copy was actually done: a branch or a tag. Using Subversion makes no difference because a directory is a directory and a file is a file, and that's it. The structure is mainly for users to know where to find what, and often it is easier to follow the common standard of having the directories trunk, branch, and tag. You also need to decide whether you want these directories to be repositorywide or whether you want to create them for each project or design.

Connecting to Subversion

Before you can use Subversion and see it in the Versions browser, in Data Modeler you must create a connection to the Subversion repository. To create a connection, choose Team | Create Connection or go to the Versions browser, right-click, and choose Create Connection. Then select whether you want to create it manually (Manually Create A Subversion Connection) or automatically by importing a connection somebody else has created (Import Subversion Connections) either with Data Modeler or with Oracle SQL Developer. Now you will create it manually and a bit later you will see how to export and import connections. Select Manually Create A Subversion Connection. In Repository URL, enter the full and valid URL for a Subversion repository. The following are the possible choices, which depend on where the repository is located and which protocol you need to use:

- **file:///**   Direct repository access to a repository on a local disk

- **http://**   Access via the WebDAV protocol to an Apache server

- **https://**   Same as http:// but with Secure Sockets Layer (SSL) encryption

- **svn://**   Access via custom protocol to an svnserve server

- **svn+ssh://**   Same as svn:// but through an SSH tunnel

For instance, I have a repository on my local computer, and I define the URL file:///C:/Users/Heli/DataModeler/SubversionRepository. Remember to replace the backward slash (\) with a forward slash (/) in the path.

Then define the connection name. If you leave it blank, the name of the connection will be the whole URL of the repository location. If you have created users and granted privileges to the repository, enter your username (User Name) and your password (Password). If your repository does not demand these, leave them blank. If your repository is a production repository, it should have user privileges defined. Remember that usernames and passwords are case sensitive. You can test the connection by clicking the Test Read Access button. If it works, you are ready to start working with Subversion. If you get an error message, fix what is needed and try again.

To make a copy of your connections, you can use the export/import functionality. To export your connections, go to the Versions browser, right-click, and choose Export Connections. Select the directory to export the file with the Browse button and enter the name of the connection file. Select the connections you want to export from the list and click OK. To import connections to your new Data Modeler installation, go to the Versions browser, right-click, and choose Import Connections. Select the file that has the connections with the Browse button and click OK. The file created during export includes also usernames and passwords, so this file should not be shared with other users. The password is encrypted in the file.

Using Subversion in Oracle SQL Developer Data Modeler

The main concept while using Subversion is the working copy on your local computer. Your working copy of the design will exist there, and all the changes you make will be saved to your local working copy when you save the design. You commit your changes to version control always through the working copy (outgoing changes) and update changes other users have made from version control (incoming changes) to your working copy. Only one design can be located in one working directory, so you must have one working directory for each design.

NOTE
Remember to save! Your changes will be visible in
Pending Changes only after a save operation.

You use Check Out when you get the files from Subversion for the first time and define the working directory for the design. Check Out brings the design files from Subversion to your working directory and creates the .svn directory for Subversion. Check Out has nothing to do with locks (unless you defined that in Preferences), and there is no concept of "checking in" like in many other version control tools. Subversion can be used with locks, but it is not recommended by Subversion or Data Modeler. Locking is complicated and makes working with Data Modeler more difficult. My recommendation is not to use locking, and all my advice and working models on this chapter are based on that. If you want to use locking, make sure you have studied Subversion and how it works well enough before using it.

When you are ready with your changes, you commit them to the Subversion repository. Remember to always commit as soon as you are ready to prevent conflicts.

When you continue working with a design you have worked before, always refresh the incoming changes first to see whether there are any changes in Subversion and then click Update Working Copy to get those changes to your local working copy. Update Working Copy also updates your .svn directory to the same status at the Subversion repository. If you get any errors about mixed versions or something that indicates that your local working copy is not on the same level with Subversion, try clicking Update Working Copy first.

TIP
If you make changes outside the tool, for instance removing the .svn directory, restart Data Modeler since many things are in cache.

Exploring the Oracle SQL Developer Data Modeler Tools for Subversion

The main tools when working with Subversion are the Versions browser, Pending Changes, and the Team menu. Also, by right-clicking an element in the Browser pane, you can choose Versioning and some operations related to versioning.

In the Versions browser, you can see all the definitions for existing Subversion connections. By double-clicking the connection name or right-clicking and selecting Properties, you can edit the connection definitions. If you right-click a design directory name in the Versions browser, you get the following operations allowed for a directory:

- New Remote Directory creates a new directory in Subversion.

  - The URL will define where the directory will be created. It will be automatically defined as the location in the navigation tree where you have selected New Remote Directory. You only need to fill in the Directory Name and Comments fields. Comments can be based on a template.

- The Delete button deletes the directory or the file.

- Copy URL copies the URL for the location you are at, and you can paste it where needed.

- Refresh refreshes the Versions browser.

- Show Log starts the Log Browser that shows the revisions of the selected file or directory.

  - You can see the revision number (Revision), action, date and time of the change, and author of the change for the revisions on a list. You can limit the list with these parameters: Stop On Copy, Show All Revisions, and Next 20 Revisions. In Comment, you can see the comments written for a revision. If you select a revision from the revision list, you can see all the changes for it, as shown in Figure 9-1.

■ Check Out gets a design from Subversion and puts it in the location you define in Destination and defines that as your working directory for this design. You can get the latest version (HEAD Revision, which is the default), or you can select one of its revisions. You can get the whole design (Infinity: Fully Recursive) or parts of it.

■ Export gets a design from Subversion and puts it in the location you define in Destination Path. You can get the latest version (HEAD Revision, which

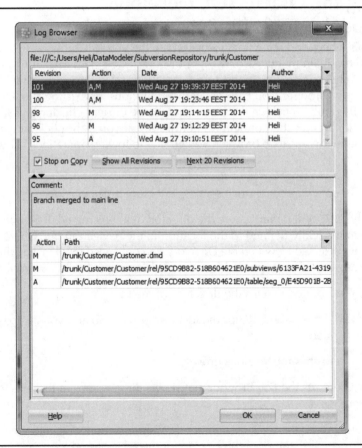

FIGURE 9-1. *Log Browser showing all revisions*

is the default), or you can select a revision. No link to Subversion and the selected destination is created.

■ Branch/Tag creates a new branch or tag of the latest version (HEAD Revision, which is the default) or a selected revision in Subversion. The source (From) will be the directory where this operation was activated in the Versions browser. You select the revision wanted and the destination (To) in Subversion where the new branch or tag will be created. It is recommended to write a comment to describe this branch or tag.

■ In Properties you can see the Repository URL option, last changes information (revision, date and time, and the user), lock information (owner, created, and comment), and user-defined Subversion properties.

In Pending Changes (Figure 9-2), you can see the options Incoming Changes, Outgoing Changes, and Unversioned Files. Incoming changes can be seen only after you have clicked Refresh Incoming Changes, and Outgoing Changes can be seen after you have saved the design as well as the unversioned files. There is also a Refresh button for the Outgoing Changes and Unversioned Files tabs.

■ Incoming Changes lists the changes made for the same design by someone else. This person committed them to Subversion, but you have not yet updated them to your working copy.

  ■ You can refresh the Incoming Changes list by clicking the Refresh button or the list sign beside it and selecting either Refresh Incoming Changes or Refresh All.

  ■ You can update your working copy by clicking the Update Working Copy icon.

■ Outgoing Changes lists the changes you have made and saved locally but not yet committed to Subversion.

  ■ You can refresh the Outgoing Changes list by clicking the Refresh button or the list sign beside it and selecting either Refresh Outgoing Changes or Refresh All.

  ■ You can commit your changes to Subversion by clicking the Commit icon, or you can cancel them by clicking the Revert Working Copy icon. If you decide to reverse the changes, Data Modeler asks you, "Do you really want to discard your changes in the working copy?" If you click Yes, the revert is completed. When you commit the changes to Subversion, you can add a comment to each revision. Comments can be used when finding the right revision, so it is important to create a

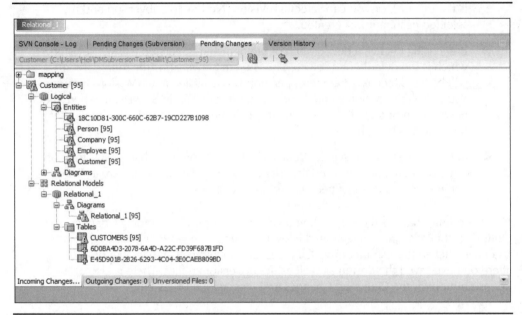

FIGURE 9-2. *Pending Changes list*

thorough comment for every revision. You can also use templates when creating comments, as explained earlier in this chapter. Defining a template (or templates) is good for standardizing the comments.

■ On the Unversioned Files tab, you can see files that have not yet been added to Subversion.

   ■ You can refresh the Unversioned Files list by clicking the Refresh button or the list sign beside it and selecting either Refresh Unversioned Files or Refresh All.

   ■ You can add a file by clicking the green plus sign or remove it by clicking the red X icon.

In Pending Changes you can also right-click a change in any of the panes and get operations allowed at that point. Interesting operations might be, for instance, the following: Compare With, Version History, View Subversion Properties, Add Subversion Property, and Properties. Properties might be things such as Name, ID, Text Status, Property Status, Revision, and Path (which shows the location of the file and its name in the working directory). If there are any problems with Subversion, the SVN Console – Log pane will appear (unless you have prevented it with Preferences), and you can see what the problem is and fix it.

There is also the Team menu that includes operations for Subversion. Most of these operations are explained elsewhere in this chapter. Versions opens the Versions browser, and Pending Changes opens the Pending Changes pane. The operations Check Out, Commit, Commit Design Update, Revert, and Update Design are also available in the Team menu. If you are using locking, you can find Lock and Unlock operations in the Team menu. Cleanup Working Copy removes locks in the working copy and resumes unfinished operations. You can see version histories of different viewpoints with Version History, Version Tree, System Files Version History, and Design Version History.

TIP
If the operations in the Team menu are dimmed,
click the Pending Changes pane to try again.

If you right-click an item in the Browser pane and select Versioning, you can lock and unlock that item, see the version history or the version tree for it, and view or add Subversion properties.

NOTE
Starting from version 4.1 the Versioning status
indicators will be visible also in the design tree.

Adding a Design to Subversion

On your local computer you should have specified a directory to serve as the parent for design-specific working directories when you specified the Default Designs Directory preference (see Chapter 2 for more information). Under that directory you should create directories for all your designs as their working copies. For instance, say you want to create a design called Customer and need to create a directory called Customer under the default design directory to serve as a working copy directory for the design Customer. If you have not created the connection to the Subversion repository yet, you must do it before you can use Subversion.

Now is the time to add the design to Subversion. There are two ways of doing it: You can save the design to a directory that has been defined as the working copy directory, or you can import the design to version control. Oracle recommends only the save-as method because the import method also adds .local files to Subversion, which is not recommended.

To save a design to a working directory and add it to version control (the save-as method), follow these steps:

1. Create your design and save it to some other location than the working copy directory. Close the design.

2. Go to the Versions browser and create a new remote directory for the design.

3. Check out the design to your working copy directory (Data Modeler will create a directory for you if needed). The .svn directory is created in it for Subversion to keep control of everything in that directory.

4. Open your design.

5. Use File | Save As to save your design to the location you just specified as the working copy directory.

6. Data Modeler will ask you, "Add design to version control system?" Click Yes.

If you want to use the import method, this is how to do it, but remember that this is not recommended. I will describe this method since it can be found in the Team menu and most likely will be supported in future. If your design is open, close it before doing anything else. If the design is open while importing to Subversion, locks created by Data Modeler will prevent a successful import. Here are the steps for importing the design to Subversion (the import method):

1. Select the connection from the Versions browser. If you do not see the Versions browser, go to the Team menu and select Versions.

2. Create a new remote directory by right-clicking the directory name and choosing New Remote Directory. You might want to name it the same as your working directory.

3. Choose Team | Import Files to open the Import To Subversion Wizard.

4. Select the right connection from the Repository Connection list. Then select the Destination as your newly created directory and click Next.

5. Select the working directory as a source directory. You can also type a comment or use a predefined comment template for that. It is always good to write a clear comment because that will help you later if you want to find a particular revision. Then click Next.

6. In the Filters dialog, you can define file types by their extension not to be imported to Subversion. You can also create new filters by clicking the New button. If you do not have any you want to leave out, just click Next.

7. In the Options dialog, there are two parameters: Do Not Recurse and Perform Checkout. If you select Do Not Recurse, only the directory you selected as a source and its content will be imported to Subversion, not any of its subdirectories and their contents. If you select Perform Checkout, the imported files will be checked out after import. Click Next. On the Summary screen, you can see what has been selected for the import.

8. If you want to change something, click Back; if you want to complete the import, click Finish. If you want to cancel it, click Cancel.

Whichever way you choose, your design has now been added to Subversion successfully, and a new directory (.svn) has been created for your working copy directory for Subversion to keep track of changes. If you want to continue working with the design, open the local copy as usual (File | Open) and start working.

Note that adding a new design to version control always takes time, and the bigger the design, the more time it takes. The reason for this is that it needs to add all the files for a design, and each design has several files, as mentioned earlier. If the preference Show Log Messages In Subversion Console is selected in SVN Console – Log, you can see the progress of the process and the text "Committed revision xyz" when everything is done. If the preference is disabled, you cannot see the SVN Console – Log pane at all. If you used the save-as method instead of importing the files, you can see in the Message – Log pane something like this:

2014-09-14 10:44:44 - Start adding files
2014-09-14 10:44:57 - End adding files
2014-09-14 10:44:58 - save properties - start
2014-09-14 10:45:03 - save properties - end

If you used the importing files method, not even the Message – Log will tell you about the progress. So, if you prefer to use the import files method, always remember to select the Show Log Messages In Subversion Console preference and then exit and restart Data Modeler before starting the import to be able to see the progress in the log panes.

Making Changes to a Design You Have Worked with Before

To start working with a design, open it from its working copy directory as usual (choose File | Open). How do you know if there are any changes that other users may have made to the design? Go to the Incoming Changes tab in Pending Changes (shown earlier in Figure 9-2) and select Refresh Incoming Changes. You can see exactly what has been changed compared to your local copy by right-clicking the element in Pending Changes and selecting either Compare (Figure 9-3) or Compare As Text (Figure 9-4). Then select Update Working Copy by clicking the icon on the right of the Refresh icon. Now you will have the latest version of the design in your local working directory.

If you made changes before and forgot to commit them in Subversion, you will see them on the Outgoing Changes tab in Pending Changes. Commit them. If there is a conflict in design versions, you must solve it. To avoid conflicts, always commit to Subversion before leaving the tool.

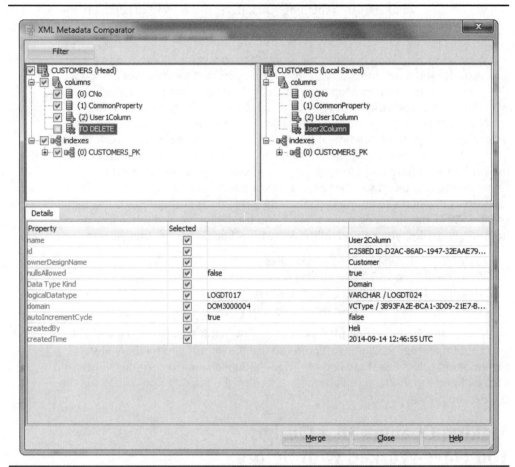

FIGURE 9-3. *Comparing two revisions, XML Metadata Comparator*

Now you are ready to work with your design. Make changes as usual and save them. When you are ready to commit your changes to Subversion, choose Pending Changes | Outgoing Changes and commit. Remember that Pending Changes will show your changes only after you have saved your design. If you see files on the Unversioned Files tab in Pending Changes, that means you have added a file to your working directory that should be added to Subversion. You can add it on the Unversioned Files tab in Pending Changes. Select the file and click the green plus sign to add it. If you do not want to add it, select it and click the red X button. If you want to see the changes in Subversion, you can check them from Versions. Refresh Versions, go to the subdirectory where the file should be located, and check the changes.

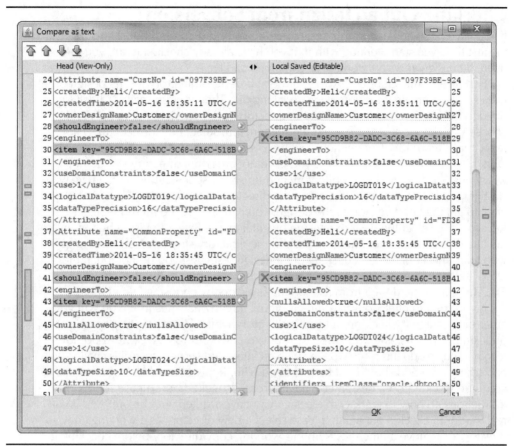

FIGURE 9-4. *Comparing two revisions as text*

TIP
Always save your design to see changes you have made in Pending Changes and Outgoing Changes, and always commit your changes to Subversion when you are done. Do not leave the commit until after lunch or tomorrow, for instance. Committing right after the change is easier than solving conflicts later. Remember, you have a version control tool, so if you committed something you want to roll back, you can do this easily.

Checking Out a Design from Subversion

If you have not worked with this design before, you must check it out from Subversion the first time you start working with it. If you have already checked it out, you just open the design and start working as explained earlier.

First, create the subdirectory in your default designs directory for the design or let Data Modeler create it for you when checking out. Then choose Team | Check Out, or go to the Versions browser, select the directory for the design, right-click, and choose Check Out. If you are using the Team menu, select the correct Subversion repository (Repository Connection) and the correct directory (Path). Then select the working directory in Destination. If you have not created a directory yet, do not worry; just specify the desired directory and finish the specification with a backward slash (\), and Data Modeler will create the directory automatically. If you do not want to get the latest version of the design, you can specify the revision. Select Revision and select the desired revision by clicking the Select Revision button. In the Depth list, you can define how deep in the directory structure you want to go with your checkout. When checking out a design, I suggest you do not touch the Depth selection but go with Infinity: Fully Recursive, which is the default. Click OK. Then open the design from its working directory by choosing File | Open.

If you tried to check out to a directory that already has files in it, you will get an error message: "Checking out into a directory which is not empty may cause undesirable results. Are you sure you want to checkout to C:\...\...?" I do not recommend you do this since working with an integrated version control is challenging enough by itself and should not be interfered with. Reply No to this. If you wanted to continue working on a design you have already checked out, please follow the instructions on how to work with a design you have worked with before. And if you really want to check it out again, please select a new directory as a working copy directory or remove all the files from this working copy directory before checking it out. Data Modeler will create a new directory for you automatically and suggest a name for it (MyDesign_0, MyDesign_1, and so on).

Solving Conflicts

A conflict (Figure 9-5) means you have made changes to a version that has been changed by someone else after you updated your working copy. In other words, you have changed a version that is not the latest version, and you have changed something that conflicts with other changes. Usually that happens if one of the users does not commit immediately after making changes but then does it later. So, you do not see the other person's changes in your Incoming Changes list (because they have not been committed to Subversion) and therefore cannot update them to your local copy, and you continue working without knowing about the changes. When you both finally commit to Subversion, that situation is called a *conflict,* and it must

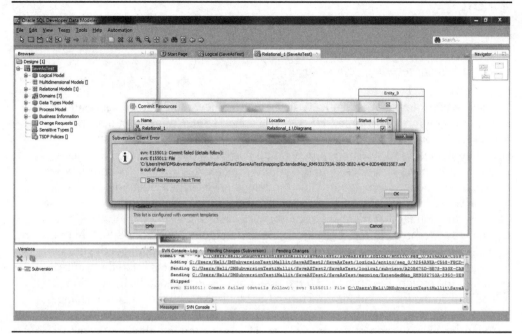

FIGURE 9-5. *A conflict*

be solved by the person who committed last. Conflicts are shown in red in Pending Changes. Solving a conflict must always be done manually; it cannot be done automatically. As in real life, you cannot have a pattern solution for every conflict.

When a conflict arises, you can see both incoming changes and outgoing changes at the same time. If you accept the changes made to version control, you simply commit the incoming changes and get those updated to your working copy. You can select the change from the list, right-click it, and choose either Update or Update All. Or you can click the Update Working Copy icon or the arrow beside it and select Update All. Then you decide what to do with the outgoing changes: commit or revert. Remember, everything in red is still in conflict and must be solved before you can continue.

If you do not want to accept the changes somebody has committed to version control, you see them one by one (double-click the change in Incoming Changes) and merge them as you want by clicking Merge when comparing (XML Metadata Comparator). Clicking Merge brings the change selected to your local working copy. This way, you build the version wanted piece by piece in your local working copy and finally commit it to Subversion as it is.

NOTE
To avoid conflicts, remember to save and commit your changes after you have finish working with them. Never leave Data Modeler without either committing or reverting your changes.

Here is an example of a conflict: User2 creates a new table named user2 and adds a new column to the table CUSTOMERS called User2Column but does not remember to commit it to version control. Meanwhile, User1 comes and adds a new table named user1 and adds a new column to the table CUSTOMERS called User1Column in the same design and commits the changes to version control. Now User2 comes back to work, opens Data Modeler, and sees their outgoing changes. Because User2 knows the process, the next thing User2 does is click Refresh Incoming Changes and notices that there are also incoming changes. User2 can now see that the changes are shown in red, both incoming and outgoing, and knows that there is a conflict. If User2 does not realize it and tries to commit, User2 will get the error message shown earlier in Figure 9-5. What User2 must do next is build the wanted version of the design. Because the Merge preference is set to Locally, the version will be built in the local working directory. User2 will start with the incoming changes. As shown earlier in Figure 9-3, User2 can see that there is a new column to be added to the local version of the design (User1Column) and that the local copy has a column (User2Column) that does not exist in the version in Subversion. User2 now must decide the following:

- Is the column User1Column correct, and should it be added to the local version?

- Is the column User2Column correct, or should it be removed?

If User2 wants to keep the column User1 (User1Column), User2 lets it be selected on the XML Metadata Comparator screen. If User2 does not want to keep it, User2 will disable it. If User2 still wants to add the column User2Column, it should be disabled on the XML Metadata Comparator screen. But if User2 does not want to add it anymore, it should be selected. After User2 has made up their mind on what to do with the columns, User2 clicks Merge and then saves the design. Now the local working copy has been built the way User2 wants.

User2 still sees red text in Incoming Changes because there is still the issue about the new table. Like with the columns, User2 must now decide what to do with the table that User1 added and what to do with the table User2 added. After making the decision, User2 clicks Merge and saves the design. If there are still some changes on the Incoming Changes tab but not in red, User2 updates them to the working copy and saves the design. Now the complete version is in User2's working directory. User2 will commit all the changes to Subversion on the Outgoing Changes tab, and User1 will see them the next time User1 opens the design and checks Incoming Changes. There might be a real-life conflict after that when User1 realizes that User2 removed the table User1 added earlier. User1 can see the changes on the Incoming Changes tab and can add the table again based on their local working copy or later restore the table from previous revisions.

TIP
Remember that if you have not committed to version control yet, you can always cancel the changes either by right-clicking the outgoing change in the Pending Changes pane and selecting Revert or Revert All or by choosing Team | Revert. You can also use these options when trying to solve a conflict that is too complicated.

Making Changes Based on an Older Revision

You can also change your design based on an older revision. The change can be just a single change or several changes, or you can go back to the design from a certain point in time. If you want to change just an element or one thing, go to that element in the Browser pane, right-click, and choose Versioning | Version History. In Version History, select the two revisions you want to compare, right-click, and choose Compare or Compare As Text. Now you can see the differences between the two revisions and can decide whether something should be merged to the current revision from the older one. If you want to revert to an old revision, either permanently or temporarily, you can select either Check Out or Export in Versions, as explained earlier. You might want to get the DDLs or see the logical model of a certain version of the design. If you want to unlink the working directory with version control, remove the .svn directory.

TIP
If you want to recover a deleted element from previous revisions of a design, you can choose Team | Design Version History.

Understanding Branches, Changes, and Synchronizing

Some development teams like to keep a certain version of the design untouched and easily available so they save it in the tags directory (remember to document that in Comment), and some teams want to have two separate development tracks (trunk and branch) that can be merged afterward. A separate track from the main track will be saved in the branch directory. As explained earlier in this chapter, you can create a new branch or tag by right-clicking the source location in the Versions browser and selecting Branch/Tag, and depending whether you save it to the tag or branch directory, this gives the meaning of a version being a tag or a branch. The other possibility is to select the source location in the Versions browser and then choose Team | Branch/Tag.

If you want to merge a branch to the main line design totally or partially, there are many ways to do it. You can use the Merge Design functionality found in the Teams menu to compare and merge the changes from the version in Subversion to your local working copy, or you can use the compare/merge functionalities to merge two local working versions of the designs and then commit the changes to version control.

If you want to use Merge Design first, open the main version (trunk) of the design in Data Modeler. Then follow these steps:

1. Get all the incoming changes, and even if there might not be any available, still select Update Working Copy in Pending Changes. That is because even though you might not have changed the trunk version of the design, you have changed the branch version of it, and therefore Subversion and your local working copy of the design are not synchronized.

2. Make sure you have committed all outgoing changes and saved the design.

3. Choose Team | Merge Design.

4. Select the URL for the design in the branch directory (the branch version of your design) and click OK.

5. In the Merge Design pane, you can now see all the revisions for the version of your design in that branch. Select the revision wanted (if you have written good comments in Comment when saving the revision, selecting should be easy).

6. In the Action pane, you can see each change in that revision. Right-click the change and choose Compare And Merge. If you know you want to merge everything, you can also select the revision from the revision list, right-click, and choose Merge.

7. In the XML Metadata Comparator, you can see what the differences are, and you can select which of the changes to bring to the local working copy of the latest version of the trunk version of the design. Select the changes and click Merge.

8. Save your design. Commit all the outgoing changes, and you will have a merged version of the design in version control as your latest revision.

TIP
*After merging or updating, always close and reopen
the design. Sometimes things stay in cache, and not
all changes are shown without closing and opening.*

The Merge Reintegrate functionality is for the final merge of a branch into the trunk. After using this functionality, you should delete the branch and not use it anymore.

TIP
*If you get an error message saying that something
cannot be done because the local version is not
up to date or it is a mixed version, then go to the
Incoming Changes tab of Pending Changes and
select Update Working Copy.*

The way Data Modeler works can sometimes cause conflicts when merging two designs. As mentioned earlier, Data Modeler has directories for each element type (table, entity, subview, and so on), but the directory is created only when the first of that kind of element is created, and therefore a conflict may arise. For example, let's assume there is the trunk and the branch, and in both revisions a new element type has been created for the first time; let's say it's a view. So, somebody creates a view for the branch, and somebody else creates another view for the trunk. Now the directory for views has been created in both versions for the first time. You try to merge the designs and get an error saying there is a conflict. That is correct; there is a conflict: A directory for views has been created in both versions, and you must decide which one is the correct one. What you need to do now is to remove the directory from the local target design by right-clicking the row in Action screen below the Revision screen in Merge Design and choosing Delete Local Folder. If there are outgoing changes, commit them and then update the working copy. Now there should be no more conflict, and the merge can be completed. Everything is OK except you must get back what was in the local directory you deleted. You can do this by choosing Team | Design Version History. Select that and then restore the view file that was in the removed directory. After that you should have a complete merge done to the trunk.

Every element-type directory includes a subdirectory called seg_0, and if there are more than 70 elements of the same type, a new subdirectory of the same level is created (seg_1). In other words, a directory can have only 70 files. This is for performance reasons. Data Modeler creates the new subdirectory when needed and removes it when a Save As is performed if there is no need for that subdirectory anymore. This is a little complicated when merging the designs. There can be two subdirectories in one design and one subdirectory in the other. In addition, merging might cause the number of elements to exceed 70, or other situations like this can sometimes cause a conflict when merging designs.

Sometimes instead of using Subversion revisions, it is easier to use the comparisons and get the changes wanted from there. If you want to compare two designs and make the changes based on that process, there are two ways of doing it: Tools | Compare/ Merge Models or File | Import. We will talk more about comparisons in Chapter 12. If you decide to use Tools | Compare/Merge Models, this is how to do it:

1. Make sure you have the latest version of both designs in your working directories since the comparison will be done based on the designs in your working directories, not the ones in Subversion.

2. Open the original design (target).

3. Choose Tools | Compare/Merge Models. Select the branch design (source) on the Import Design screen.

4. Select the relational model to be compared for both the source and the target. Click OK.

5. In the tree view, you can see the changes, as shown in Figure 9-6.

6. In the tabular view (Figure 9-7), you can generate a report to see exactly what has been changed, as shown in Figure 9-8.

7. If you want to delete a table while merging, select the table; otherwise, it will not be deleted. The default for deletion is No. If you want to add it, select the table. The default for insert is Yes.

8. To merge, click Merge.

9. Choose File | Save to save the changes in the local copy.

10. Commit the outgoing changes to Subversion in Pending Changes.

NOTE
If you use the tabular view, remember that it does not behave like the tree view. For instance, if you want to change only one column, remember to select not only the column but also the table it is related to. If you select only the column, no changes are performed on your target design.

Now you have merged the changes in a branch to the main line of the design. You can use this same method any time you want to merge two designs. The only limitation of this method is that you can compare only relational or physical models,

FIGURE 9-6. *Compare Models dialog in tree view*

but the good thing is that you can also get the scripts (Alter DDLs) for the target database to be changed as desired (DDL Preview). If you also want to compare the logical model to another logical model and merge changes from there, you should use the File | Import method, as explained here:

1. Make sure you have the latest version of both designs in your working directories since the comparison will be done based on the designs in your working directories, not in Subversion.

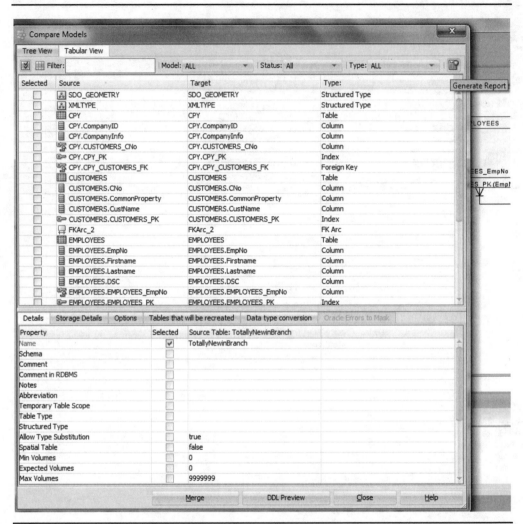

FIGURE 9-7. *Compare Models dialog in tabular view*

2. Open the original design (the target).

3. Choose File | Import | Data Modeler Design. Select the branch design (source) in the Import Design dialog.

4. Select the logical model (Selected) if you want to compare that and the relational model if you want to compare that too. For the relational model, you can select it to be imported to a new relational model (New Relational),

Compare Models

Design Name	Customer
Source Model	Relational_1
Target Model	

Objects

Sorce Name	Target Name	Type	Status
TotallyNewinBranch		Table	New
	NewinOriginal	Table	Deleted

FIGURE 9-8. *Report based on comparing two models*

or you can select from a list one of the relational models in the target design. Click Next. Click Finish. The Compare Oracle SQL Developer Data Modeler Designs dialog will open.

5. In the tree view, you can see the changes, as shown earlier in Figure 9-6.

6. In the tabular view, you can generate a report to see the differences between the two models.

7. If you want to delete an element from the target design, select it; otherwise, it will not be deleted. The default for deletion is No. If you want to add an element, select the element. The default for the insert is Yes.

8. To merge, click Apply.

9. Choose File | Save to save the changes in the local copy.

10. Commit the outgoing changes to Subversion in Pending Changes.

If you are not familiar with Subversion and how it works, I advise you to use either of the two latter ways of comparing the local working copies and committing the locally built version to Subversion. During the merge design process, there might be conflicts, and you must understand the reasons for the conflicts and know how to solve them to be able to have the merge take place correctly. For instance, if you merged some of the changes earlier and try to merge everything again, the changes committed before will cause a conflict that must be solved.

Sharing Files

Chapter 2 discussed files that might be good to save in version control and share with other users from there. Now you will see one option of how to do that.

Create a directory in Subversion for the files you have decided to share with all users (preferences, domains, RDBMS sites, design properties, glossaries, report templates, and so on) by right-clicking the location wanted and selecting New Remote Directory. Name the directory and click OK. Then create a directory on your computer and collect all the files there. Go back to Data Modeler and choose Team | Import Files. Use the Import Wizard to import the files to Subversion. You can, of course, do this with the Subversion client as well.

Decide the name for the directory, such as SharedFiles, on every computer where the shared files will be exported and create it. Go to the Versions browser in Data Modeler and navigate to the SharedFiles directory. Right-click the directory and select Export. Select your local SharedFiles directory as the destination path and click OK. Now the files will be on your local computer. Then import and copy files where needed as explained in Chapter 2 to be able to use them in Data Modeler. For example, import the preferences and copy the RDBMS sites file (defaultRDBMSSites. xml) to the directory defined as your default system types directory in Preferences.

When there are changes to these files, first export or copy the changed files to the working directory. Then you can use either the Subversion client or SQL Developer to insert the changed files to Subversion. You can use SQL Developer for this because in SQL Developer you can work with individual files. This is one way to do it with SQL Developer:

1. If you use SQL Developer, open the file from the working directory.

2. Choose Team | Subversion | Commit and remember to write a description.

3. Advise your users to export the files again with Data Modeler and proceed with the files that have been changed.

If you use the Subversion client, then insert the files into Subversion and perform step 3.

Working in a Multiuser Environment with Microsoft Excel

As will be explained in Chapter 11, you can generate reports with the search functionality and save them in Microsoft Excel format. These reports can be edited in Microsoft Excel and then imported back into Data Modeler, and the related information in Data Modeler will be updated. This is useful if you want the end users to edit the descriptions, for instance, but you do not want them to have to learn how to use Data Modeler. This can be used with the logical and relational models.

First generate the report you want as explained in Chapter 11. Figure 9-9 shows an example of a report of entities. If you want, you can modify the report using the

	A	B	C	D	E	F	G
1							
2							
3							
4	**Name**	**Based on structured type**	**Comment**	**Comment in RDBMS**	**Complete subtypes**	**Create surrogate key**	**Created tim**
5	Company				false	false	2014-05-16 18:34:3
6	Customer				false	false	2014-05-16 18:31:3
7	Employee				false	false	2014-05-17 06:16:0
8	Person				false	false	2014-05-16 18:34:1
9							
10							
11							
12							
13							
14							

FIGURE 9-9. *An entity report for Microsoft Excel*

tools Microsoft Excel offers to allow only certain cells to be edited. Then give the report to the end user for editing. In Figure 9-10 you can see an example of an edited report. When the user is done with the changes, open the design in Data Modeler. Then right-click either the logical or relational model in the Browser pane, depending on which level of report you are uploading, and select Update Model With Previously Exported XLS (XLSX) File, as shown in Figure 9-11. Select the report from the list and click Open. The view log will show you what has been updated. You can save the log if you want by clicking Save and close it by clicking Close. Now all changes have been saved to the design. See Figure 9-12 for an example of changes on the entity Customer and its comments.

	A	B	C	D	E	F	G
1							
2							
3							
4	**Name**	**Based on structured type**	**Comment**	**Comment in RDBMS**	**Complete subtypes**	**Create surrogate key**	**Created tim**
5	Company		Heli's comment in Excel		false	false	2014-05-16 18:34:3
6	Customer		This is a Customer who makes orders and pays		false	false	2014-05-16 18:31:3
7	Employee		Our own employees		false	false	2014-05-17 06:16:0
8	Person		Definition of a person...		false	false	2014-05-16 18:34:1
9							

FIGURE 9-10. *An edited report*

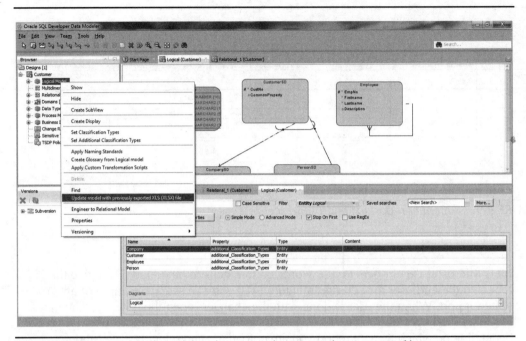

FIGURE 9-11. *Updated model with previously exported XLS (XLSX) file*

FIGURE 9-12. *The entity Customer and its comments property updated in Microsoft Excel*

Summary

You need to make a few decisions before starting to use Subversion, specifically, about privileges, the number of Subversion repositories, and the structure for Subversion directories. Also, it is valuable to create templates for comments that will be used when committing changes to Subversion to make finding the right revision easier.

Data Modeler offers integration with Subversion, which means that you can use Subversion in Data Modeler fluently. Subversion can be used for both version control and to enable a multiuser environment. In fact, Subversion can be used to version the database designs the same way the application design is versioned. Every design must have a working copy directory where changes are saved and then committed to Subversion. Every committed change in Subversion creates a new revision. In Pending Changes, you can see both incoming and outgoing changes as well as new files that should be added to Subversion.

If there are conflicts, someone must resolve them; they cannot be resolved automatically. Conflicts are resolved by merging, committing, or reverting, depending on the desired outcome. Conflicts often can be avoided by saving and committing right after you have finished making a change.

You can let end users edit the designs in Microsoft Excel and then upload those changes to Data Modeler easily.

CHAPTER
10

Documenting an
Existing Database

I t is important to have documentation for your databases. If you do not understand your data, you cannot keep it up to date, secure, of good quality, and so on. In addition, changing the data structures based on current requirements is impossible if you do not understand what you are changing. Documentation is also vital when addressing problems related to data, such as poor performance.

Surprisingly, often databases don't have any documentation. This could be because the database came with an application product and the vendor did not deliver any documentation for the database. In these cases, it might be possible not to have documentation for the database because all the changes, problem solving, and so on, are done by the vendor; still, it is good to know what you have bought. In some cases, you might have some documentation for a database that was created during the software development process, but it was not maintained, and now it would be too much work to bring it up to date. In other cases, the documentation was handwritten and cannot be used, for instance, to generate data definition language (DDL) scripts. There are usually many reasons why there is no documentation or why it is too expensive to create documentation.

You could, of course, document an existing database manually from scratch, which can be expensive and a lot of work, but Data Modeler offers several other possibilities that are far more efficient and cost effective. It allows you to document an existing database by reverse engineering the database from the data dictionary or from existing DDLs. Or you can use the documentation you might have on a third-party modeling tool and import that into Data Modeler. You can also combine these methods.

Setting Preferences and Properties

Data Modeler has some preferences that will change the result of reverse engineering or importing from a third-party modeling tool. Choose Tools | Preferences to open the Preferences dialog.

On the Data Modeler | DDL tab, you can define two preferences for the import process: Replace System Names During Import and Create Domains During Import. If Replace System Names During Import is not selected, the constraint names are imported from the dictionary as they have been defined (SYS_). If it is selected, the name is changed during the import according to the naming standards defined in the design properties. If Create Domains During Import is selected, domains are created from data types during the import operations. If it is not selected, no domains are created.

On the Data Modeler | DDL | DDL/Storage tab, you will see the DDL Storage Options for Import And Export options. Here you can define which storage parameters are imported and which are not. And on the main Data tab, you can define the default directory for imported files (Default Import Directory). If you select Show Log After Import, you will always see the log after every import operation.

On the Data Modeler | Model | Relational tab, the Default Foreign Key Delete Rule preference defines the delete rule when a new foreign key is created. If you create a design by importing a DDL script or scripts, then ensure the option is set as required before the import.

You can also define in the Preferences dialog whether the OCI8 (thick) driver is used, instead of the JDBC (thin) driver, by default for Oracle Database connections if it is available. You set this on the Data Modeler tab with the preference Use OCI/ Thick Driver.

Reverse Engineering an Existing Database

If you have a database that has no documentation in another modeling tool, there are two ways of documenting your database: You can reverse engineer from the data dictionary, or you can import the DDLs that were used for creating the database. If you want to start designing the changes to the database with Data Modeler, after importing the physical and relational models, you can use the Engineer To Logical Model functionality to generate a logical model. Then you are ready to maintain the logical model, forward engineer them to the relational model, and export the DDLs or get the ALTER DDLs by synchronizing with the model as explained in Chapter 12.

Reverse Engineering from a Data Dictionary

You can reverse engineer from Oracle, but you can also import from other supported relational database management systems (RDBMSs). At the moment, the supported databases are Microsoft SQL Server 2000 to 2012, IBM DB2/LUW v7–v10, IBM DB2 for OS/390, DB2 Mainframe/zOS up to DB2 11, and ODBC/JDBC-compliant data dictionaries. The non-Oracle drivers are not included in the Data Modeler installation. To be able to import from non-Oracle databases, you need to download the drivers required and add them in the Preferences dialog. Specifically, after downloading the drivers, you must open the Preferences dialog, select Data Modeler | Third Party JDBC Drivers, and add the drivers by clicking the green plus sign. You will see the non-Oracle database as a new tab in the New / Select Database Connection dialog, and you can create a new connection.

For instance, if you added Microsoft SQL Server, you will see a new tab called SQLServer beside Oracle and JDBC in the New / Select Database Connection dialog, as shown in Figure 10-1. Depending on the RDBMS selected and the version of Data Modeler, there might be some other thing you must do to get the connection

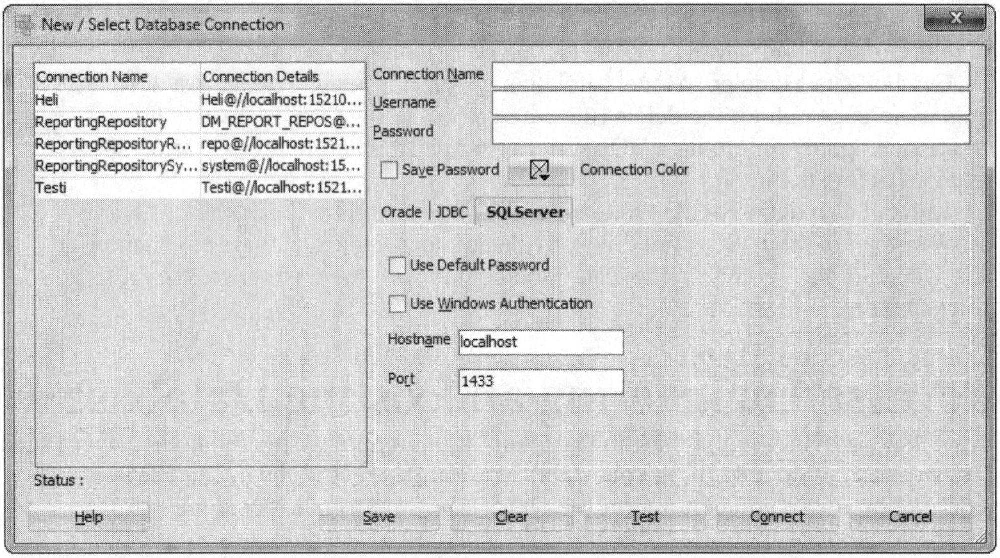

FIGURE 10-1. *Connection to Microsoft SQL Server*

working, such as with Java settings, but in general the process is downloading the drivers, extracting them, and setting the Data Modeler preferences for third-party drivers.

Reverse Engineering from an Oracle Database

To reverse engineer from an Oracle database, choose File | Import | Data Dictionary. Then select the connection wanted from the connection list in the Data Dictionary Import Wizard, as shown in Figure 10-2. Or click Add to create a new connection using the New / Select Database Connection dialog shown in Figure 10-3.

You can create an Oracle connection or a connection based on JDBC drivers. Since Data Modeler 4.0.3, you can make the connection using Secure Shell (SSH) tunnels, and the proxy connection was moved to the same place within the settings. To create an SSH tunnel, click the Advanced button in the New / Select Database Connection dialog to be taken to the Advanced Properties dialog. Select the SSH tab and then fill in the information needed for an SSH connection:

■ Select Use SSH to define an SSH tunnel to be used.

■ Type the SSH server for Host.

■ Type the SSH port for Port. The default port is 22.

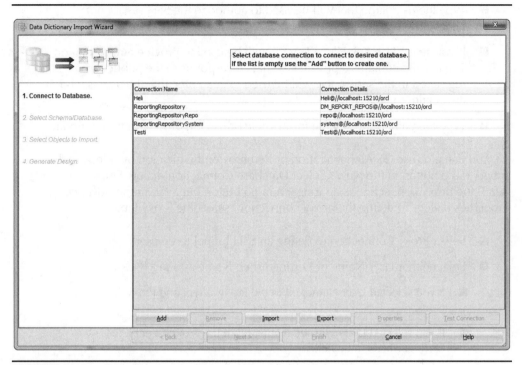

FIGURE 10-2. *Data Dictionary Import Wizard*

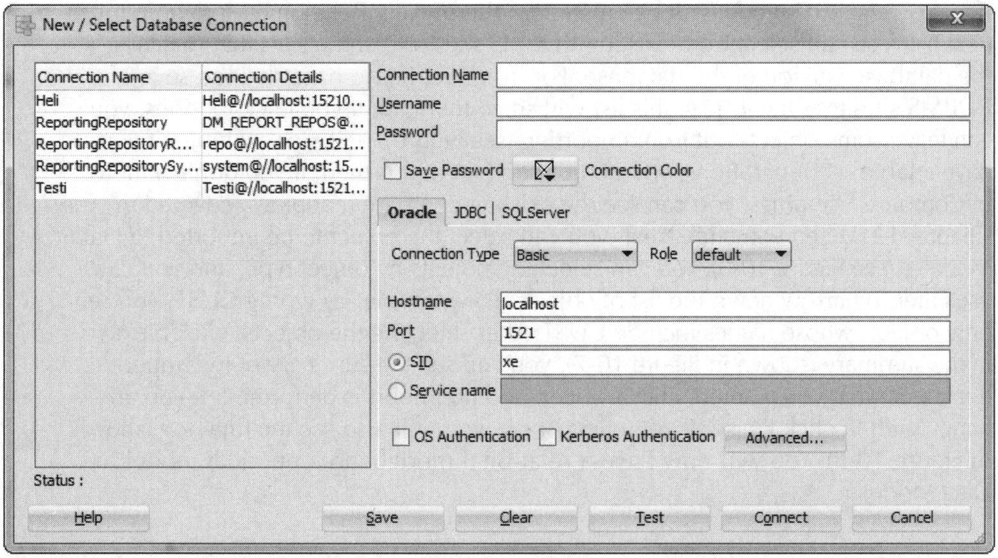

FIGURE 10-3. *New/Select Database Connection dialog*

■ Type the username that will be used to authorize the SSH session for Username.

■ If you select Use Key File, a key file will be used to provide authentication. The key file contains a private key that corresponds to the public key registered in the server and will be used to guarantee that the user is who they claim to be.

■ Type the path to the key file for Key File or use the Browse button to find it.

You can also use OS Authentication or Kerberos Authentication by selecting the proper radio button in the New / Select Database Connection dialog. Since version 4.0.3, the proxy connection is no longer a radio button but a tab in the Advanced Properties dialog. To define the proxy connection, select the Proxy tab.

■ Select Proxy Connection to define an SSH tunnel to be used.

■ Select either User Name or Distinguished Name as a proxy type.

   ■ If you selected User Name, fill in the Proxy Client and Proxy Password fields.

   ■ If you selected Distinguished Name, fill in the Proxy Client and Distinguished Name fields.

After you have selected the connection, select the schema or schemas wanted for the reverse engineering (see Figure 10-4). You can set the options under Import To if the objects will be imported to an existing relational model (Relational_1) or if a new relational model will be created for them (New Relational Model); in the next list, you can select from existing RDBMS sites one of the sites that matches the database version of the database. For instance, if you have defined several RDBMS sites for Oracle 11*g*, this list will show them all. If you click Options, you can leave some objects out from importing (see Figure 10-5). For example, if you have a large set of partitions, you do not need to import them if you don't want to. In Compare Mappings, you can see the existing compare mappings, covered in Chapter 12. When you click Next, you can select the object to be imported to Data Modeler (see Figure 10-6). You can select the objects by object type, and you can use Filter to narrow down the list of objects. For example, by typing **CUST**, you see only objects whose names include CUST. After selecting the objects, click Next. In the summary (shown in Figure 10-7), you can see the summary of the import. If it is not what you wanted, click Cancel, and no import is performed. If you are happy with it, click Finish. If you click Finish, you will also see the final log (shown in Figure 10-8). You will now have a relational model and a physical model in Data Modeler.

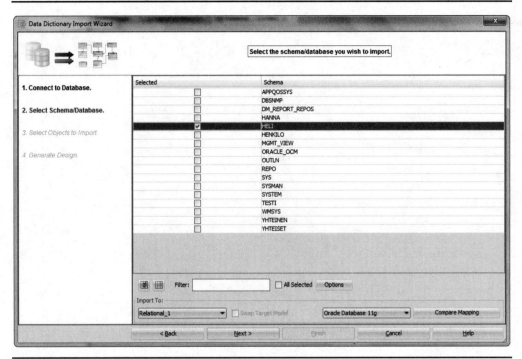

FIGURE 10-4. *Selecting schemas*

NOTE
If you bring several schemas from the data dictionary, Data Modeler will automatically create a subview for each.

FIGURE 10-5. *Optional Import and Processing options*

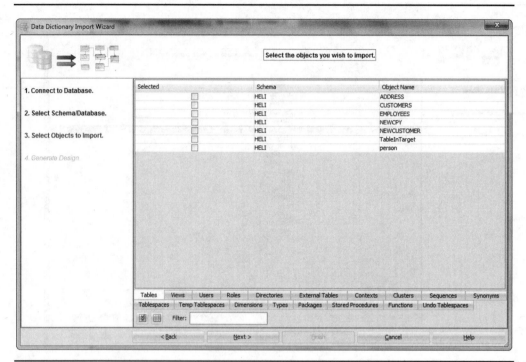

FIGURE 10-6. *Select Objects to Import screen*

NOTE
Storage templates (see Chapter 6) are defined automatically when importing from a data dictionary or a DDL file that defines one or more tablespaces with common storage properties.

Since version 4.0.2, Data Modeler (and since version 4.0.3, SQL Developer) supports Oracle Big Data SQL and Hive. This support allows you to connect to Hive and reverse engineer Hive tables, use SQL Developer to query the Hive tables with any other Oracle tables, design/create/alter Hive tables, and generate the DDLs for Big Data SQL-enabled Oracle external tables.

To be able to create a connection to Hive, you must first download the JDBC drivers and connectors. Data Modeler integration was first developed on Hortonworks Sandbox 2.0, and it supports those JDBC drivers as well. Hive integration in SQL Developer works only with the JDBC drivers from Cloudera. You can download the

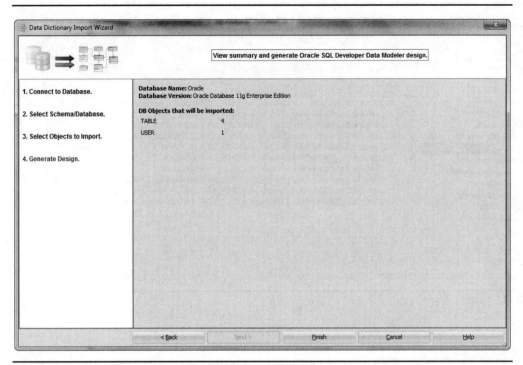

FIGURE 10-7.   *Data Dictionary Import Wizard summary*

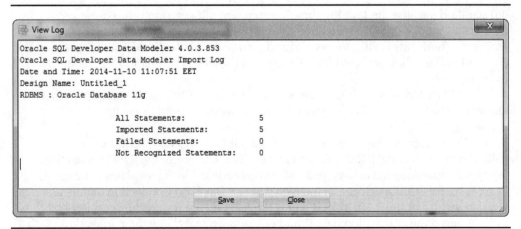

FIGURE 10-8.   *Data Dictionary Import Wizard log*

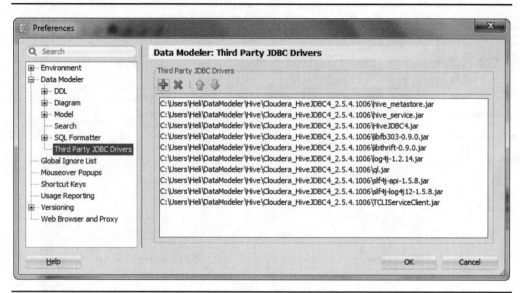

FIGURE 10-9. *Preferences for a Hive connector*

Cloudera JDBC drivers from www.cloudera.com/content/cloudera/en/downloads
.html. The Cloudera JDBC drivers for Hive are delivered in two .zip files: Cloudera_
HiveJDBC3_<version>.zip and Cloudera_HiveJDBC4_<version>.zip. These files
compile with the JDBC 3.0 and 4.0 standards. Extract the files in Cloudera_
HiveJDBC4_<version>.zip. SQL Developer and Data Modeler are using the JDBC
4.0 standard because the Java Runtime Environment (JRE) version is 6.0 or newer.
Start Data Modeler or SQL Developer. Choose Tools | Preferences and select Data
Modeler | Third Party JDBC Drivers and add the drivers on the list. Click the green
plus and find the files extracted from Cloudera_HiveJDBC4_<version>.zip, as shown
in Figure 10-9.

Close Data Modeler or SQL Developer and restart it. Choose File | Import | Data
Dictionary and click Add in the Data Dictionary Import Wizard to create a new
connection.

For Data Modeler, the Hive connection is a JDBC connection, so just select the
JDBC tab and define the JDBC URL and Driver Class settings for the JDBC connection.
When you download the drivers, you will also get a PDF file that explains what to
insert here. For SQL Developer, in the New / Select Database Connection dialog, as
you can see in Figure 10-10, there is a new tab named Hive for creating connections
to Hive. Insert the connection details and click Test to make sure the connection
works. Then click Save to save the connection settings. Now you can import (reverse
engineer) from Hive to Oracle using this connection.

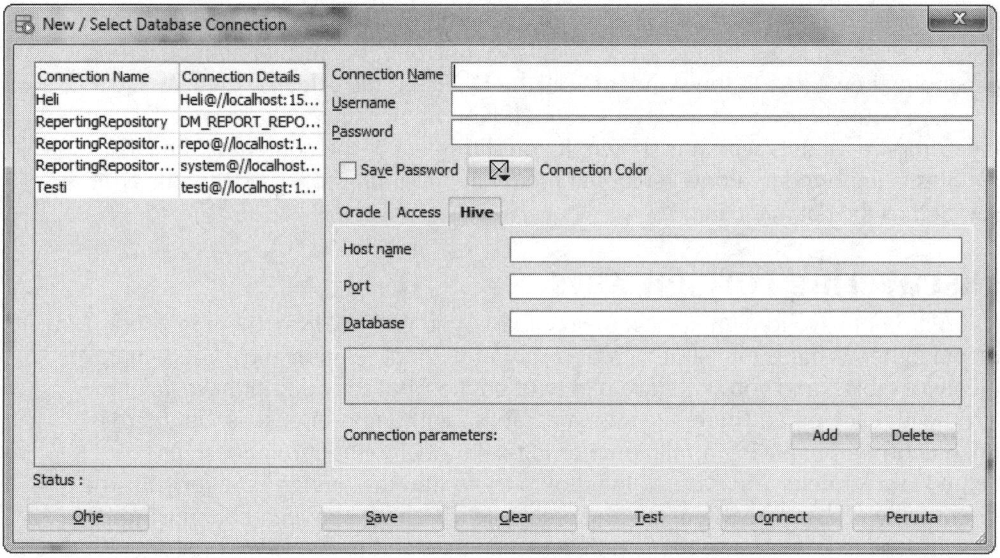

FIGURE 10-10. *Hive connection in SQL Developer*

Importing a DDL File

One way to document a database is to find the DDL files for generating the database and import them to Data Modeler. To do this, choose File | Import | DDL File. Click the green plus sign to select the correct DDL files or click the red X button to remove them from the list. If you have CREATE and ALTER DDLs, make sure to run them in the right order. You can, for instance, run the CREATE TABLE DDLs first and then restart the importing DDLs for the ALTER clauses. In the Options section, you can select whether you want to import to (Import To) an existing relational model or to create a new relational model (New Relational Model). If you select a new model, the Skip Merge Dialog option is no longer dimmed. If you select Skip Merge Dialog, the Relational Model dialog will not be displayed during the import operation. If you select an existing model, the Swap Target Model dialog is no longer dimmed. If Swap Target Model is not selected, the content of the script is merged to the relational model, and on the Compare Models screen the content of the script is shown on the left and the relational model is shown on the right. If Swap Target Model is selected, the content of the relational model is merged to the content of the script, and on the Compare Models screen, the relational model is shown on the left and the content of the script is shown on the right. You can read more about compare models in Chapter 12. View Compare Mappings will show the existing compare mappings, as covered in Chapter 12.

After setting the parameters the way you want, click OK. Next you must select the databases in the Database Sites dialog (covered in Chapter 6). Make sure to select the correct RDBMS site. If you select a wrong one, the result might be wrong, depending how close to the standard SQL the DDL and the selected RDBMS site are.

Then you will see the View Log screen. If you did not select Skip Merge Dialog, the Compare Models screen is shown. If you did select it, the content of the DDL file/files is imported to a new relational model and to a physical model of the type selected as the database site.

Discovering Foreign Keys

If you did not have foreign keys in the database, you will not have them in your model either. What is the value of a data model without relationships? You will have plenty of tables, and you will have plenty of entities, but they do not have anything to do with each other. There might be a database without foreign keys, but there is not much point in having a relational or logical model without relationships.

In Data Modeler you can ask the tool to try to find the foreign keys for you. The discovering is based on the name and data type matching between columns. You specify foreign key column name policies to be used in the discovery process. Go to the Browser pane and select the relational model. Right-click and select Discover Foreign Keys; the Create Discovered Foreign Keys screen opens. In the dialog you will see a list of primary keys that could be used in foreign keys. You can select and unselect them. In the list you can see the referred table, the referred key, the table, and the column. With Column To Filter, you can select the element to be used in filtering (table, column, referred table, or referred key), and in Filter, you can type a string to restrict the list. You can, for example, restrict the list to only table names starting with *LNK*. If Single Use Of FK Column is selected, a foreign key column can be bound to only one foreign key. You can define the naming policy for selecting the foreign key candidates by setting the FK column name policy. The possible values are Referred Column, FK Column Template, Referred And Template, or Template And Referred.

- If you select Referred Column, Data Modeler will look for a foreign key column that has the same name as the referred column.

- If you select FK Column Template, Data Modeler is looking for columns with the name generated using the foreign key template.

- If you select Referred And Template, Data Modeler first applies the Referred Column policy and then the FK Column Template policy.

- If you select Template And Referred, Data Modeler applies first the FK Column Template policy and then the Referred Column policy.

For example, you have two tables: Customer and Order. In Customer, you have defined a primary key called CustNo. In Order, you have two potential foreign key columns CustNo and Customer_ID. If you know that the name of the foreign key column in this database is always the same as the name in the parent table, you simply select Referred Column as the FK column name policy, as shown in Figure 10-11.

NOTE
If you have some foreign keys in your model before adding the discovered foreign keys, it is possible that you will have duplicates of foreign keys with different foreign key names. Make sure to remove the extra ones manually.

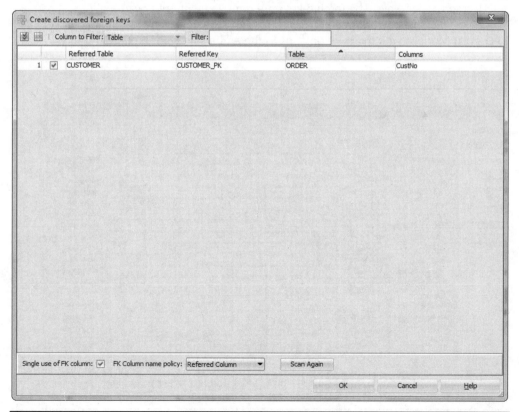

FIGURE 10-11. *Create Discovered Foreign Keys dialog, same name*

If you know that in this database the foreign keys are always called ParentTable_ID, you simply go to the design-level properties and change the template setting for the foreign key column, as shown in Figure 10-12, and in Discover Foreign Keys, you select FK Column Template as the FK Column Name Policy option, as shown in Figure 10-13.

If you know that both of these are possible, you can select either Referred And Template or Template And Referred depending on which one is preferred. In this example, if you select Referred And Template, Order.CustNo will be defined as the foreign key, and if you select Template And Referred, Order.Customer_ID will be defined as the foreign key for the Order table.

Clicking the Scan Again button refreshes the screen based on the changed parameters. If you click OK, the discovered foreign keys are created. If you click Cancel, no foreign keys are created. All discovered foreign keys have a dynamic property called createdByFKDiscoverer attached to them and can be easily found using that. If you want to remove the discovered foreign keys, choose Edit | Remove Discovered Foreign Keys. The foreign keys are removed without a warning.

When you have created the discovered foreign keys, remember to click Engineer To Logical Model to get the relationships to the entities as well. Note that the

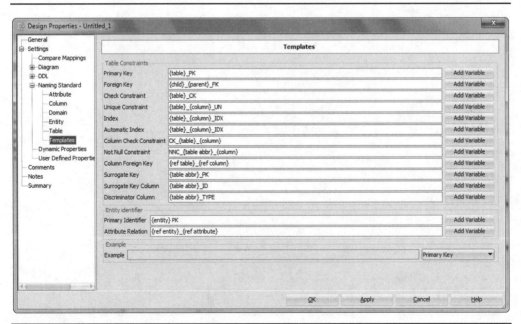

FIGURE 10-12. *Template setting for a foreign key column*

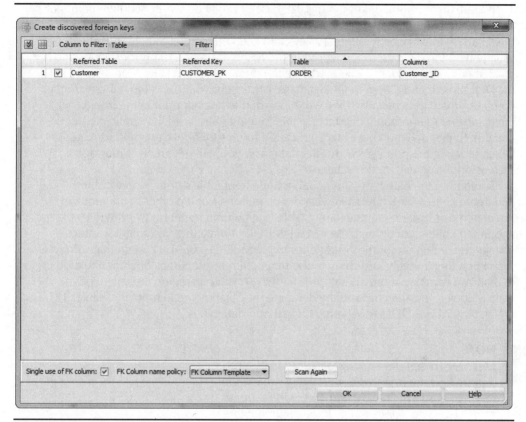

FIGURE 10-13. *Discovering foreign keys based on the template*

dynamic property createdByFKDiscoverer is not engineered to the relationship in the logical model. If you decide to remove the discovered foreign keys for some reason, remember to click Engineer To Logical Model again so that the relationships will also be removed.

TIP
You can use Create New Models Based On Schema Names to get a relational model for each schema. It might help to make finding the right foreign keys more controlled. Right-click the relational model name and choose Create New Models Based On Schema Names.

If there are no primary keys in the database, it might be worth defining them, not just for getting the Discover Foreign Keys functionality to work but also for getting the database to work better. Primary keys will keep the data quality high and will usually help the database optimizer to improve the execution plans for queries and make them more efficient. You can define the primary keys in Data Modeler and get the DDLs for creating them in the database. Make sure you really know these are the correct primary keys because they will block duplicate data from being inserted in the database. You probably need to see the data in tables, read the application code, and talk to people who know this application to be sure about the primary keys. When creating the primary key for the database, you will get an error message if there is duplicate data in the database.

Sometimes the date types are equal in the parent table's primary key column and in the child table's foreign key candidate column but the other definitions do not match. For instance, in the parent table, the column might be NUMBER(16,0), and in the child table, it might be just NUMBER. In that case, you might want to change the definition for the child tables to NUMBER(16,0). You can do that using the search functionality and using the setting common properties operation related to that. You can read more about it in Chapter 11. After changing the date type in Data Modeler, you can compare the design to the database (read more in Chapter 12) and get the ALTER DDLs for altering the column date types.

NOTE
Discover Foreign Keys works only if primary or unique keys are defined for the parent table and if the columns in the parent and child tables are of same date type. For instance, if the column name matches the primary key column name in the parent table but the date type is different for it in the child table, this column is not included as a foreign key candidate.

Engineering to the Logical Model

When you have imported from the data dictionary or DDLs, remember to use the Engineer To Logical Model button (see Figure 10-14) to get a logical model if you want to start designing the changes in data structures with Data Modeler. From now on, you can make the changes to your logical model, forward engineer them to the relational model, and export the DDLs as explained in Chapters 3 through 7 or get the ALTER DDLs by synchronizing with the model, as explained in Chapter 12.

Of course, there are situations in which you do not need the logical model, and therefore there is no point in creating it, such as if the database structures are maintained by a software vendor or if the changes are very small, such as when adding a single column to a table. In these cases, you simply add columns to tables

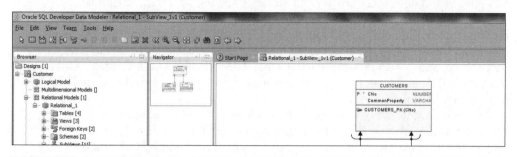

FIGURE 10-14. *Engineer To Logical Model*

and get the ALTER DDLs for adding the columns to the database, and no logical model is needed. If you are making larger changes or changes that will use transformation scripts to add columns to new tables or other changes like that, having a logical model is definitely worth it.

If you do decide to create the logical model and start maintaining the database objects with Data Modeler, the logical diagram might not look exactly the way you want it to after the reverse engineering. If you want to change the layout, either you can move the elements in the diagram to the places you want or you can use the functionalities Data Modeler offers for automatically making the layout look better. Specifically, right-click the canvas and choose Layout. You might also want to create subviews or layouts, as explained in Chapters 3 and 4.

The relationship names are after engineering the foreign key names in the database. Depending on how the database was designed and created, those names might be completely technical, making no sense to the human eye. In those cases, it might be worth renaming the relationships manually to something more meaningful.

Importing Documentation from a Third-Party Modeling Tool

You might have databases that already have documentation and you would like to get that documentation into Data Modeler so you don't have to start from scratch. You can, of course, insert the design into Data Modeler manually, but there are other possibilities too. You might have the documentation in a VAR file that has been created from Sterling COOL (DBA v2.1 or Sterling Bsnteam v7.2), Cayenne Bsnteam v7.2, Rational Rose, Together, JDeveloper, MEGA, or PowerDesigner v.12. Or you might have it in ERwin 4.1 or 7.3 or in Oracle Designer. Or you might have your data warehouse documentation in Cube Views metadata or Microsoft XMLA. There is support for many other modeling tools in Data Modeler. The tools include Oracle

Designer 9*i* and newer, CA Erwin Data Modeler 4.x and 7.x, Sterling COOL: DBA v2.1, Sterling Bsnteam v7.2, and Cayenne Bsnteam v7.2. For multidimensional models, there is support for IBM DB2 Cube Views and XML for Analysis (XMLA) metadata. XMLA is designed for universal data access to any standard multidimensional data source, and it is an industry standard maintained by the XMLA Council. XMLA is a Simple Object Access Protocol (SOAP)–based XML protocol, and it is used, for instance, by Microsoft.

To import a VAR file or one from ERwin 4.1 or 7.3, Cube Views metadata, or Microsoft XMLA, choose File | Import and then select the appropriate importing option. In all these cases you are asked for a filename to be imported, and by following the instructions, you will get the documentation imported to Data Modeler.

In some cases, it is possible that not all the documentation will be brought into Data Modeler, so it is important you check the result manually. In other words, compare the source to the target. And if there is any information missing, add that manually. One of the things standards do not usually handle is the layout of diagrams. So, most likely you will need to change the layouts of the diagrams manually or using the functionalities Data Modeler offers to make the diagrams easier to read. You might also want to consider creating subviews after the import to make the diagrams easier to read and understand. See Chapters 3 and 4 for more information.

You will learn a bit more about how to import from Oracle Designer in the next section.

Importing from Oracle Designer

Before starting to work with Oracle Designer, make sure that the designs in Oracle Designer are valid and there is nothing you do not want to import to Data Modeler. Also check that you really want to import them all; if not, document which ones you will not import and why. It is better to avoid importing old information into Data Modeler.

NOTE
If you have versioning enabled in Oracle Designer, only the latest version of objects is imported.

Open Data Modeler and save the empty design. Choose File | Import and select Oracle Designer Model. First you need to create a connection to the Oracle Designer repository using a username that has enough privileges to see all the objects needed. Click Next. Select work area and click Next. Select the application you want to import. It is probably logical to make one Data Modeler design from one Oracle Designer application. Select all the objects you want to import and click Next. You will see a summary of database objects that will be imported into Data Modeler in the Oracle Designer Import Wizard. If you are happy with the result, click Finish.

Otherwise, click Cancel. The View Log dialog will show the final log for importing. You will now have all the information you want imported into Data Modeler. You might have two relational models: Relational_1 and another named after the Oracle Designer connection. All the elements have been imported to the one with the connection name. In that case, you can delete the empty Relational_1 model and maybe rename the other relational model. Save the design. In my opinion, the import works well and is definitely worth doing.

NOTE
During an import from the Oracle Designer repository, the short name for an entity in Oracle Designer is used for both the entity short name and the table abbreviation of the mapped table in Data Modeler. The Oracle Designer Plural property for the entity is mapped to the Preferred Abbreviation property of the entity in Data Modeler.

At the moment, Data Modeler does not import tablespaces, stored procedures, packages, functions, and data flow diagrams from the Oracle Designer repository. Most of these can be added from the data dictionary, as described next. Every version of Data Modeler gets better at importing from Oracle Designer.

NOTE
The import functionality does not import the original layouts of the diagrams in the other modeling tool. After the import, you need to change the layout in Data Modeler to meet your needs either manually or using the functionalities Data Modeler offers for automatic layout setting.

Now, you might realize that not all the information needed is in your design. There are several reasons for that. Possible reasons might be that you have been using database features that are not supported by Oracle Designer, maybe you did not add all the information to Oracle Designer (for instance, data files), or maybe it is because of the limitations of the Data Modeler conversion. There's no need to panic. You probably have everything implemented in your database, and you can connect to your data dictionary and import all the missing information from there. Choose File | Import | Data Dictionary. Select the connection to the database or create a new one. Make sure you have enough privileges to be able to see all that you need. Click Next. Select the schema that contains the information for this design. Click Next. Select all the objects you want to import. Click Next. You will see the summary of the import. Click Finish. Now you will see the Compare Models screen (read more about it in Chapter 12). Select the changes you want to implement in your design and click Merge. Remember that there are a lot of parameters in the Compare Models dialog that make selecting the right changes easier. For instance, maybe you do not want to replace a comment for a table with an empty one from the data dictionary. Now you should have the complete documentation of your database. You might want to check your model with design rules (see Chapter 2) or maybe even add new rules to check with. Next you might want to add your design to version control. See Chapter 9 for more information.

NOTE
The import does not import the layouts of the diagrams. You must edit them manually after the import.

Summary

You can document an existing database either manually, by using the documentation from other modeling tool, or by importing the information from a data dictionary or from a DDL file.

Data Modeler has support for importing designs from many tools, including Oracle Designer 9*i* and newer, CA ERwin Data Modeler 4.x and 7.x, Sterling COOL: DBA v2.1, Sterling Bsnteam v7.2, and Cayenne Bsnteam v7.2 formats. For multidimensional models, there is support for Cube Views metadata and XMLA. A database that has no documentation can be reverse engineered into Data Modeler by importing either from a data dictionary or from a DDL file. At the moment, the supported databases are Microsoft SQL Server 2000 or 2005, IBM DB2/LUW v7 or v8, IBM DB2 for OS/390 and z/OS, and ODBC/JDBC-compliant data dictionaries. If the database has no foreign keys, you can use Discover Foreign Keys to try to guess the possible foreign keys. After importing the physical and relational models, you can use the Engineer To Logical Model functionality to generate a logical model if needed. Then you are ready to maintain the logical model, forward engineer the changes to the relational model, and export the DDLs or get the ALTER DDLs by synchronizing with the model as explained in Chapter 12.

CHAPTER
11

Generating Reports
and Using Search

Reporting functionality is a must when selecting a tool for database design. If you can't create reports using the tool, it is not worth using. There are so many different needs for reporting: auditing, quality reviews, documenting, talking with end users, informing internally, and so on. Data Modeler has strong reporting functionalities. In Data Modeler, you can generate reports from designs that are open or from the optional reporting repository on all designs uploaded to the repository. You can generate reports with the reporting functionality or by using the search feature and generating the search results as a report. Reports can be used, for instance, to create documentation for tables, entities, domains, glossaries, structured types, distinct types, collection types, change requests, or measurements. You can also print a diagram by choosing File | Print Diagram. You can print the diagram either to an image file (To Image File) or to a PDF file (To PDF File). A user can create templates for the reports easily, and SQL can be used to query the reporting repository. You can find useful information on reporting in datamodeler\ datamodeler\reports\.

Data Modeler uses a standardized transformation to produce reports from the source Extensible Markup Language (XML) files. Extensible Stylesheet Language Transformation (XSLT) defines the syntax and semantics for transforming XML documents to other document formats or other XML documents. Data Modeler uses XSLT 1.0 by default, but you can also download the Saxon XSLT 2.0 processor and use that in report generation. Version 2.0 is more advanced and supports, for instance, large PDF reports and multibyte characters in Rich Text Format (RTF) reporting. If you know that you will be producing large PDF reports or will be running RTF reports from designs including multibyte characters, using the Saxon XSLT 2.0 processor will be essential.

You can generate PDF reports with Apache Formatting Objects Processor (FOP) v0.95. The Apache FOP configuration file is called fop.xconf. The file contains only the basic fonts and default settings but automatically adds fonts from the default system fonts directory. If the PDF report does not support the fonts you need, edit the fop.xconf file as explained in datamodeler\datamodeler\reports\Reports_Info.txt.

When Data Modeler generates reports, it first creates a file called report_data .xml (or report_data_rs.xml if the reporting repository is used). In the directory\ datamodeler\reports\xslt\, there are two subdirectories for templates: 10 and 20. If you are using the default XSLT 1.0, then templates are in directory 10, and if you have XSLT 2.0 in use, the templates in directory 20 are used. All template files are named based on the element type and output format, such as AllTablesDetails_rtf. xslt or AllTablesDetails_pdf.xslt.

A report can be run and saved in different formats depending on the settings. PDF and HTML formats are usually always supported. PDF is a good format when you want to send reports that no one should edit, for instance during a review. HTML is useful as a custom web page that could be, for instance, used as an online data dictionary on an internal web site or for technical people who want to see the information without installing Data Modeler. RTF is a good format if you want to let the receiver edit the report, but in that case, probably the best choice is Microsoft Excel, since some information edited in the Microsoft Excel report can be imported into Data Modeler as explained later in this chapter. You can read more about Data Modeler and reporting in datamodeler\datamodeler\reports\Reports_Info.txt.

NOTE
Starting from version 4.1, you can insert your corporation's logo or any picture into your diagrams and reports.

Setting Preferences and Properties

There are no properties that affect the reporting functionality, but there are two preferences that do. In Preferences (choose Tools | Preferences), go to the Data Modeler | Reports tab to define the Default Report Directory setting where the reports will be saved by default. If you have downloaded the Saxon XSLT 2.0 processor and want Data Modeler to use it for generating reports, you can define the path for it in Path To Saxon XSLT 2.0 JAR File. If you do not specify the path, Data Modeler uses XSLT 1.0 in report generation. Since version 4.1, you can also define your Company Name to be used in reports and decide whether a page break will be added after each object.

There are also some preferences in the Preferences dialog that will affect the search functionality that can be used for reporting. You can find them by going to the Data Modeler | Search tab. You can define whether the search will start after ENTER has been pressed or while typing. If you want it to start while typing, you can also define the number of symbols ignored before starting the search. The default is three characters. You can also predefine search profiles to be used while searching. With version 4.1, you can also define search profiles to be used while searching. A Search Profile can be used to narrow down the scope for a search operation.

Generating Reports Based on Open Designs

You can run a report by choosing File | Reports. The report will open automatically and be saved to the directory specified in Preferences (Default Reports Directory). The Messages – Log pane will tell you when the report is ready and where it is saved. There are three sections in the Reports dialog for defining the scope and format for the report: Reports, Templates, and Designs. See Figure 11-1.

In the Reports section, you can specify the following:

- In Available Reports, you select the element type for the report: Tables, Entities, Domains, Glossaries, Structured Types, Distinct Types, Collection Types, Change Requests, or Measurements.

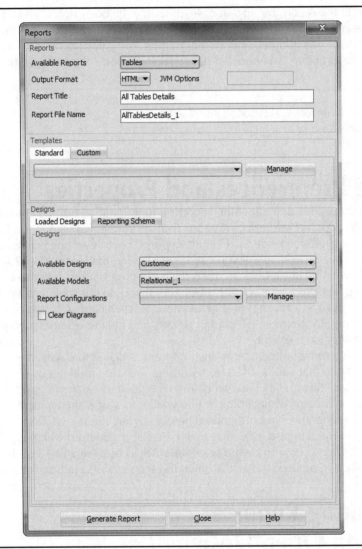

FIGURE 11-1. *Reports dialog*

■ For Output Format, you can select HTML, PDF, or RTF for standard templates and HTML, PDF, XLS, or XLSX for custom templates. For an HTML report, several files are generated; other formats have only one file. Both XLS and XLSX reports can be imported into Data Modeler as described in the "Search" section later in this chapter.

- In JVM Options, you can specify the memory allocation for PDF reports if needed. The default that Data Modeler suggests is -Xmx768M. PDF reports, especially with XSLT 1.0, consume a lot of memory, and you might need to either raise the value for memory allocation or consider using XSLT 2.0 in generating reports if you have problems getting the PDF reports to run.

- In Report Title, you can define a name for the report. The name will be shown in the header of the report.

- In Report File Name, you can define the name for the report file. Data Modeler automatically looks after the uniqueness of the filename by adding a sequence number at the end of the filename. If you manually change the name to be not unique, Data Modeler gives a warning: "The file … already exists! Are you sure you want to overwrite?"

In the Templates section, you can specify whether you want to use a standard template or a custom template. Standard templates have a somewhat fixed and limited set of options to choose from, whereas custom templates will give you extensive control over the elements that are in the final report. Depending on which you choose, the list of available templates is different, and the choices for creating a template are different. Standard report templates are saved in a file called report_templates.xml, and custom report templates are saved in a file called custom_report_templates.xml. Both files are saved in the directory defined in the Default System Types Directory setting in Preferences. You can share and version templates as explained in Chapter 9 using Subversion. If you want to use an existing template, you select it from the list. If you want to edit or delete an existing template or create a new template, click the Manage button.

To create a new standard template, click Add. You must give the template a name (Template Name), but the elements to choose for the report template depend on the element type chosen for the report. For instance, if you have selected Tables for Available Reports and create a new standard template for it, the choices are shown in the Report Templates Management dialog, as shown in Figure 11-2. You enable the elements you want to have in the report template and disable the ones you do not. When you are done, click Save. This template will be shown in the list of standard templates and can be used. To share it with other users, simply share the file report_templates.xml with other users. They should save it to their default system types directory.

To create a new custom template, click the Add icon (green plus sign). Then give the template a name (Name) and a description (Description). The elements to choose for the report template depend on the element type chosen for the report. For instance, if you select Tables for Available Reports and create a new custom template for it, the choices are shown in the Custom Reports Template dialog, as

FIGURE 11-2. *Report Templates Management dialog for standard templates*

shown in Figure 11-3. In Available Collections, you can see a list of relevant information that can be added to the report layout for this type of element. Use the arrow icons to add and remove the information from the Report Layout section. In Custom Name, you can define a name for that element in the report. The Report Layout section shows which information will be included in the report template. In Available Properties, there is a list of available properties for the selected Report Layout element. Use the arrow icons to add and remove the information from the Report Columns section. In Report Columns, you can see the columns for the report template. If you want, you can change the column names for the report in Column Name. In Column Width, you can set the width for the column. If you do not change it, the best width will be defined automatically. In Data Sort Order, you can specify sort order values for individual columns. You set 1 to the one that will be first, 2 to the second, and so on. On the right of the screen, there are arrows that can be used to reorder the elements. When you are done, click the Save icon. This template will be shown in the list of custom templates and can be used. To share it with other users, simply share the file custom_report_templates.xml with other users. They should save it to their default system types directory. If you are using a

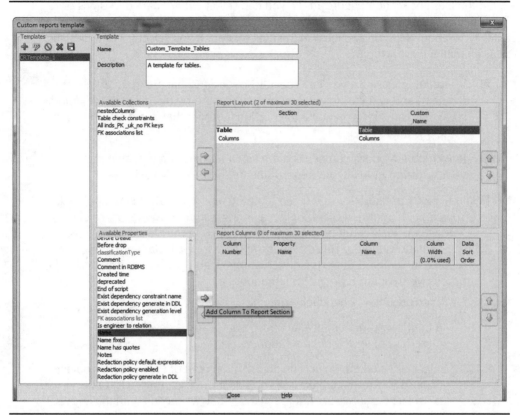

FIGURE 11-3. *Custom Reports Template dialog for custom templates*

custom template for your report, you can also select Replace Boolean Values to specify values for True (Y, YES, y, yes) and False (N, NO, n, no) in a report.

TIP
You can use the Custom Name and Column Name fields in the Custom Reports Templates dialog to get a different name for the element in a report than is defined in the model. You can do this, for instance, if you want to have your report template in Finnish.

NOTE
You cannot create a template for glossaries; the report is run based on Available Report glossaries.

In the Designs section (Figure 11-1), you can select either Loaded Designs or Reporting Schema. You will now see the choices if you select Loaded Designs and learn more about Reporting Schema in the next section. If you select Loaded Designs, you can define these settings:

- In Available Designs, you can see a list of designs that are open at the moment, and you can select the one you want to be the base for the report. Note that you cannot execute a report on a design that is not already open using this method.

- In Available Models, you can see the list of models of a type that matches your selection in Available Reports and are in the design selected.

- In Report Configurations, you can limit the report to only a certain object. You can either leave it blank, select a configuration from the list, or click Manage to create, edit, or delete configurations in the Standard Reports Configurations dialog. This dialog is the same for both standard and custom reports. In Standard Reports Configurations (Figure 11-4), you can add, edit, or remove standard reports configurations.

  1. To create a new one, click Add.

  2. In the Report section, give a name (Name) and a description (Description) for the configuration.

  3. Select either all the objects (Include All Objects) or only subview objects (Choose Subview(s) Objects). If you select Choose Subview(s) Objects, you can select the subviews wanted in the Subviews section with the arrows. Selected subviews appear on the right, and possible subviews appear on the left. Using subviews is an efficient way of getting only the wanted elements to the report, which is much faster than selecting one by one.

  4. In the Object section, you can select and deselect objects to be included in the report.

- The reports will use the diagrams from the directory. When generating reports, the diagrams are saved and can be reused to save time and resources. If Clear Diagrams is not selected, those diagram files are reused and not generated again. If it is selected, the existing diagram files are deleted, and new ones are created. Selecting Clear Diagrams might affect the performance dramatically, and if the diagrams have not been changed, there is no need to create the files again.

When you have selected all these and are ready to run the report, click Generate Report. Data Modeler will notify you in the Messages – Log pane when the report is ready and where to find it. When it is ready, the report will open automatically.

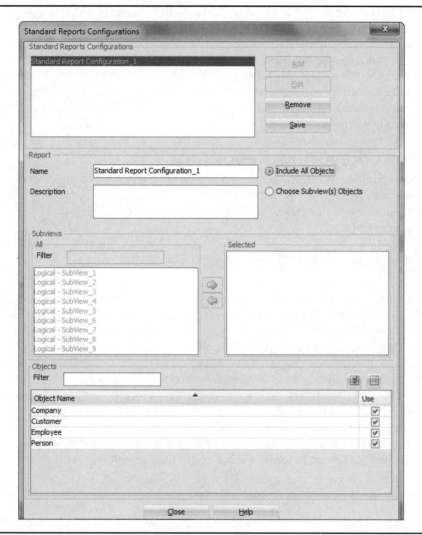

FIGURE 11-4. *Standard Reports Configurations dialog*

Introducing the Reporting Repository

The Data Modeler reporting repository is a database schema with database objects for storing metadata and data about Data Modeler designs. You can decide which designs to export to the repository, and when needed, you can remove designs from the repository. The reporting repository is useful as a database for all the information you want to share with users who do not have access to Data Modeler. For users with access to Data Modeler, the value is having all the information in one place, having the ability to generate reports for all designs, and using SQL for querying the reporting repository. In datamodeler\datamodeler\reports\Reporting Schema diagrams, you can find the descriptions of the reporting repository structures. The reporting repository is a read-only repository. Any changes to the content must be done with Data Modeler and exported to the repository. A user can be granted a read-only access to the reporting repository to be able to run SQL scripts directly on the reporting repository.

Creating a Reporting Repository

To create a reporting repository, you should first create a repository owner (schema) in your database. This is not mandatory (you can use any schema), but having a dedicated repository owner makes maintaining the repository easier.

Here's an example:

```
create user DM_REPORT_REPOS identified by password;
```

Then find the file Reporting_Schema_Permissions.sql in datamodeler\datamodeler\
reports. You can use this file for granting privileges to the repository owner and for defining the OSDDM_REPORTS_DIR directory for the report generation to use as a temporary directory at runtime. Edit the file and replace every <USER> instance with your username (for instance DM_REPORT_REPOS) and replace <OS DIRECTORY> with a directory path and name of a temporary directory in the server where the repository database runs. This directory will include files for the runtime of a report: osddm_reports.log and report_data_rs.xml. The value cannot be longer than 30 characters, for example /home/oracle/Reporting. Then go to that computer or server and create the directory. Now run the edited script Reporting_Schema_
Permissions.sql in your database. Your script might look something like this:

```
CREATE OR REPLACE DIRECTORY OSDDM_REPORTS_DIR AS '/home/oracle/
Reporting';
GRANT READ, WRITE ON DIRECTORY OSDDM_REPORTS_DIR TO DM_REPORT_REPOS;
GRANT CREATE SESSION TO DM_REPORT_REPOS;
GRANT RESOURCE TO DM_REPORT_REPOS;
GRANT CREATE TABLE TO DM_REPORT_REPOS;
GRANT CREATE SEQUENCE TO DM_REPORT_REPOS;
GRANT CREATE VIEW TO DM_REPORT_REPOS;
GRANT CREATE PROCEDURE TO DM_REPORT_REPOS;
```

The first time you export a design to the reporting repository, the reporting schema is created automatically. Make sure you log in as the schema owner.

TIP
You can create additional users in the reporting repository with only read access using the script CreateExtraUserForReporting.sql in the /reports directory.

Exporting a Design to the Reporting Repository

When you export the first design to the reporting repository, all the database objects needed for the repository will be created automatically. To export a design to the reporting repository, first open the design in Data Modeler and then choose File | Export | To Reporting Schema. Then you will either choose an existing connection or create a new one (Figure 11-5). To create a new connection, you click the green plus sign; the New / Select Database Connection dialog will open, as shown in Figure 11-6. Fill in the information needed. Remember to log in as the schema owner. Then click Test to see that the connection works. The status should show

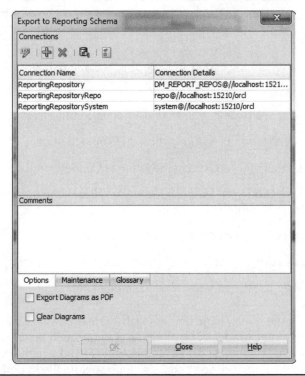

FIGURE 11-5. *Export To Reporting Schema dialog*

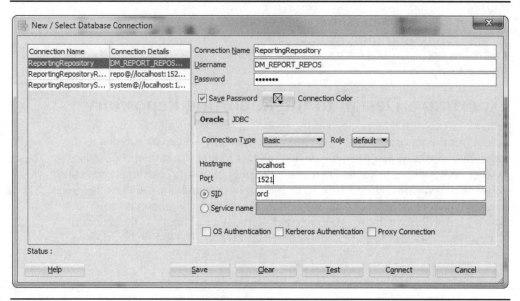

FIGURE 11-6. *Defining a database connection*

Success. Then click Save. In the Export To Reporting Schema dialog, in the Connections section, you can do the following:

- Edit a connection by clicking the Connection Properties icon

- Add a new connection by clicking the Add Connection icon

- Remove a connection by clicking the Remove Connection icon

- Import a connection from SQL Developer by clicking the Import SQL Developer Database Connections icon

- Test the connection by clicking the Test Connection icon

- Edit the connection by double-clicking the connection name

- Write a description (Comments) for each connection

On the bottom of the screen there are three tabs: Options, Maintenance, and Glossary. In Options, you can specify whether the diagrams will be exported to the repository in PDF format or not (Export Diagrams As PDF) and whether the diagrams will be cleared from the directory first and reproduced before the import. Remember that if you select Clear Diagrams, exporting will take longer.

On the Maintenance tab, you can drop the reporting repository, delete designs, and enable and disable indexes. If you drop the repository, all the database objects and all the content of a repository will be deleted. When you click the Drop Repository button, Data Modeler will ask, "Are you sure you want to drop the reporting repository?" If you decide to drop it, after the deletion is done Data Modeler says, "Reporting repository has been dropped successfully." If you click the Delete Designs button, you can select which designs to delete from the repository. From each design you can see the date and time of exporting, the name, and the comments. If you want to delete a design, select Selected for that design and click Delete Selected. Now the repository is not deleted; only data of selected designs is deleted. If you click Enable Indexes, the indexes for the repository database objects will be rebuilt, and if you select Disable Indexes, the indexes will be set to Unusable. If the indexes are valid, the reports will be generated faster.

On the Glossary tab, you can export a glossary to the reporting repository by clicking the Export Glossary button, and you can delete a glossary from the repository by clicking the Delete Glossary button. To export a glossary, you select the glossary file and click Open, and to delete a glossary, you select Selected for the glossary in the repository and click Delete Selected. It might sound strange to also export glossaries, but remember that there might be users without access to Data Modeler, and they might be interested in glossaries as well. Exporting all the information to the reporting repository gives them the chance to see all the information related to Data Modeler designs.

To export the design that is open, click OK, and it will be exported to the repository that can be found in the connection selected. Data Modeler will inform you that the design has been exported successfully.

Running Reports from the Reporting Repository

When you have the reporting repository created and designs exported, you can run reports from the repository, or you can use SQL to query it. The reports will be saved to the directory defined as Default Reports Directory in the Preferences dialog. To run a report from the reporting repository, choose File | Reports. Running the report is the same as explained earlier in this chapter, but now you select Reporting Schema instead of Loaded Designs. Specifically, you select the repository connection wanted in the Reporting Schema section. In that section you can edit, add, remove, and test a connection. Click Reload Design And Models to get the Available Designs and Available Models lists populated with the information from the reporting repository. Then you can select the available design, available model, and report configuration from the lists, as explained earlier. The values in the lists depend on the selected Available Report setting and the selected Reporting Schema setting. You can also select Clear Diagrams if you want the diagrams to be created again. You can edit, add, and delete report configurations by clicking Manage and defining them in the Standard Reports Configurations dialog, as explained earlier in this chapter. When you are done with the report configuration, you click the Generate Report button.

TIP
If there are several people running repository reports constantly, the temporary directory on the server might get busy. You can define a different directory when starting the report by entering the directory in the Directory Path field in the Reports dialog. Remember that you must have privileges to the server to create directories; otherwise, it will not succeed.

TIP
In SQL Developer there are several reports for Data Modeler's reporting repository. Go to SQL Developer, run the report, get the SQL, and use that as the basis for your own SQL query.

Using Search

Data Modeler has strong search features. The improved search features were introduced in version 3.3. You are able to search in many ways and on many search levels. At the end of the search, you can produce a report from the search result. The Search operation will look only inside the scope selected. A global search will search the whole design and a model search will only search the model. You can find the Search operation in both the Edit (Find) and View (Model Search) menus, as well as in the right-click menu of a logical or relational model in the Browser pane. There is also a Search icon on the toolbar for the logical and relational models. In the View menu, you will also find Global Search, which will search throughout the whole design.

You can use search for searching, but you can also use it for reporting and setting common properties. You can make searches in two different modes: simple or advanced mode.

Reporting with Search

The search functionality offers fine-tuned possibilities for first finding the information needed and for then turning that into a report. You can search in a selected scope, with a word or part of it, and with negation, or you can search for an empty value. You could, for instance, look for all the columns that are of type XMLTYPE and create a report from them. Or you could find all the tables without a unique key and get a report of those. In the Results pane (see Figure 11-7) for a search operation, you'll see a Report button. The Report button will be available as soon as you have selected the model from the Model list or when starting the search and the object

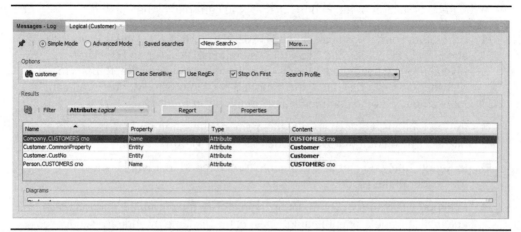

FIGURE 11-7. *Search result and starting the report*

from the Object list if there are any objects to report. Custom reports can include only one type of object at a time, which is the reason why the Report button is dimmed unless an object type has been selected.

Click Report to run a report; the Reports dialog box (see Figure 11-8) for generating Data Modeler reports opens.

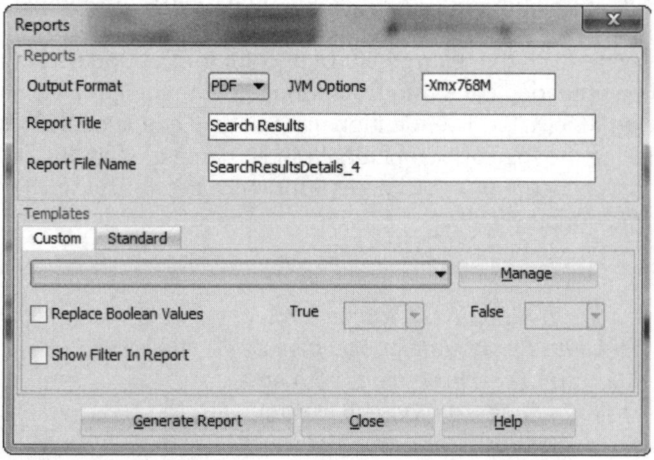

FIGURE 11-8. *Configuring the report*

In the Reports section of the Reports dialog, you can specify the following:

- For Output Format, you can select HTML, PDF, or RTF for standard templates and HTML, PDF, XLS, and XLSX for custom templates. For an HTML report, several files are generated; other formats generate only one file. Reports in XLS and XLSX can be edited and imported back into Data Modeler. You can, for example, edit the comments and comments in RDBMS.

- In JVM Options, you can specify the memory allocation for PDF reports if needed. The default that Data Modeler suggests is -Xmx768M.

- In Report Title, you can define a name for the report that will be shown in the header of the report.

- In Report File Name, you can define the name for the report file. Data Modeler automatically looks after the uniqueness of the filename by adding a sequence number at the end of the filename. If you manually change the name to be not unique, Data Modeler gives you this warning: "The file … already exists! Are you sure you want to overwrite?"

In the Templates section, you can specify whether you want to use a custom template or a standard template. The templates can be used and defined as described earlier in this chapter.

Reports in XLS or XLSX format can be edited in Microsoft Excel excluding the read-only properties. Some properties even have a list of values in the Microsoft Excel report where you can select the value wanted. Those properties are, for instance, domains, any kind of true/false property, and logical data types. Changes in the data type for a foreign key attribute/column in a Microsoft Excel report will not be implemented in Data Modeler because these types of attributes/columns inherit their data types from the referred attribute/column. The updated Microsoft Excel report can be uploaded back into Data Modeler with the Update Model With Previously Exported XLS (XLSX) File functionality that you can access in the Browser pane by right-clicking the logical or relational model name, depending on which kind of report it is. See Figure 9-9 in Chapter 9 for more details. A log will be generated about the updates.

TIP
You can edit reports in XLS or XLSX format and import them back into Data Modeler. You can, for example, use Microsoft Excel in sessions with end users to write notes in Notes, or you can ask an end user to write a description in Comments.

Simple Mode

In simple mode, you can search using strings, or you can use regular expressions as the search criteria. You can also run a report based on the search result or change common properties for the search result set.

To start a search in simple mode, select the Simple Mode radio button and enter a string to be searched for in the box with the binoculars sign, as shown earlier in Figure 11-7. Depending on what you selected in Preferences, the display is updated either as you type or when you press ENTER.

TIP
If you want to search everything, just type an asterisk
(*) in the search field.

Select either All or one of the object types in Filter to limit the search. If you select Case Sensitive, the search will also check the case sensitivity. If you select Stop On First, only the first occurrence of the result is displayed if there are duplicates under Name.

In Results, you can see the objects that fulfilled the criteria. If you double-click an element in the list, you can see and edit the properties for that element. You can change the column order in Results by dragging and dropping the columns headers, and you can sort the result set by clicking the column header.

In Diagrams, you can see the diagram or diagrams where the object can be found. If you double-click the diagram name, the diagram will open.

If you want to save the search, go to Saved Searches in the <New Search> field, enter a name for the search, click More, and select Save. If you select Clear for More, the search result will be cleared. If you select Delete, the saved search will be deleted. Before deleting it, Data Modeler asks, "Are you sure you want to delete saved search?" If you want to use one of the saved searches, click the list button next to <New Search> and select the desired search from the list. You can pin the search by clicking the pin icon, and if another Find operation is started, it will be on its own tab.

If you select Use RegEx, you will have an enormous number of possibilities for searching the content in open designs with regular expressions. You can, for example, search for anything in open designs that have some indication of having a URL (includes any of these strings: http:, https:, ftp:, or ftps:) by searching (f|ht)tps?:. The parentheses, (…), group the pattern elements into a single element, and the pipe symbol (|) says that one of the alternatives should match (f or ht). The question mark (?) says that the preceding pattern (s) is optional. Thus, the preceding regular expression matches the http:, https:, ftp:, and ftps: strings. Figure 11-9 shows an example of a search with a regular expression. The search returns the Comment property of an attribute EMPLOYEES.Information that has the value http:\\.

The characters | and ? are called *metacharacters,* and using them makes regular expressions powerful. Another example of a metacharacter is {}, which means an interval. {1} means exactly one, {1,} means at least one, and {1,7} means between 1

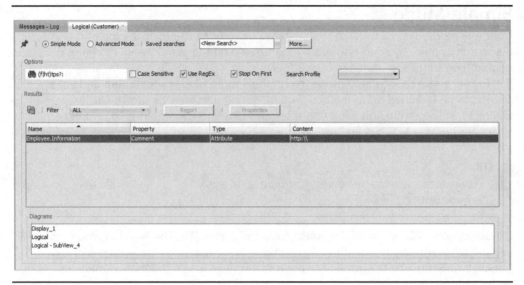

FIGURE 11-9. *Global search with regular expression*

and 7. Using this you can find, for example, anything that has two p's in it with p{2} or at least two p's with p{2,}. This search would return, for instance, humppa.

Curly braces, {}, are called a *quantifier*. Other quantifiers are as follows: * meaning 0 or more, + meaning 1 or more, and ? meaning 0 or 1. As mentioned earlier, (…) is a group. The square brackets, […], indicate a range. For instance, [abc] means "a or b or c," and [^abc] means "not a or b or c." [1-9] means "any digit between 1 and 9," and [a-q] means "a letter between *a* and *q*." Ranges are inclusive. There are plenty of other metacharacters that can be used as well. You can use all the basic elements to create complex and powerful patterns. For instance, ((?=.*/d)?=.*[a-z])(?=.*[A-Z]).{8,15}) can be used to check that the string includes at least one digit, one lowercase letter, and one uppercase letter, and is 8 to 15 characters long.

TIP
You can read more about regular expressions at http://docs.Oracle.com.

Advanced Mode

Advanced mode has more features for searching than simple mode. In advanced mode, you can search by object properties, and you can specify ORs and ANDs in the search logic. Select the Advanced Mode radio button to enable those features.

The upper part of the screen in advanced mode is the same as in simple mode; the difference is in the lower part of the screen. In advanced mode you also have another tab beside Results: Options. The Options tab is where you add object property criteria for the search. First you select the object type that will be used in the search, and then you click the Add Property button to be able to select the wanted property for the object type. From the Searchable Properties list, select the property you want to search again and insert the search criteria in the field next to it. If you want the search to be a negation, select Not. If you want this compare to be case sensitive, select Case Sensitive. You can add as many properties as desired by clicking Properties and selecting the property and the criteria. On the right you can decide with a radio button whether the separate properties and their criteria will be combined with OR or AND. If you want to remove a property from the search, click the red X button next to the property line. When you want to perform the search, click the Find button next to Add Property. You can see the result of the search on the Results tab.

You can find, for example, all the attributes that are deprecated (see Figure 11-10) or all the entities that have the property Create Surrogate Key selected. Or you can find all the domains with the VARCHAR data type or all the relationships with attributes. In short, you can search based on any property you have entered in the design. This tool is powerful, and it gets even more powerful when you add the regular expressions to the search criteria explained earlier. The sky is the limit regarding what you can search for with this tool.

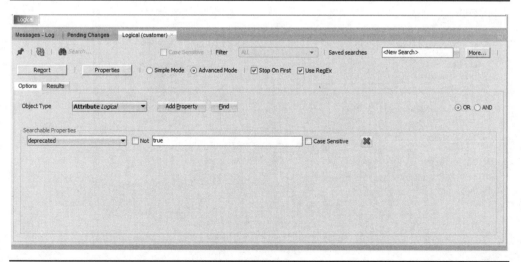

FIGURE 11-10.   *Advanced mode search for attributes with the property deprecated=true*

Remember that every search result can be saved in a report. The report can be in different formats, with different templates, and new templates can be built easily. And the search result can be used for updating the common properties for the result set.

Setting Common Properties

If you have selected an object type in Object, both the Report and Properties buttons appear. By clicking the Properties button, you can see the common properties for the result set and set them, as shown in Figure 11-11. In the Set Common Properties dialog, you can change a property for the whole set. In Old Value, you can see the current value of that property, and in New Value you can enter a new value or select a value from the list (marked with …) as the new value for all the items in the result list. Double-click the New Value field for the property name to enter the new value. When you click Apply, this new value is changed for all the items.

FIGURE 11-11. *Setting common properties*

For example, if you want to associate the same schema name for all the tables in the relational model, start the Search operation for the relational model wanted, type * in the search field, and select Table Oracle Database 12*c* (or whatever the RDBMS site is) in Filter. Then click Properties, go to Property Name User, and click the list to select the value for a schema name. Click Apply.

TIP
If you want to replace an existing value with an empty value, click the left-pointing arrow at the end of the property name setting and select Empty String.

Summary

You can generate reports by choosing File | Reports or by using the search functionality. You can also print a diagram by choosing File | Print Diagram. You can generate reports from Data Modeler designs that are open at the time, or they can be generated from the Data Modeler reporting repository. A user can create standard and custom templates to get the reports to look like they need to and to include the information wanted. Customer reports can be generated in Microsoft Excel format, and the changed information can be imported back into Data Modeler to either a logical or relational model. Reports can be generated in different formats for different needs.

The reporting repository is a database that can be accessed with SQL. A user can have read-only access to the reporting repository to be able to query it with SQL. The reporting repository is a read-only repository, and all changes to the content must be done with Data Modeler.

Data Modeler has strong search features to find any possible detail in a design. A search can be performed in simple or advanced mode. Also, regular expressions can be used in searches. The search functionality can be used not only for searching but also for reporting and setting common properties in the result set.

CHAPTER
12

Comparing Designs
and the Database

There are many situations when you need to compare either two designs with each other or the design with the database. You can compare two designs either by choosing File | Import | Data Modeler Design or by choosing Tools | Compare/Merge Models. The main difference between these two methods is that in Compare/Merge Models you can compare only the relational and physical models, whereas via Import | Data Model Design you can compare everything in a design. On the other hand, via Compare/Merge Models you can also preview and influence the DDLs that will be generated. A design and a database can be compared with either Synchronize Model With Data Dictionary or Synchronize Data Dictionary With Model, and the actual comparison will be done in the Compare Models dialog. A comparison to a design can also be done based on DDLs or data dictionary. This comparison also takes place in the Compare Models dialog.

In all comparisons, you always have a target and a source, and the possible changes are always performed on the target. The source is shown on the left, and the target is shown on the right in the comparison screens. A target in a design comparison is the one that is open in Data Modeler when the comparison starts. In synchronization, in Synchronize Model With Data Dictionary the target is the model, and in Synchronize Data Dictionary With Model it is the database. The best part of comparisons and synchronizations is that you can select any differences you want from the source and implement them in the target telling the tool you want it to be implemented in the target.

Setting Preferences and Properties

There are some preferences that will affect the comparisons—not what objects will be compared but what features will be compared. You can find them in the Preferences dialog by selecting Data Modeler | DDL | DDL/Comparison. The DDL Comparison Options section includes the preferences for adjusting the comparisons.

- A Data Type Kind comparison is always done, but if you select the Use 'Data Type Kind' Property In Compare Functionality preference, the difference will be enabled for merging automatically. Data Type Kind means that if a column on one side of the comparison is VARCHAR (10) and on the other side is defined as VARCHAR (10 CHAR), these definitions differ. Or if a column has been defined as Logical Type (VARCHAR) and on the other side as Domain (NameFirst), even though they both are of the same data type and length (VARCHAR(30)), they differ from each other in Data Type Kind.

- Use 'Schema' Property In Compare Functionality defines whether the different schema definition is a reason to show a difference when comparing two objects, and if this is selected and, for instance, the same table on one side

is on schema TEST and on the other side is on schema PROD, Data Modeler
suggests you create a new table because it sees this as a new table.

■ The column order for each table is always checked, but if Use 'Columns
Order' Property In Compare Functionality is selected, then the difference
in the column order on the Details tab will be automatically selected for
merging. If it is not selected, the difference is not enabled for merging but
can be selected manually if desired.

■ Case Sensitive Names In Compare Functionality defines whether the names
are case sensitive in comparisons. If this is selected, then, for instance, the
tables CUSTOMER and Customer will not be the same. The tool will suggest
removing one or adding the other.

■ If you select Include System Names In Compare Functionality, the system-
generated constraint names are compared. That is not usually wise since
the generated name is random and most likely different in different databases.

If you do not have a specific reason to change these preferences, you should
leave them at the default settings.

There are also some preferences that will affect the result only when importing
DDLs or synchronizing with the database. These preferences define what objects
will be taken from the database for comparison. All objects from the design are
always compared. In Preferences, you will find them in the Preferences dialog on
the Data Modeler | Model | Relational tab. There is a category called Database
Synchronization that includes the following preferences:

■ If you select Use Source Connection, the username and connection defined
for the database connection are the main criteria for selecting objects for
comparison. Only those objects from the source that have been defined in
the physical model to be included in that user schema are included in the
comparison. For instance, if your connection is via username Heli, only
objects that have been defined in the schema of the user Heli in the physical
model of the design will be included from the database side for the comparison.
All the objects that have no owner in the physical model will also be included
in both cases. All the objects from the design are included. If you used
several connections to import objects, the same or a different database, or
the same or a different user, you can use this option to filter out objects that
are imported with connections not selected in the synchronizing dialog.

■ If Use Source Schema is not selected, only those objects from the source
that have the same owner (schema) as in the design will be included in
the comparison. All the objects from the design are included. If Use Source

Schema is selected, all the objects from the source schema that exist also in the design will be included, no matter if they have the same owner. Objects in the database that do not exist in the design are not included. All the objects that have no owner in the physical model will also be included in both cases.

■ If Use Source Object is selected, the comparison is made only to objects that exist in the database when connecting using the connection. All the objects that have no owner in the physical model will also be included in both cases.

■ If Synchronize The Whole Schema is selected, all the objects that exist in the database and all the objects that exist in the design are shown in the list.

If none of these is selected, the objects that have the same owner will be included from the database for comparison. If all of them are selected, you will see all the objects from the database and all the objects from the design.

Comparing Two Designs

There are two ways to compare two designs: You can choose File | Import | Data Modeler Design, or you can choose Tools | Compare/Merge Models. The Import | Data Modeler Design method is for comparing two designs in every level: logical models, relational models, physical models, and so on. The Compare/Merge Models method is only for comparing the relational and physical models. The Compare Models dialog where the comparison is done in the latter case is the same dialog that will be used when importing DDLs, importing from a data dictionary, or when using the database synchronization.

Importing a Data Modeler Design

If you want to compare the logical models, in addition to the relational and physical models, and apply changes from there, you should use the File | Import | Data Modeler Design method. Open the target design (target) in Data Modeler. Then choose File | Import | Data Modeler Design. Select the source design on the Import Design screen. Select Selected for the Logical Model setting if you want to compare logical models and the relational model if you want to compare that too. For the relational model, you can select it to be imported to a new relational model (New Relational), or you can select an existing relational model from the list of relational models in the target design, as shown in Figure 12-1. You can use New Relational to create a new relational model under the logical model without affecting the existing relational model. But if you want to compare the relational model to an existing relational model, select that model. Click Next and then Finish. The Compare Oracle SQL Developer Data Modeler Designs screen, shown in Figure 12-2, will open.

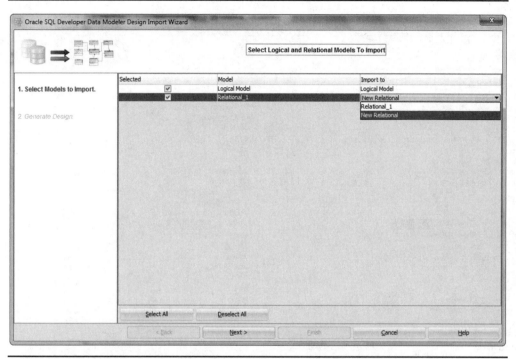

FIGURE 12-1. *Selecting the logical and relational models to import*

As mentioned earlier, the source design is always on the left, and the target design is always on the right; any changes based on the source are made to the target, and the source will remain untouched. There are once again two ways of seeing the differences: tree view and tabular view. In the tabular view, you can run a report (HTML, PDF, RTF) of the differences, and by selecting Separate Objects By Status, you can have them listed by their status (modified, new, deleted). In both of those views you can see the differences in the Details pane under the comparison. The details are shown from the selected element. The yellow triangle shows that there is something different in those two designs. If you select that element and view the details in the screen, you can see what has been changed. A red *X* shows that something has been deleted, and a green plus sign shows that something has been added. When applying the differences to the target model, the default for a deletion is always disabled, and for an addition it's selected. Remember to always check that you have selected and disabled the differences the way you want before clicking Apply. If you Apply and then realize something was not correct, you can always close the design without saving it. When you have selected which changes you would like to make to your target design, you can run a report of the changes and

FIGURE 12-2. *The compare screen*

then apply the changes to your target design. When you have clicked either Apply or Cancel, the Compare Oracle SQL Developer Data Modeler Designs screen will close, so if you want to run the report, run it before applying or closing.

In the tabular view, you can select/deselect everything with one click, and you can select only the model whose elements you want to see: ALL, Data Types Model, Logical Model, or Relational Model. In both views you can select by the status (New, Deleted, or Modified), but in the tabular view you can also select unchanged elements. In the tabular view you can select the type: ALL, Arc, Attribute, Column, Entity, Entity View, FK Arc, Foreign Key, Index, Key, Relationship, Structured Type, Subview, or Table. To me, the tree view is easier to read, but in the tabular view you can see, for instance, columns and nothing else, which can be useful. I recommend you learn to use both views because they are both excellent, and depending on your needs, one might be better than the other in a particular case. In my experience, though, when finally applying the changes to the target design, it is safer to use the tree view. For instance, if you want to implement a change to a column NAME and select it in the tabular view, no change is performed. You must also select the table CUSTOMER to get the column changed, and that is easier done and noticed in the tree view.

Comparing/Merging Models

This method is for comparing the relational and physical models. The target design must be open in Data Modeler. Choose Tools | Compare/Merge Models. Select the source model you want to use to compare from the Import Design dialog that will open. Note that you must also have the source design in your working copy directory. If you have several relational models, select the one you want to compare. If you have several physical models in your target model's relational model, select the one you want to compare. If you do not select any, the relational database management site (RDBMS) that has been defined as the default in Design Properties for the *source* design is used. If you select an RDBMS site that does not exist in your physical models of the target design, one will be created for you during the comparison. Click OK.

In the Compare Models dialog, you can see exactly how the two models differ. The source design in always on the left, and the target design is on the right. There are once again two ways of seeing the differences: tree view and tabular view. The yellow triangle shows that there is a difference. If you select that element and view the details in the screen, you can see exactly what has been changed. A red *X* shows that something has been removed, and a green plus sign says that something has been added. The default for a deletion is always disabled, and for an addition it's selected. Remember to always check that you have selected and disabled the elements the way you want before clicking Merge. If you merge and then realize something was not correct, you can always close the design without saving it. When you have selected which changes you would like to make to the target design, you can see the DDLs it would generate by clicking DDL Preview and check that is what you wanted and merge the changes to the target design. When you have clicked either Merge or Close, the Compare Models screen will be closed, so if you want to run a report or get the DDLs, do that before merging or closing.

In both of those views, you can see the differences on these tabs: Details, Storage Details, Options, Tables That Will Be Recreated, and Data Type Conversion. If you have selected either of the Advanced DDLs settings in Options, you will also see Oracle Errors To Mask.

On the Details tab, you can see all the details related to the element type selected in either the tree or tabular view. You can see the value for that detail (for instance, the column name) in the source and in the target. If there is a difference in the values, it will be marked in red. In Selected, you define whether this detailed change will be performed on the target element. You could say in the tree view that the change will be performed on the columns, and in Details you can select that only some of the changes suggested will be performed. For example, you can specify to change only the name, but not the data type, as shown in Figure 12-3.

On the Storage Details tab, you can see the storage values for the source and the target for elements that have storage values, such as a table. If there are differences, they are marked in red. Storage details are, for instance, a tablespace or any of the parameters in the storage clause.

FIGURE 12-3. *Compare Models dialog, Details tab*

On the Options tab, you can define DDL Options, DDL Storage Options, Compare Options, Properties Filter, Storage Properties Filter, and Date/Time Format. Let's see them more carefully:

- In DDL Options, you can specify the following:

    - You can specify the elements that will be included in DDL clauses. In Preferences (Data Modeler | DDL), you have specified the values for all these parameters except Include Comments (see Chapter 7). The preference can be overrun for the comparison by setting it differently in Compare Models | Options. The Preferences setting will overrun this parameter setting the next time you start Data Modeler.

        - The parameter Include Comments controls whether comments are included in the comparison.

        - The parameter Include Default Settings controls whether default settings are included in generated DDLs. It will add all DDL keywords for the object created in the generated DDL statements. This option is useful if you want to see the syntax for an object DDL.

        - The parameter Include Logging controls whether the logging information is included in the generated DDLs.

        - The parameter Include Schema controls whether object names are prefixed with the schema name in the generated DDL statements, such as PROD.CUSTOMER instead of just CUSTOMER.

        - The parameter Include Storage controls whether storage information is included in the generated DDLs. If the storage is not included, in Oracle the storage setting of the tablespace where the object is saved is used. Storage settings are, for instance, PCTFREE, PCTUSED, INITRANS and MAXTRANS, INITIAL, NEXT, MINEXTENTS, and MAXEXTENTS.

        - The parameter Include Tablespace controls whether tablespace information is included in the generated DDLs.

    - You can select the type of the DDL, as mentioned in Chapter 7. The possible types are Regular DDL, Advanced Interactive DDL, and Advanced CL (command-line) DDL. Both Advanced Interactive DDL and Advanced CL DDL create a script. Both scripts are interactive, and the advanced CL DDL script can be run from the command line. Both scripts include input parameters such as start step, stop step, log file, and log level (1, 2, or 3). If you want to run the advanced CL DDL script in SQL*Plus, the syntax is as follows: SQL> sqlplus user/password@ name @script_name start_step stop_step log_file log_level.

■ If the parameter Replace Existing Files is selected, Data Modeler will automatically replace any existing DDL files.

■ You can also specify Unload Directory. That is a directory on the server side that is used if anything goes wrong when performing the operations. For example, if the database runs in Linux, this directory is a Linux directory. For instance, space could run out on a tablespace where a table was supposed to be re-created. This can be used only with Advanced Interactive DDL or Advanced CL DDL, and the backup strategy is set to unload. Regular DDL uses only a rename of the table for backup.

■ In DDL Storage Options, you can change the values you have set in Preferences for what to include in the DDL clause (see Chapter 7). You can either include or exclude these parameters from the storage clause in DDL: PCTFREE, PCTUSED, INITRANS, INITIAL, NEXT, MINEXTENTS, MAXEXTENTS, PCTINCREASE, BUFFER_POOL, FREELIST, FREELIST GROUPS, and OPTIMAL.

■ In Compare Options, you can specify the same parameters introduced earlier in this chapter for preferences: Use Data Type Kind Property, Use Schema Property, Use Column Order Property, Case Sensitive Names, and Include System Names. The values will come from Preferences, but you can change them for the comparison. After changing these parameters, click Refresh Tree to get the upper part of the screen updated, and these parameters take effect for the current comparison.

■ In Properties Filter, you can select properties to be included or excluded while comparing. There are settings for elements such as arcs, columns, foreign keys, primary key and unique key constraints, structured types, tables, and views. Select Included for all the properties for the element type you want to be included. For instance, you can exclude comments and notes for a table when you are comparing a model that has the comment to another model created from the database that does not have the comment and can be sure the comment will not be overwritten.

■ Storage Properties Filter has content if the element is of a type that has storage properties. You can exclude some of the storage properties from comparison. You might want to exclude tablespaces from comparison if you know they are different for tables in the source versus the target and it is on purpose.

■ In Date/Time Format, you can set the date format, timestamp format, and timestamp time zone format.

On the Tables That Will Be Recreated tab, you can define the backup strategy (rename/none), data restore (restore/none), script execution (continue), and unload directory for each table that will be re-created. A table might need to be re-created, for example, if a column is changing a data type, and depending on whether the tables have data or do not have it, you might want to select a different backup strategy.

On the Data Type Conversion tab, you will see what column will be converted and its current and new data types. You can define whether the table will be re-created. If the table is empty, it can be just dropped and created, but if it is not empty, it must be re-created. You can also define the conversion expression.

If you have selected either Advanced DDL or Advanced CL DDL, you can specify on the Oracle Errors To Mask tab some Oracle errors to be ignored during script execution. For example, you can specify -942 for ORA-00942.

TIP
You can change the column order on the Tables That Will Be Recreated and Data Type Conversion tabs by clicking a header and moving it to where you want. The change might make the screen easier for you to read.

Quite often people ask me which one is better, the tree view or the tabular view. My answer is that they complement each other, and it depends on what you are doing. In the tabular view, you can select/deselect everything with one click, and you can select only the model whose elements you want to see: ALL, Data Types Model, and Relational Model. In both views you can select by the status (New, Deleted, or Modified), but in the tabular view you can also select Unchanged. In the tabular view, you can select the type: ALL, Column, FK Arc, Foreign Key, Index, Structured Type, or Table. To me, the tree view is easier to read, but in the tabular view you can see, for instance, indexes and nothing else, which can be useful. I recommend you learn to use both views because they are both excellent, and depending on your needs, one might be better than the other in a particular case. I would also advise you to use the tree view when finally merging since the logic in the tabular view for merging might not be so obvious. In either view, you can run a report (HTML, PDF, RTF) of the differences. And by selecting Separate Objects By Status, you can have the differences listed by their status on the report.

Comparing a Design to the Database

A design and a database can be compared with either Synchronize Model With Data Dictionary or Synchronize Data Dictionary With Model. In all comparisons, you always have a target and a source, and the possible changes are always performed on the target. In Synchronize Model With Data Dictionary, the target is the model, and in Synchronize Data Dictionary With Model it is the database. If you do not want to use the synchronizing functionality to compare the database, there are a couple other options: either import DDLs or import from a data dictionary.

The difference between these methods is at the beginning of the process: All these methods end up at the same Compare Models dialog introduced in the previous section. The only difference is in Synchronize Data Dictionary With Model because the Compare Models screen for that also includes a Sync New Objects button.

If you are using the synchronization functionality to compare the design to the database, you need to create a connection to the database if you have not done so before. There is no particular place to really create a connection, but it can be done with Import. Choose File | Import | Data Dictionary. Then click Add to create a new connection and insert the information needed for the connection. Test that the connection works by clicking Test, and when you are done with it, click Save. Now the connection is created, and you do not need to continue with the importing anymore, so click Cancel.

With the Synchronize Model With Data Dictionary button, you can view what has changed in the database and get those changes to your model. Click the arrow pointing to the left, as shown in Figure 12-4. Select your connection from the Redirect Connection list and click OK. Now you will see the Compare Models dialog again. Data Modeler suggests that the objects that exist only in the database should be added to the design, and the objects that exist only in the design and not in the database should be removed from the database. You can use this comparison to get changes made directly to the database to the design as well. Select the changes you want to perform. You can view the DDL preview before clicking the Merge button to make sure your model will be updated the way you want. You can also use the DDL script Data Modeler gives you to alter the database. Check the design before saving it to be sure it is what you wanted.

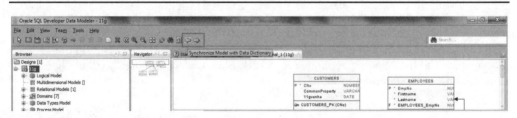

FIGURE 12-4. *Synchronize Model With Data Dictionary and Synchronize Data Dictionary With Model buttons*

With the Synchronize Data Dictionary With Model button, you can see what has changed in the design and make those changes to the database. Click the arrow pointing to the right, as shown in Figure 12-4. Select your connection from the Redirect Connection list and click OK. You will see the Compare Models dialog again. Data Modeler suggests that the objects that exist only in the database should be deleted from the database and the objects that exist only in the design should be added to the database. You can use this comparison when you have made changes to the design but have not implemented them in the database yet. Note that the Merge button is not disabled in Figure 12-4 because there are no changes that can be performed in the design. Note also that there is a new button called Sync New Objects when synchronizing the data dictionary with the model. Select the changes you want to perform and open the DDL preview. Check that the script is correct and save it. Run the script in the database. This is the ALTER script to change your database to match the model. Depending on what you have selected, this script can include elements for creating new objects in the database and for deleting or altering existing objects.

You can also use the DDLs that were used for creating the database to make comparisons against the design. Choose File | Import | DDL File to do that. You can either compare to the existing relational model in the open design (target) or create a new relational model based on the DDLs. If you want to have the DDL design as the target, during the import you can select Swap Target Model to change the model from the DDL as the target. Then you need to select the database site (RDBMS site) to be compared to. After that, you can view the log in the View Log dialog and save it if desired. The same Compare Models screen will open that you have seen before. Another option is that you import from the data dictionary. Select the desired connection and select the schemas to import, the relational model where to import them, and the RDBMS site. If you want, you can select Swap Target Model as explained earlier. Then select the objects you want to import. The Compare Models screen will open.

For example, say somebody has changed the name and data type of a column in the database. The Compare Models dialog does not know that. It shows that there is a column in the design that does not exist in the database, and vice versa. Select the column on the source side and right-click. Select Map To Existing Column and select the column that it should be mapped to. You have just created a compare mapping, and Data Modeler will remember it the next time you do a comparison. This is only for comparisons between the design and a database, a DDL script, or a data dictionary. If you compare two designs, Data Modeler recognizes it is the same column, and there is no need to create a compare mapping. You can see the existing compare mapping in Design Properties, as shown in Figure 12-5. If you want to perform the operation (change the name and data type), click Merge.

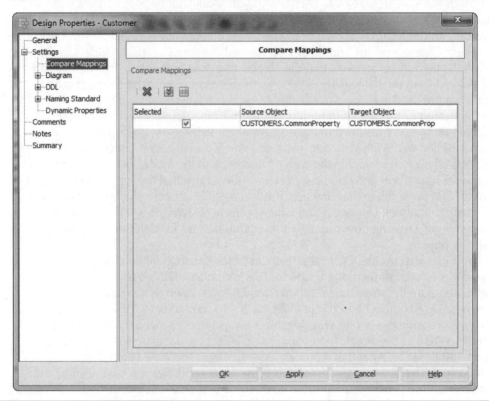

FIGURE 12-5. *An example of compare mappings*

Summary

There are several ways of comparing designs to each other and comparing a design to a database. As a result of a comparison, you can also change the design or the database accordingly.

Designs can be compared either with the Import functionality or with Compare/Merge Models. Import compares all the elements a design has, whereas Compare/Merge Models compares only the relational and physical models.

A design and a database can be compared either with synchronization or by importing the DDLs for creating the database or importing them from a data dictionary. The comparisons on the design and database are done with the Compare/Merge Models dialog. During the comparison you can either change the model or get the DDLs to change the database. You can also get ALTER DDLs, for instance, when renaming a table or changing a data type of a column. There are several parameters that can be used to get the kind of DDLs you want. Remember to always check the DDLs before running them on your database.

Index

T

Join the Largest Tech Community in the World

 Download the latest software, tools, and developer templates

 Get exclusive access to hands-on trainings and workshops

 Grow your professional network through the Oracle ACE Program

 Publish your technical articles – and get paid to share your expertise

Join the Oracle Technology Network
Membership is free. Visit oracle.com/technetwork

@OracleOTN facebook.com/OracleTechnologyNetwork

Reach More than 700,000 Oracle Customers with Oracle Publishing Group

Connect with the Audience that Matters Most to Your Business

Oracle Magazine
The Largest IT Publication in the World
Circulation: 550,000
Audience: IT Managers, DBAs, Programmers, and Developers

Profit
Business Insight for Enterprise-Class Business Leaders to Help Them Build a Better Business Using Oracle Technology
Circulation: 100,000
Audience: Top Executives and Line of Business Managers

Java Magazine
The Essential Source on Java Technology, the Java Programming Language, and Java-Based Applications
Circulation: 125,000 and Growing Steady
Audience: Corporate and Independent Java Developers, Programmers, and Architects

For more information or to sign up for a FREE subscription:
Scan the QR code to visit Oracle Publishing online.

Beta Test Oracle Software

Get a first look at our newest products—and help perfect them. You must meet the following criteria:

- ✔ **Licensed Oracle customer or Oracle PartnerNetwork member**

- ✔ **Oracle software expert**

- ✔ **Early adopter of Oracle products**

Please apply at: pdpm.oracle.com/BPO/userprofile

ORACLE®

If your interests match upcoming activities, we'll contact you. Profiles are kept on file for 12 months.